Impacts of Faith-Based Decision Making on the Individual-Level Legislative Process:

Emerging Research and Opportunities

Karla Drenner
Kaplan University, USA

A volume in the Advances in Public Policy and Administration (APPA) Book Series

IGI GLOBAL
DISSEMINATOR OF KNOWLEDGE
www.igi-global.com

Published in the United States of America by
IGI Global
Information Science Reference (an imprint of IGI Global)
701 E. Chocolate Avenue
Hershey PA, USA 17033
Tel: 717-533-8845
Fax: 717-533-8661
E-mail: cust@igi-global.com
Web site: http://www.igi-global.com

Library of Congress Cataloging-in-Publication Data

Names: Drenner, Karla, author.
Title: Impacts of faith-based decision making on the individual-level legislative process : emerging research and opportunities / by Karla Drenner.
Description: Hershey : Information Science Reference, 2017.
Identifiers: LCCN 2017001213| ISBN 9781522523888 (hardcover) | ISBN 9781522523895 (ebook)
Subjects: LCSH: Christianity and law. | Legislation--United States. | Christianity--Influence. | United States--Church history.
Classification: LCC BR517 .D74 2017 | DDC 270.0973--dc23 LC record available at https://lccn.loc.gov/2017001213

This book is published in the IGI Global book series Advances in Public Policy and Administration (APPA) (ISSN: 2475-6644; eISSN: 2475-6652)

British Cataloguing in Publication Data
A Cataloguing in Publication record for this book is available from the British Library.

For electronic access to this publication, please contact: eresources@igi-global.com.

Advances in Public Policy and Administration (APPA) Book Series

ISSN:2475-6644
EISSN:2475-6652

MISSION

Proper management of the public sphere is necessary in order to maintain order in modern society. Research developments in the field of public policy and administration can assist in uncovering the latest tools, practices, and methodologies for governing societies around the world.

The **Advances in Public Policy and Administration (APPA) Book Series** aims to publish scholarly publications focused on topics pertaining to the governance of the public domain. APPA's focus on timely topics relating to government, public funding, politics, public safety, policy, and law enforcement is particularly relevant to academicians, government officials, and upper-level students seeking the most up-to-date research in their field.

COVERAGE

- Political Economy
- Public Administration
- Urban Planning
- Politics
- Public Policy
- Resource Allocation
- Law enforcement
- Government
- Public Funding

IGI Global is currently accepting manuscripts for publication within this series. To submit a proposal for a volume in this series, please contact our Acquisition Editors at Acquisitions@igi-global.com or visit: http://www.igi-global.com/publish/.

The Advances in Public Policy and Administration (APPA) Book Series (ISSN 2475-6644) is published by IGI Global, 701 E. Chocolate Avenue, Hershey, PA 17033-1240, USA, www.igi-global.com. This series is composed of titles available for purchase individually; each title is edited to be contextually exclusive from any other title within the series. For pricing and ordering information please visit http://www.igi-global.com/book-series/advances-public-policy-administration/97862. Postmaster: Send all address changes to above address.

Titles in this Series

For a list of additional titles in this series, please visit:
http://www.igi-global.com/book-series/advances-public-policy-administration/97862

Therapeutic Jurisprudence and Overcoming Violence Againt Women
Debarati Halder (Centre for Cyber Victim Counselling (CCVC), India & Unitedworld School of Law, India) and K. Jaishankar (Raksha Shakti University, India)
Information Science Reference • ©2017 • 344pp • H/C (ISBN: 9781522524724) • US $230.00

Public Sector Entrepreneurship and the Integration of Innovative Busines Models
Mateusz Lewandowski (Jagiellonian University in Kraków, Poland) and Barbara Kożuch (Jagiellonian University in Kraków, Poland)
Business Science Reference • ©2017 • 309pp • H/C (ISBN: 9781522522157) • US $190.00

Handbook of Research on Citizen Engagement and Public Participation in the Era of New Media
Marco Adria (University of Alberta, Canada) and Yuping Mao (California State University Long Beach, USA)
Information Science Reference • ©2017 • 503pp • H/C (ISBN: 9781522510819) • US $265.00

Global Perspectives on Development Administration and Cultural Change
Gbenga Emmanuel Afolayan (Murdoch University, Australia) and Akeem Ayofe Akinwale (University of Lagos, Nigeria)
Information Science Reference • ©2017 • 277pp • H/C (ISBN: 9781522506294) • US $170.00

Handbook of Research on Managerial Solutions in Non-Profit Organizations
Vojko Potocan (University of Maribor, Slovenia) Mustafa C. Üngan (Sakarya University, Turkey) and Zlatko Nedelko (University of Maribor, Slovenia)
Information Science Reference • ©2017 • 609pp • H/C (ISBN: 9781522507314) • US $300.00

Achieving Open Justice through Citizen Participation and Transparency
Carlos E. Jiménez-Gómez (Department of Justice of the Autonomous Government of Catalonia, Spain) and Mila Gascó-Hernández (Institute of Public Governance and Management, ESADE Business and Law School, Spain)
Information Science Reference • ©2017 • 296pp • H/C (ISBN: 9781522507178) • US $190.00

For an enitre list of titles in this series, please visit:
http://www.igi-global.com/book-series/advances-public-policy-administration/97862

IGI GLOBAL
DISSEMINATOR OF KNOWLEDGE

www.igi-global.com

701 East Chocolate Avenue, Hershey, PA 17033, USA
Tel: 717-533-8845 x100 • Fax: 717-533-8661
E-Mail: cust@igi-global.com • www.igi-global.com

Table of Contents

Preface vii

Acknowledgment xvi

Introduction xviii

Section 1
Historical Development of American State Legislatures

Chapter 1
Introduction to Faith in State Legislatures: Land of the Brave and the Home of the Free – The Star-Spangled Banner 1

Chapter 2
Emergence of Faith and Politics at the State Level 26

Section 2
Intersection of Religion and Politics

Chapter 3
The Use of Faith in Legislative Decision-Making: Bill Sponsorship 63

Chapter 4
The Holy Wars of Marriage 92

Section 3
State Battle Grounds and Emerging Research Opportunities

Chapter 5
Defenders of Faith 118

Chapter 6
The Implications of Religious Liberty....................143

Related Readings....................163

About the Author....................184

Index....................185

Preface

I have served in the Georgia General Assembly since 2001 as a State Representative and have been involved in legislative battles that involved both same-sex marriage and religious freedom policy issues. This both informs my research and has also contributed to my understanding of the moral complexity of these issues. My research and writing on legislative decision-making is more than a professional affair; having served as a member of the body for 16 years it is from this intense participant observation perspective that I draw from. In being elected to the House and serving as its first openly gay member made me wonder why, some legislators felt compelled to introduce some types of bills and others did not? I understood my personal decision-making process and was curious as to my colleagues.

My assumption was that legislators, who were Protestant evangelicals, were more likely to sponsor bills that restricted gay rights. This piqued my interest, both because of my background, and also because it surprised me as to that the passion and determination that came with passing certain types of bills. Though my own point of view and experience provided the impetus for this book, the research design and methodology focuses on identifying patterns in data sources.

Simply put, standpoint theory holds that different individuals or groups in society possess significantly different perspectives (or standpoints) that shape their views of reality (Wood, 1993). This theory posits that people are situated in specific social standpoints; that is, they occupy different places in the social hierarchy. Thus, individuals view social situations from particular vantage points. By necessity, each vantage point provides only a partial understanding of the social whole. Standpoint theory in this book sheds light on my own experience of particular moments in Georgia legislative history and illuminates the complexities that shape the views of other participants in legislative debates. The design and findings of this book reflect in part the standpoint of this researcher. I have experienced being a legislator from multiple vantage points: that of a legislator, a Democrat, a woman, a mother, a member of the majority and minority parties, and the South's first openly gay state legislator.

The introductory remarks to a speech I gave on February 16, 2004, during the first floor debate on Senate Resolution 595, a constitutional amendment to ban same-sex marriage make clear my ideological perspective regarding the same-sex marriage.

I am going to tell you before I go into my prepared remarks; I have a few things to say about some of the comments that I heard today. First of all, I came here to be a legislator and I want to be a good legislator. I have worked extremely hard and when I came here I did something different than what you all did. I did not just run a campaign; I had to come out about my personal life as a result of running for office. And I did that not without trepidation, but I did that with pride because I am who I am. I make no apologies for that whatsoever. I am who God made me to be and I will tell you that the way I was raised was not to be gay. I was not raised any differently than any of you all here in this room. I had two parents, they loved me, they gave me food, and they paddled my back when punishment was still acceptable. I was raised a Southern Baptist. I know what it is like to be a Baptist[1].

Followed by a segment of the speech I gave on March 3, 2016, during the floor debate on House Bill 757, an enhanced version of a bill to protect religious freedom.

I must note that the irony of debating a bill that licenses prejudice against my community in the "City Too Busy to Hate," is not lost on me…I oppose House Bill 757 as amended by the Senate and I oppose it for any number of reasons…It says that my rights under the Constitution, under the law, and under God are not inalienable, but rather are subject to the opinions of others…Freedom is an all or nothing principle, there are no shades of liberty. And when I am not as free as my neighbor, we all lose…. (Georgia Public Broadcast Media, 2016)[2]

This book comes from my attempt to wrestle with the internecine conflicts that exist in the Georgia legislature. The rise of conservative Christians into the field of political power is a product not just of elites at the top, but evangelicals at the grassroots level, advocating in the churches, for the righteousness of their causes. These evangelical legislators have had much success; the voices of liberal Protestant legislators have been all but silenced in red states within many legislative chambers across America. Correspondingly, so with evangelical legislators in blue states; each group has been disparately affected by single party dominance, paving the way to enact far-reaching conservative and liberal policies.

The author attempts to demonstrate that the clash of cultures is real between these groups, but not simple. The faith worldviews of each of these groups share common structural features, though often reaching very different conclusions. Moreover, in the process of analyzing these worldviews I found myself seeing strengths and weaknesses in both and coming to a grudging respect for each perspective. And, of course, I have my own perspective and motivations that I bring to this project.

LEGISLATIVE DECISION-MAKING

In recent years, state legislatures in the United States have been transformed based on the social identities of their membership. The partisan proclivities and ideological diversity among state legislators combined with significant changes has reshaped state legislatures. These changes are portrayed by both demographics and geographical location and characterized as either "red" or as "blue" states or areas based on a set of values that translate into legislative decision making and electorate voting behavior (Pallay, 2013). This Red State/ Blue State dichotomy illustrates the polarity which extends beyond politics and includes divergent social and religious worlds.

The idea of red (Republican) and blue (Democrat) states or areas has become commonplace; the general idea is that blue states tend to be more liberal politically, while red states are more conservative. Conservatives in red areas emphasize and adhere to traditional family values, and are often opposed to social differences that require cultural accommodation, such as homosexuality. In contrast, progressives or liberals that reside in blue areas stress the importance of choice and diversity. Supporters of both perspectives feel threatened and are critical of the others points of view, voting for individuals and policies that reflect these differences. Brought about by demographic and economic shifts the relationship between family, home and the marketplace, has redefined gender roles. During this time, the purpose of marriage began to shift. These competing groups struggle for dominance in American political culture and to define the role of religion in government, irrespective of geographic boundaries and individual lives (Wuthnow, 1988).

The association among these constructs forms the foundation for a broader perspective of what Hunter (1991) refers to as the "cultural wars." This theoretical interpretation asserts that faith and politics in America today are best understood by recognizing the existence of deep social divisions over changing values and lifestyles. State legislators are on the front lines of the culture wars. Ideologically legislators from red and blue states have developed different worldviews; that shape their decision-making.

THE DESIGN

The theoretical framework of this study is social constructivism; the primary research tool involves an interpretative approach to this phenomenon. Blumer (1969) notes two elements involved in the interpretative case study approach to the study of social phenomena. The first element is exploration, which he defines as an exploratory description, rigorously conducted, of the phenomena under study. The second element of the interpretative method is inspection, which consists of "an intensive focused examination and the empirical content of whatever analytical elements were used for purposes of analysis, and this same kind of examination of the empirical nature of the relations between such elements." Empirical content consists of those phenomena that appear in the area of study, and the analytical elements are those items employed in analyzing the subject matter (Gilsinan, 1987, 1989 & 1991).

Social construction theory requires a different definition of the term "hypothesis" than the one typically found in traditional, deductive science. The deductive approach begins with a theory and then deduces, from this theory, a hypothesis that describes what may be expected under a given set of conditions. Since the deductive approach is ill suited to a social constructionist framework for investigation, this book uses an inductive approach that allows for the emergence of the concepts and relationships throughout the process of the research, with the goal of representing the changing reality of the situation.

Through the use of social construction, this book explores the tension between religious freedom and rights for the Lesbian, Gay, Bisexual, and Transgendered (LGBT) community, explaining through a historical lens how the conflict developed and summarizing legislator's attempts to mitigate threat of same-sex marriage. One of the challenges the author faced in preparing book relates to the very nature of American religion-its continued pluralistic evolvement, its diverse regional and ethnic bases, and its generational differences. These characteristics preclude the possibility of any single definition of religion. Rather, the author defines religion or faith as a social construct. Within constructionist thought, a social construct refers to a concept or practice, which appears to be natural and obvious to those who accept it, but is actually an invention or artifact of a particular culture or society (Hacking, 1999). A social constructionist framework reveals the ways that individuals and groups participate in the creation of their social reality. An example of a social construct is an individual's faith is around the issue of same-sex marriage.

This book suggests that the legislator's social construction of faith has led to bill sponsorship. The emphasis of this book is to explore how faith operates among state legislators while describing the nature of values that have effect on their political beliefs and behaviors.

ORGANIZATION OF THE BOOK

The book is organized into three sections containing six chapters. A brief description of each of the chapters follows:

In Section 1, the author endeavors to strike a balance between providing enough information and cluttering the narrative with endless nuance. The historical background is an essential part of this context, so Chapter 1 is devoted to historical roots in addition to providing historical details elsewhere in the text. The big picture may seem to oversimplify at times. I do not try to document all of the interesting differences between states or individual legislator.

Chapter 1 of this book begins with thematic interpretation of faith and politics at the state level. This complex history of the relationships between faith, politics and culture, in state legislatures is organized around three ideas: separation, demography and polarization. In particular the author identifies the factors that play a role in the continued debate that rages across America regarding the role of faith in government and the related problems with single-party control over state legislatures.

In order to sort out the influences among politics, faith, in the molding of American state legislative cultures, a sense of history is required. The objective of this chapter is to sort out the influences, around the themes of separation, demography and polarization. The association among these constructs forms the foundation for a broader perspective of what Hunter (1991) refers to as the "cultural wars." This theoretical interpretation asserts that faith and politics in America today are best understood by recognizing the existence of deep social divisions over changing values and lifestyles. The author endeavors to strike a balance between providing enough information and cluttering the narrative with endless nuance. The historical background is an essential part of this context, so Chapter 1 is devoted to historical roots in addition to providing historical details elsewhere in the text. The big picture may seem to oversimplify at times. I do not try to document all of the interesting differences between states or individual legislator.

Chapter 2 begins the exploration of the legislative process rather than the outcomes, by describing the context rather than specific variables, in discovery rather than confirmation (Merriam, 1998). Through the use of Wellman's (2008) approach to understand the moral terrain and faith worldviews of individual legislators offers broad insight into how a legislator's moral core propels an issue onto the formal agenda. Based on this research, several propositions are developed as to how moral worldviews function at the individual legislator level concrete examples provided. The political views of legislators are linked to a moral worldview; their opinions, values, and convictions are not merely tools that they use, but are part of a moral worldview out of which arises their faith and political perspectives.

Section 2 invites the reader into the intersection of faith and political culture, and especially the role that faith plays in fostering the values, norms and decisions of state legislators.

Chapter 3 describes the emergence of same-sex marriage as a national political issue. As a result, state legislators have sponsored and passed statutes on an array of issues directly related to this topic. Bill sponsorship is an important legislative activity because a policy must be proposed before it is legislatively enacted. To the extent that gay issues represent a cultural cleavage between religious traditionalism and progressivism, I expect legislator decision making to be strongly influenced by phenomena that inform culture.

Chapter 4 reviews the history-the debate over same-sex marriage. Legislators have responded to the promotion of same-sex marriage by sponsoring and passing bills claiming that it contravenes their faith based principles. Despite vigorous opposition, same-sex marriage protection continued to spread across the country, and LGBT anti-discrimination laws rapidly increased, causing many states to fear that a court decision could guarantee broad civil rights for the LGBT population. Consequently, state RFRA laws became the legal missile targeted at marriage equality. What followed in conservative states was the proliferation of increasingly robust mini RFRA laws. As the judiciary continued to invalidate bans on same-sex marriage, and as municipalities adopted LGBT-protective antidiscrimination laws, states continued to push back with the adoption of robust religious freedom laws.

Section 3 summarizes how faith moral worldviews have been applied throughout the nation and offers for an understanding of the legislative arena.

Chapter 5 illustrates the tensions between religion and LGBT rights, discussing the heightened lawmaking efforts by legislators that are more inclined toward religious claims due to their opposition to homosexuality.

Chapter 6 concludes with framework for resolving the tension between religious liberty and LGBT rights. The impact of the court's decision to legalize same-sex marriage has left many unanswered questions. Due to the near absence of state antidiscrimination protections for LGBT individuals in the areas of employment, housing, and public accommodations and the increase in legislation that restricts public accommodations on the basis of sexual orientation and gender identity. The LGBT community is face with future concerns.

CONCLUSION

In conclusion, this book posits that the courts must undertake a delicate balancing act in managing the tension between equality and religious freedom claims. The purpose of this analysis is to show the power of faith worldviews, and, in particular, how they work and function at the individual legislative level. Most, important, is for outsiders who wish to understand the inner workings of these individuals. My hope is to expand the understanding, not simply to encourage a bland tolerance of or create a false consensus, but to inspire respect for differing truth claims. In this sense, agreement is not necessary, but the understanding of difference and the recognition of strongly held faith convictions, and equality concerns on both sides is important. By Illuminating the role of faith as it operates in government among state legislators while exploring the nature of values that have so much effect on their political beliefs and behaviors. Only by doing this may the dynamics of faith in state houses across America is fully appreciated. Wellman (2008) states that scholarship is a "moral enterprise," seeking to explain the truth about the data and on occasion, allow it to changes one's perspective; I invite readers to read carefully the faith worldviews and then make up your own mind.

The book is for those who do not know, but are interested in knowing about the legislative process and how faith plays a role. By describing these phenomena, I hope to contribute to the understanding of the process of constructing social realities and, more specifically, to the understanding how these realities impact the legislative decision-making process.

Karla L. Drenner
Kaplan University, USA

REFERENCES

Blumer, H. (1969). *Symbolic interactionism: Perspective and method.* Englewood Cliffs, NJ: Prentice-Hall.

Georgia Public Broadcast Media. (2016 March). *Legislative Day 38, 2016* [Video]. Retrieved from http://www.gpb.org/lawmakers/2016/day-38

Gilsinan, J. (1989). They is clowning tough: 911 and the social construction of reality. *Criminology*, *27*(2), 329–343. doi:10.1111/j.1745-9125.1989.tb01035.x

Gilsinan, J. (1991). Public policy and criminology: Historical and philosophical reassessment. *Justice Quarterly*, *18*(2), 201–216. doi:10.1080/07418829100091001

Gilsinan, J., & Valentine, J. (1987). Bending granite: Attempts to change the management perspective of American criminologists and police reformers. *Journal of Police Sciences and Police Administration*, *15*, 196–203.

Hacking, I. (1999). *The social construction of what?* Cambridge, MA: Harvard University Press.

Hunter, J. D. (1991). *Culture Wars*. New York: Basic Books.

Merriam, S. B. (1998). *Qualitative research and case study applications in education*. San Francisco, CA: Jossey-Bass.

Pallay, G. (2013). *Who Runs the States?* Academic Press.

Wellman, J. K. (2008). *Evangelical vs. liberal: the clash of Christian cultures in the Pacific Northwest*. Oxford, UK: Oxford University Press.

Wuthnow, R. (1988). *The Restructuring of American Religion*. Princeton, NJ: Princeton University Press.

ENDNOTES

1. This information is provided to the reader to fully disclose that the researcher is a current member of the House of Representatives and prior to the 2004 same-sex marriage issue had other legislative battles regarding gay issues with members of the Georgia Religious Right organizations. These issues included the Boy Scouts use of public facilities; Gay Straight Alliances in schools; and Gay parental adoption rights.
2. [Video] Georgia Public Broadcast Media. (2016 March). Legislative Day 38, 2016 Retrieved from http://www.gpb.org/lawmakers/2016/day-38

Acknowledgment

Upon completion of this I would like to sincerely acknowledge and recognize all the people involved in helping me see this project through to completion. Specifically, to the publisher for welcoming my idea and giving me the opportunity to explore and present this subject matter I am passionate about. I would like to express my sincere appreciation for IGI Global's support throughout the publication process of this research insights book. The reviewers provided important feedback and without their support, this book would not have become a reality.

There are many who contributed along the way my friends Kim Jones, Greg Creech, who assisted with technology challenges; Kathleen Wright and Tracy Cartledge and Kim Bernstein who provided unending encouragement and support.

State Representative Dr. Betty Price for facilitating a meeting with Reverend Bryant Wright and the willingness of Pastors Dr. Ken Samuels and Victor Belton to participate in this important discussion regarding the faith implications of the legalization of same-sex marriage. I greatly appreciated the dialogue and the insights.

To the National Federation for Women Legislators who allowed me the opportunity to briefly interrupt the conference to solicit assistance from the elected woman participants with this research.

To my legislative colleagues especially the members of the DeKalb House delegation who have filled in for me when I could not attend meetings (because I was working on "my book")-State Representatives Michele Henson, Howard Mosby, and Pam Stephenson and Senator Steve Henson.

Despite our differing worldviews to someone that I immensely respect, House Speaker David Ralston for your willingness to listen and to lead with compassion; to Leader Stacy Abrams for the support and guidance along the way; and to any of you that I may have over looked, thank you.

To one of my dearest friends State Representative Sam Teasley, to an outsider our apparent differences should have prohibited us from being friends...but then they don't understand that it's the willingness to bridge those differences world a better place. Thank you for unwavering friendship.

Lastly, and most importantly I want to thank my FAMILY....my mother June Butterfield, my partner Candice Campen, my sister Kitti Summey, and my extended family Bobbie Bassett, Lynn and Nancy Campen. All who stood by me through this journey, in particular their understanding of my limited availability and my need to sacrifice my time with them to "work on my book."

I look forward to sharing this accomplishment with them and engaging in thoughtful dialogue with all of those who are interested in the issue of faith.

Thank you GOD for all the blessings of this life!

Introduction

In recent years, legislatures in the United States have undergone great changes in the social identities of their membership both within and across legislatures from a number of viewpoints these include: the impact of increased diversity within legislatures; the consequences of declining ideological diversity among partisans; and the impact of changing social norms.

Bill sponsorship is an important legislative activity because a policy must be proposed before it is legislatively enacted. To the extent that gay issues represent a cultural cleavage between religious traditionalism and progressivism, I expect legislative decision making to be strongly influenced by phenomena that inform culture.

This book explores the tension between religious freedom and rights for the Lesbian, Gay, Bisexual, and Transgendered (LGBT) community, explaining through a historical lens how the conflict developed and summarizing legislator's attempts to mitigate threats of same-sex marriage. As in American society, religious convictions among state legislators vary widely, sometimes even within the same religious tradition or denomination. These expressions of belief and devotion often provide insight into a member's political actions.

This book's contribution to the legislative behavior literature is to show that faith traditions influence legislative activity even outside of the roll call arena. Primarily, scholars have searched for evidence of electoral influence by asking whether vulnerable members take more positions by sponsoring to cosponsoring —than safe members. This book shifts the locus of the search for electoral influence from the volume of a member's legislative activity to the content of that activity. This shift yields greater support for the notion that legislative activity is motivated by faith convictions.

Karla Drenner
Kaplan University, USA

Section 1

Historical Development of American State Legislatures

America's faith history is woven into the social and political fabric that shapes state legislatures.

Chapter 1
Introduction to Faith in State Legislatures:
Land of the Brave and the Home of the Free - The Star-Spangled Banner

ABSTRACT

This chapter introduces the complex history of the relationships among faith, politics and culture in state legislatures. Each of these concepts is explored by organizing them into three themes: separation, demography and polarization. The direction and content of public policies across the United State are influenced by these elements contributing to either the support or opposition to social change. State legislators are on the front line of these ideological divides. These variations by region contribute to the increase in single party control and have generated pronounced policy differences.

INTRODUCTION

Religion has played a role in political activity in America since its founding. The role of religion in the making of public policy has always been a subject of great debate. The debate persists in part because of those who argue against the advocacy of organized religion in the body politic as a conflict between the separation of church and state; and those who claim its part of America's Judeo-Christian faith tradition. In order to understand American politics, an appreciation of the enduring tension between the church and state

DOI: 10.4018/978-1-5225-2388-8.ch001

is imperative. The American story of relating and separating religion and politics is paradoxical; church and state are legally separated but are intimately related. This historical intimacy between faith and the political has affected our culture, shaping the operation of its institutions and participants.

Since colonial days, faith has played a profound role in molding American culture. The American Constitutional Republic was forged through an intermingling of faith and political imperatives to create a form of government in which the people are the ultimate source of authority, electing representatives to make laws that advance the common good. Through the creation of a Constitution and a Bill of Rights asserting that each individual possesses unalienable rights, this unique type of democracy implemented a form of democratic republicanism, not a pure democracy (Reid, 2003).

This constitutional democracy is predicated upon the belief in the sanctity of the individual and requires the protection of individual rights against governmental encroachments. Among the widespread political ideas in eighteenth-century America was the concept that people can shape their government, community and society in accordance with the laws of nature. Associated with this belief is the conviction that government does not grant rights. Rather, rights are inherent, part of what makes people human and referred to as natural rights (Woll & Binstock, 1984); and whenever possible, government exists to protect these rights. In the United States, these rights and freedoms cover a broad spectrum, including the freedom to speak, to write, to associate in groups; and to practice religious faith as one pleases. These individual freedoms and rights are at the heart of American democracy and are based on an underlying set of values or beliefs which has created the dominant political culture in the United States and consists of: individualism, democracy, liberty, property rights and religion, all tied together by the value of equality (Coleman, Goldstein, & Howell, 2011). This set of beliefs has been labeled, the American Creed (Hartz, 1955; Ericson & Green, 1999; Lipset, 1997). Americans embrace these concepts in the abstract; however, these values frequently clash with one another separating Americans into two categories: conservatives and progressives. James Hunter (1991) in *Culture Wars* describes the differences between these factions by distinguishing "orthodoxy[1]," between conservativism (conservative, the Right) from progressivism (liberals, the Left) which embodies contemporary life. These differences are rooted in their contrasting attitudes toward change and produce the struggle to define which direction America takes in the future. These competing groups struggle for dominance in American political culture and to define the role of religion in government, irrespective of geographic boundaries and individual lives (Wuthnow, 1988). The association among these constructs forms the foundation for a broader perspective of what Hunter (1991) refers to as the "cultural wars." This theoretical interpretation asserts that faith and politics in America today are best understood by recognizing the existence of deep social divisions over changing values and lifestyles. The emphasis of this book is to explore how faith operates among state legislators while describing the nature of values that have so much effect on their political beliefs and behaviors.

BACKGROUND

The colonization of the United States was fueled in part by the European upheavals unleashed by the Protestant Reformation. The Pilgrims were the first of the European immigrants who fled the volatile political environment in England looking for religious freedom. They established the Plymouth colony in 1620 becoming the second successful English settlement in North America (after the founding of Jamestown, Virginia in 1607). Unlike the Plymouth colony, the settlement at Jamestown, Virginia was comprised mostly of noblemen and was not a family-oriented community. The Jamestown settlement was used as an economic front for the London Company. These two British colonies came to the United States for different reasons and with dissimilar ideologies. In 1630, another religious group left England in search of religious freedom, where they could worship the way they wanted without fear of persecution. This group was called the Puritans[2]. Both Pilgrim and Puritan migrants were dissenters from the Anglican Church of England motivated to create a new church in the colonies. The Pilgrims held Calvinist religious beliefs similar to the Puritans. However, unlike many Puritans, Pilgrims maintained that their congregations needed to be separated from the English state church. This desire for separation was based on the belief that the Church of England was too corrupt to ever be purified. In contrast, the Puritans believed that the Church of England was the true church in need of major reforms from within.

Throughout Americans history, the sense of who we are has been profoundly influenced by our religious beliefs and practices. The colonist thought of themselves as a chosen people, living in a land of the free and the home of the brave, and defenders of faith. Our identity as a nation is still marked by this truth. The involvement of religion gets creates differences that are reflective in historic teachings and deeply held patterns of belief and practice. These beliefs and practices cannot easily be disconnected from questions about truth and morality. Believing that one's faith is correct and behaving in ways that reflect this, presents many personal and societal challenges when confronted with differences; it is these contrasts that this Chapter explores.

THE WALL OF SEPARATION

The beginning of the churches involvement in American politics predates the founding of this nation. It was religion; at least in part, that gave birth to America. It is no exaggeration to say that religious concerns went into the founding of every one of the original colonies. Having fled religious persecution, the leaders in the New World enforced their own interpretation of theological law and banished those that did not share their views. The Pilgrims' story is a central theme inherent in the history and culture of the United States.

As illustrated by Roger Williams who arrived in America in 1631, preaching absolute liberty of every sect (including heretics and infidels); he realized that this blessing could never be realized without a complete separation of church and state (Longacre, 2016). Rejecting Puritanism, Williams embraced the tenets of separatism, turning briefly to Baptist principles. Ultimately, he declared that Christ's true church could not be known among men until Christ himself returned to establish it (Williams, 1644). Based on his interpretation of the New Testament, Williams concluded that liberty of conscience or "soul liberty" was necessary since no one could know for certain which form of religion was the true one God had intended (Hartz, 1957). John Cotton stood in opposition to separatism and advocated for a strong alliance between church and state, recommending harsh punishment for heretics. Williams was exiled from the Massachusetts Bay Colony because he rejected the governing document of the colony — in part, because he objected to the charter's civil punishment of religious dissent and disobedience (McElroy, 2013). Williams corresponded with Cotton, asking for a comment about the proper relationship between church and state. Cotton responded with a lengthy letter explaining that the theological points made relative to the expulsion were based on that fact that Williams's "doctrines disturbed the peace of the church and state" (McElroy, 2013). The letters between Roger Williams and John Cotton depict contemporary church-state separation differences that are deeply ingrained in American culture. The most important impact of the exchange between Williams and Cotton was its likely influence on several

Founding Fathers. More than a century and a half later, Thomas Jefferson used the same wording as Williams. In an 1802 letter to the Danbury Baptist Association of Connecticut, Jefferson cited the First Amendment and declared the American people had erected a "wall of separation between church and state" in order to respect the intimate relationship between an individual and God. Jefferson believed strongly that religious beliefs should be solely a matter of individual conscience.

Believing with you that religion is a matter which lies solely between man and his God... that the legislative powers of government reach actions only and not opinions, I contemplate with sovereign reverence that act of the whole American people which declared that their legislature should 'make no law respecting an establishment of religion, or prohibiting the free exercise thereof,' thus building a wall of separation between church and state. (Jefferson, 1802)

That letter is widely credited with being the source of the phrase commonly used to describe the First Amendment's guarantee of religious freedom: "the separation of church and state" (McElroy, 2013). Jefferson; however, was not the only leading figure to use the phrase. In his *Memorial and Remonstrance against Religious Assessments*, written in 1785, James Madison also defended the separation of church and state describing the right of conscience "to exercise it as they may dictate" and "the care of the soul is treated as a private matter."

The Revolutionary war gave rise to the American Constitutional Republic and was forged in and through a complex intermingling of religious and political imperatives reflecting the ideals of eighteenth century enlightenment. The American framers of the Constitution drew from the works of various eighteenth-century political philosophers such as John Locke in his *Letter on Toleration* (1689) supported the belief that government and religion should have separate ends. Government exists only to secure things on earth and religion has a transcendent purpose of saving souls. For these reasons, a Republic was created where people elect representatives who are entrusted to make the laws. This Republic limited the power of the majority through a Constitutional framework and stressed the importance of liberty, thus ensuring the protection of individual rights. This Constitutional system established the key principals for the nation and was based upon sharing legislative, executive and judicial powers among three branches of government.

Each branch addresses distinctly different interests and is given specific powers to this end, effectively limiting the actions of the other two (Shalhope, 1972). A directly elected bicameral legislature known as Congress which is intended to represent a state's citizens is granted the power to make law with its lower house designated as the House of Representatives and its upper house known as the Senate. The executive branch was designed to represent the interests of the nation, and was given the power to veto legislation. The third branch of government is the judiciary, which is charged with interpreting the laws passed by the legislature. This functional separation of powers is reinforced by the selection of representatives directly or indirectly by the people throughout all three branches of government, underscoring the tenet that all power flows from the people. The structure of the U.S. government, its federal system and separation of powers plays an important role in matters of freedom. The judiciary holds exclusive authority to interpret the Constitution and to nullify any laws that violate that understanding. Constitutional explanations have changed over time and will continue to change as new members of the judiciary apply the law to new contexts.

The Framers of the Constitution recognized that religious freedom was more easily stated than accomplished, and that intolerance was common. The First Amendment to the Constitution was designed to establish the basic principles regarding freedom of religion (Rodgers, 1998). These two clauses are referred to as the free exercise and the establishment clauses that form the wall of separation between the church and state. Therefore, it is appropriate to speak of the "constitutional principle of church-state separation" since the phrase summarizes what the First Amendments religion clauses do – they separate church and state (Boston, 2003). Because of this historically unique relationship between faith and the state, the United States has been described as "the oldest secular state" (Drucker, 1956). The American Constitution further distributes powers between the states and the national government creating a series of checks and balances that reduces the likelihood of economic threats, ensuring that the states serve as the primary focus of everyday governance (Robertson & Judd, 1989). Like the U.S. Constitution, state constitutions provide a framework of government that includes three branches. Despite the limited specifications for state governments in the United States Constitution, legislatures were established in all fifty states.

Legislatures dominated their newly created state governments after the Revolutionary period (Crane & Watts, 1968). These organizations were central to the growth and development of the American state, coming together in representative assemblies to produce petitions, declarations, constitutions, amendments, statutes, rules, ordinances and laws; the essence of American governance (Novak, 2008). Based on the doctrine of incorporation, the first amendment is deemed applicable to the states and must guarantee religious freedom (Constitutional Rights Foundation, 1991).

The war ended the rule of the British and the religious practices of the Church of England in the colonies. A separation from the Church of England was forced since the Church of England clergy were required to swear allegiance to the British monarch. Different denominations were consequently organized shortly after the American Revolution. The religion in the colonies adhered to the religious practices of many different denominations. Several colonies had an "established" church, which meant that local tax money was allocated to the established denomination. Freedom of religion became a basic American principle, and as a result, numerous new movements emerged. Many of the new movements evolved into established denominations in their own right.

The Puritans were an important part of the Revolution. They were in the majority in Massachusetts and Connecticut. The Puritans saw their mission as divinely ordained and believed that America had a special destiny. Based on the theological conception of church and state, the Puritans instituted a form of religious establishment that would maintain institutional separation while still allowing church and state to assist one another. The logic behind this type of collaborative relationship was that it reinforced government authority by lending some divine legitimacy to civil laws and officials that could be used to shape moral and law-abiding citizens. The state supported the church by promoting the truth of its teachings by a variety of ways. Compelling church attendance, providing financial assistance, suppressing alternate religious practices, and providing political status for prominent religious leaders represent a few of the practices designed to support organized religion. Although the colonies were characterized by religious diversity, the disproportionate puritanical principles heavily influenced life in the new land.

Notably, the Puritans enforced an institutional separation, prohibiting religious leaders from holding office. The Puritan's perception of democracy included a belief that only "the religious" or church members should be allowed to elect officials. Additionally, people could only become church members if they were likely to be destined for salvation. The colonies operated more as theocracies based on a community covenant with God, since political leaders did not derive their authority directly from God. Understanding the Puritan cultural legacy is important, serving as a basis for recognizing how beliefs surrounding sin and the need for morally instructive laws to restrain individuals are deeply ingrained in American history. With independence, religious dissenters called for an end to the Puritan religious establishments throughout the states. These dissenters- Baptists, Presbyterians, Methodists,

Unitarians, Deists, Quakers, among others; struggled for religious liberty and the separation of church and state.

The dissenters placed great importance on the voluntary component of faith. This theological rejection of coercion in matters of conscience has had political consequences. The Puritan's religious establishment constituted a direct attempt to coerce religious belief and tied the state and church together for that purpose. Based on these ideas, the establishment of religion actually weakened religion. By promoting the belief that if a plurality exists in society, it's up to God and not the state to decide which will flourish, organized religion's fate is eternally up for debate. Of course, it is important to note that during the eighteenth century, no single evangelical group was large enough to garner support for establishing its church. Evangelicals such as Roger Williams, who championed the separation of church and state by the middle of the nineteenth century dominated American religious and cultural life. One could conjecture that had the Evangelicals held commensurate political influence during the founding period, they might have been tempted to seek the establishment of some form of evangelical Christianity. The modern day confusion over the role between church and state has been debated for 200 years but while religions role in government evolves, the government role in religion has always been clear except if those who control government are opposed to social change.

THE POLITICS OF DEMOGRAPHY

In recent years, state legislatures in the United States have been transformed based on the social identities of their membership. The partisan proclivities and ideological diversity among state legislators combined with significant changes in the rules and structures of their institutions has effectively reshaped state legislatures. These changes are portrayed by both demographics and geographical location and characterized as either "red" or as "blue" states or areas based on a set of values that translate into electorate voting behavior (Pallay, 2013). This Red State/Blue State dichotomy illustrates the polarity which extends beyond politics and includes divergent social and religious worlds. The idea of red (Republican) and blue (Democrat) states or areas has become commonplace; the general idea is that blue states tend to be more liberal politically, while red states are more conservative. Conservatives in red areas emphasize and adhere to traditional family values, and are often opposed to social differences that require cultural adaptation, such as homosexuality. In contrast, progressives or liberals that reside in blue areas stress the importance of choice and diversity. Supporters of both perspectives feel threatened and are critical of the other point of view, and then vote for individuals and policies that reflect their worldview. The realities of these differences are far more complicated than the simple contrast between red and blue. At the core of this distinction are faith differences between individuals whose values are widely disparate. These conflicting perspectives on life's basic choices affect everyone, especially state legislators and their policy decision making.

Deborah Stone (1997) argues that policy is meant to obtain objectives in light of particular goals or aims. These goals are defined by overarching concepts by which government decision makers are able to construct legitimate policy. She argues that equity, efficiency, security, and liberty are contested "goals" that are continuously constructed and reconstructed in the polity (Stone, 1997, p. 37). Each person has a different interpretation of each concept and assigns a different value to each concept in relation to the others, making these goals subject to a continuous debate in the construction of public policy. Because these goals are disputed, defining a problem is not always simple and frequently is disputed by different segments of society. Problems are "strategic representations of situations" constructed by actors who "deliberately and consciously fashion portrayals so as to promote their favored course of action" (Stone, 1997, p. 133). Problem definition is, in itself, a political process by which government officials assign importance to particular goals and values, and then frame issues to be problems deserving of government attention so as to legitimize their particular goals. It is critical to define a condition or issue as a problem in order to increase an issue's chance of promotion to the formal agendas of government (Kingdon, 2003, p. 207). Problems can be defined in several different manners, each of which has ramifications for the likelihood that people will view that issue as an important problem that necessitates government intervention. Because everyone does not agree on the importance of different goals, it is crucial for those who control the passage of public policy to convince the public that the problems they are addressing are significant and legitimate. Legislators often use focusing events to help define a problem or focus attention on a particular issue. These events can be sudden or dramatic events or, they can be subtle events that are strategically framed to demonstrate what they consider to be a pressing problem (Birkland, 1997). This book investigates the possibility that court cases involving same-sex marriage and religious freedom has served as a focusing events for legislative action.

The United States has undergone demographic conversions changing from a rural, agricultural economy to a more urban industrial one, finally shifting now towards an information economy (Cahn & Carbone, 2010). These cultural transformations have redefined the relationship between home and the marketplace, resulting in delays in child rearing, reducing overall fertility, and redefining gender roles. During this time, the purpose of marriage began to shift. Marriage was no longer overseen, as it had been in colonial America. Rather, marriage became the couple's private decision. By the early 1950s, a large percentage of households conformed to the husband/breadwinner and wife/full-time homemaker model. The '60s brought about the sexual revolution and the women's movement. As women took control of their reproductive lives by using birth control, men felt less obligated to marry the women if they did get pregnant (Akerlof, Yellen & Katz, 1996). As non-martial sexuality became more prevalent, mothers were more willing to raise children without marriage.

Conservatives decried these changes as a sign of moral decay. This clash of faith worldviews depends on different visions of the "good life." The blue family morality is cast in the language of reason and instrumental values (Cahn & Carbone, 2010). This code of ethics may be agnostic as it relates to permissive non-martial sex; however, it espouses unequivocally that unprotected sex is unwise and that having a child derails opportunities. These values are instilled by private discipline and internalized precepts to public sanction. For blue families, children follow career success, relationship stability, and are mostly in urban areas, along the coasts in Democratic areas of the country.

The red family paradigm celebrates marriage and procreation and is driven by religious teachings about sin and guilt. This philosophy is represented in communities whose social life centers on married couples with children. Red families generally are in Republican strongholds; are more religious, rural, less educated, and less mobile. The political leadership in these "red" areas is more likely to value tradition (Cahn & Carbone, 2010). The irony is that the moralistic basis of family attitudes requires and generates even stronger pressures for reinforcement. Adherents see themselves as embattled minorities where the values of each paradigm are mutually threaten.

This geographic separation along demographic lines means that the two groups have less in common, and as the two political parties have become more ideologically polarized, these different value orientations have become more partisan-making as a predictor of political loyalties in the twenty-first century. The intractability of the differences between the two perspectives dominates political debates. There have been significant differences in red and blue states with regard to same-sex marriage and civil union's legislation. For example, all of the states that have passed favorable legislation have been blue states. These cultural clashes between the right and left manifest in bills that legislators' sponsor and can be distinguished by region and faith tradition, especially related to bills that protect traditional marriage. So, demographics make a difference, but ideological views on what constitutes a family including reproduction also permeates each state culture (Wellman, 2008).

Another notable development in American politics over the last two and a half decades has been the increase in the number of minorities elected to public office. Demographer's project that whites will lose majority status in the middle of the 21st Century, due to both increased immigration and lower birth rates among native-born whites relative to other groups (Cohn et. al, 2015; Frey, 2015). Concurrently, politicians in both major parties have sought to capitalize on these demographic changes by using symbolic rhetoric and taking opposing stances on issues to cultivate political support. As a result, nonwhite Americans have begun to comprise a larger proportion of Democratic voters, while racially resentful whites increasingly identify as Republicans, over and above any broader ideological commitment to the parties (Abrajano & Hajnal, 2015; Hajnal & Rivera, 2014; Tesler, 2013).

Minority representation varies significantly by state. Southern states were once the home of Jim Crow and the poll tax. But now, they have some of the greatest diversity in their legislatures. Black legislators have the greatest presence in Alabama (24 percent), Georgia (25 percent) and Mississippi (28 percent) (Wiltz, 2015). One reason is the sheer size of the African-American population in those states;

another reason for this increased diversity was the "preclearance" provision of the Voting Rights Act (Wiltz, 2015).

Studies have shown the relative lack of minority representation in statehouses has an impact on the legislation that is debated and approved (Rocha, 2013). These representation gaps at the state level would certainly help block, or at the very least temper, punitive legislation from being enacted. Ethnic imbalance is not restricted to red states or blue states, northern states or southern states. In deep blue Delaware, whites account for 90 percent of all state legislators, and just 69 percent of the population, a 21-point disparity. In deep red Alaska, 85 percent of the legislature is white, 19 points higher than the state population. The average state's population is 77 percent white, according to the U.S. Census Bureau. The average state legislature is 82 percent white.

POLARIZATION

There are 99 bicameral state legislative chambers[3] typically consisting of a house, or lower chamber, and a Senate, or upper chamber. The formal names vary from state to state[4]. The length of terms of State Representatives in the 49 American lower chambers is either two years or four years[5] and customarily has the exclusive power to initiate taxing legislation and articles of impeachment (National Conference of State Legislatures, 2013). In contrast, term lengths of State Senators are generally longer; thirty states have four-year terms for State Senators. Within those chambers, there are 7,382 elected legislators that include 1,972 state senate seats and 5,411 house seats; each have different organizational patterns - varying in size, structure and partisan composition. Each legislature may establish its own rules of procedure. As a result, a legislative process varies—from state to state, from chamber to chamber, and from session to session.

Although, legislative processes differ among the states, they remain fairly constant within a chamber.

Within any given two-year period, there are between 5000 and 6000 state legislative elections (Moncrief, Squire, & Jewell, 2001). These elections have become more important as more policy related responsibilities devolve to the states. One of the most notable process differences between the states and Congress is the presence of legislative term limits in 15 state legislatures (Norberg & Newton, 2015).

As shown in Table 1 (see Appendix), California and Colorado in 1990 became the first states to enact term limits; with 53% of those occurring in1992 and then decreased steadily until 2000 (National Conference of State Legislatures, 2015). Legislative term limits can be categorized as either lifetime or consecutive term limit. Resulting in 26% of the state legislative seats that are term limited; this includes 562 or 28.5% of the state senate seats and 1,368 or 25% of the 5,411; this number varies per year (Kurtz, 2015).

Advocates of term limits argue that elected representatives become beholden to interest groups if allowed to serve an unlimited number of terms (Norberg & Newton, 2015). These supporters believe the ability of citizens to be represented in government decreases as incumbency advantage increases, and legislators will no longer face any real electoral challenge. To force electoral competition, term limits will kick incumbents out of office and make the institution more representative. On the opposing side of this argument is the contention that representation will not be increased and the actual process of legislating will become hampered (Carey, Niemi & Powell, 2000).

Term limits may not affect all legislators the same way. Legislators who know in advance that they are limited, are freer to pursue their own policy goals rather goals of their district. This may significantly influence legislative decision-making regarding what bills to sponsor. Because term-limited legislators face reduced electoral incentives they may make decisions based solely on personal views (Cooper & Richardson, 2006). This finding should give pause to those, who see reform as enhancing representation, when in fact the tradeoffs may lead to citizen legislators who will be more likely to follow their own consciences rather than those of their constituents. These legislators tend to produce more partisan sponsored legislation, and so when this career uncertainty blends with the political ambition that term-limited legislators still have, bipartisanship becomes a risky strategy. Their instinct is to become partisan rather than collaborative. Even with the enactment of term limits polarization at the state legislative level is real, and varies across states. In comparison to the US Congress, the majority of state legislatures are less polarized, whereas 15 are actually more polarized. California is by far the most polarized state legislature and Congress looks decidedly bipartisan by comparison (Shor & McCarty, 2011). Being a conservative in the Alabama House is quite different from being a conservative in the Massachusetts Senate (Shor & McCarty, 2011). California, Connecticut, and Massachusetts anchor the liberal end of the spectrum, whereas Idaho, Alaska, and South Dakota do the same for the conservative end. For example, the Democratic Party in Mississippi is more conservative than the relatively liberal Republican parties of Connecticut, Delaware, Hawaii, Illinois, Massachusetts, New Jersey, New York, and Rhode Island. The liberal Republicans of New York locate to the left of relatively conservative Democratic parties in Alabama, Arkansas, Kentucky, Louisiana, Mississippi, North Dakota, Oklahoma, South Carolina, South Dakota, and West Virginia. Rhode Island and Louisiana are the least polarized. In the former, Democrats are liberal, but so too are Republicans. In the latter, the opposite is true. Following the 2016 elections, Republicans picked up a net gain of two trifectas. The 2017 state legislative sessions began with six Democratic trifectas, 25 Republican trifectas, and 19 states are under divided government.

In the 1980s and 1990s, there was some debate about what voters were trying to say when they split their ticket and created a divided state government. It was widely believed that in those days that a large portion of the electorate was splitting tickets by design, giving each party a portion of control to prevent the other one from accumulating a monopoly on political power (Ehrenhalt, 2015). Divided government has lost its prominence and states have been moving into the all-red or blue category, voting for governments in which one party controls the governorship and both chambers of the legislature at the same time. During the past decade, divided government reached its low point after the 2012 election, with only 12 states fitting into the divided category (Ehrenhalt, 2015).

As Paul Posner and Timothy Conlan (2011) from George Mason University point out in a study of federalism and intergovernmental relations, politics in the states are splitting along partisan lines with one-party control of the legislature and governorship on the rise and sharp fractures developing between Washington and state capitols. This "polarized federalism" is marred with hostility and frustration. Both sides have ratcheted up the conflict. In 2009, Republicans controlled both chambers in just 14 states. Seven years later, they control more than double that number. Election turnout hit historic lows in 2014, which likely contributed to the Republican gains (Storey, 2014) equaling their post Reconstruction high of 30 in 1920. The continued increase in divided state governments has led to Washington-style gridlock.

THE CULTURAL DIVIDE

Since the first European settlements in North America in the early seventeenth century, governments in America have tried to regulate morality. The early colonists equated sin with crime. Such offenses as blasphemy (showing a lack of reverence toward God), heresy (holding a belief that conflicts with church doctrine), and adultery (sex between two adults, one of whom is married to another) were considered criminal acts and dealt with by sometimes severe punishments. Actions and behavior that do not conform to accepted standards of what is considered right or wrong are called public order crimes, vice crimes or moral offenses (Friedman & Scheiber, 1988). Such behavior is viewed as disruptive to daily life. They are also called. The colonies had "blue laws," because they were printed on blue paper, banning certain activities such as work on Sundays. The association of law and morality in early America resulted in the enactment of legislation toward the establishment morality with the abolition of ecclesiastical courts (Friedman & Scheiber, 1988). Moral law was the official guideline for the enforcement of morals in the American colonies and the basis for civil law itself. Sin and crime, divine law and secular law, the moral law and criminal law were intertwined. The essential contribution of moral law to the secular law was the equation of sin and crime. The precepts of moral law furnished the initial reasons for punishing a crime. If God had branded certain actions as seriously immoral and sinful, these normally became crimes by statute in every American colony. In a society where law and morals were so closely identified, the extent of the parallel relationship between church and state is significant. These laws based on morals differed from state to state; and if were allowed to occur in a community, then more serious criminal activity would likely follow according to those who consider moral offenses a crime. Popular opinion dictated that these offenses should remain an illegal criminal activity, which would serve to protect the moral fiber of communities (e.g. modern-day moral offenses include the sale of obscene materials, certain kinds of sexual activity, drug and alcohol abuse, gambling and homosexuality.

State legislators operate on the front lines in these moral debates. Socialization is about ideology and it is a symbolic system (a worldview that is developed throughout this book) internalized, frequently becoming the engine of reproduction that nurtures specific cultural and moral values and actions. Ideologically red and blue states influence of faith tradition is well established as integral part of shaping moral worldview, social commentary, and political activity. An important question is how this can help address a key theoretical problem identified by Scheitle and Hahn (2011, p. 914) that "the mechanisms by which messages heard in the pews are translated into actual law have not been adequately specified or evaluated." This is particularly the case with the bill sponsorship regarding anti-same-sex marriage measures by sponsored by religiously devout legislators. Controversies over abortion, same-sex marriage, parenthood and divorce are all challenges that confront many legislators' worldviews of the American family; and, have resulted in cultural divides across and within legislative bodies. Many legislators seek the return to the "Mom and Dad and Apple pie" family of the 1940's. On the other side of the spectrum, theses legislators embrace all of the variations present in modern day families across the country. These conflicting worldviews are evident as bills are sponsored based on their faith. The intractability of the differences between the two perspectives has dominated the political debate. Part of the reason for the conflict is geographic. The urban and coastal areas are increasingly democratic areas of the country. In contrast, the Republican strongholds are likely in rural areas. Geographic separation along demographic lines means the two groups have increasingly less in common, as the two political parties differ in values, become more ideological and are geographically separated.

Close examination of the faith characteristics of members of the state legislatures has shed light on the members' behavior. In a 2008, the National Conference of State Legislatures' (NCSL) analysis of the Faith of State Legislators showed that one-third of all legislators are Protestant. When combined with Catholics, this group represented one half of lawmakers. Again in 2015, the percentages of Protestants and Catholics accounted for the majority of faith affiliation. However, in both 2008 and 2015, between 42 and 43 percent of legislators chose not to report their faith preference in seventeen states. Interestingly, 80 percent or more of the state legislators in Arkansas, Tennessee, Virginia, Mississippi, Alabama, Florida, Kentucky, South Carolina, Texas, Louisiana and West Virginia listed their faith as compared to fewer than 40 percent who did so in seventeen states.

Southern state legislatures are dominated by Republicans, and less than a fifth of Republican state lawmakers nationally are women. Comparatively, over a third of Democratic legislators are women (Yee, 2016). Home to the nation's Bible Belt, the South has long been known for the important role religion plays in its society and politics. The region's state legislators continue to report higher levels of religious affiliation compared to lawmakers elsewhere. About 71 percent of Southern state legislators identify as Protestant, compared to 26 percent in non-Southern states. In Tennessee, Arkansas, Mississippi and Alabama, over 85 percent identify as Protestant. Compared to the rest of the country, relatively fewer identify as Catholic, other Christian or non-Christian (Yee, 2016).The objective of socially conservative or evangelical legislators is to transform the institutions of society into the image of Christ. This includes government and politics. The theology this idea is based on is the "cultural mandate" that directs the church to transform society for Christ (Nelson, 1991). There is a difference between establishing a Christian society and transforming a society into a Christian one.

Each side in this culture war uses the metaphor to attack the other. Strict separationists insist that the First Amendment requires removal of all references to faith in the public square of America. On the other side conservatives argue that this is a false interpretation. Some legislators favor a church and state mingling because they see no alternative believing that the public square is hostile to their faith. These individuals believe that if they don't do something to protect their faith through government, they may find themselves unable to express their faith at all. Politics in the states is split along partisan lines, with one party control of the legislature and governorship on the rise with fractures within state capitals and Washington. States have moved into the all-red or all-blue category, voting for governments in which one party controls both chambers and the governorship at the same time. A generation ago the partisan divide between the two parties was less pronounced, and politics in most legislatures proceeded largely on the basis of personal relationships, and divided government tended to work rather well. Today, the divided federal government has generated intense partisan anger and personal hostility, corroding the political process as a whole. It's fair to say that prolonged periods of divided government can generate intense partisan anger and personal hostility that tend to be corrosive to the political process as a whole. It wasn't always this way. A generation ago, when the ideological divide between the two parties was less pronounced, and politics in most legislatures proceeded on the basis of personal relationships, divided government worked rather well (Ehrenhalt, 2015).

RECOMMENDATION

Over the past several decades, it has become increasingly more likely that a state government will be under the control of one party (Pallay, 2013). More state legislatures now have both legislative chambers controlled by a single party than at any other time. State legislatures have become more polarized. As a result, policy differences and balance of power concerns have created long term disparities in state legislative control. This has all sorts of effects from the obvious (control of the decennial redistricting process) to less apparent results (a wider bench to groom future stars).

Single-party control of the redistricting process in many states is aimed at protecting current legislative majorities seems likely to perpetuate more hyper-partisan state governments. An avenue to consider is to reduce single party control both at the National and State level by implementing a process that is bipartisan in nature to change electoral districting, primary elections, and campaign finance are areas to explore. Additional changes could be directed towards legislative procedures such as those related to the filibuster, appropriations, and confirmation process to limit the opportunities for polarization to undermine government (Barber & McCarty, 2013). The only way to overcome factional control is by constructing processes that neutralize their effects.

FUTURE RESEARCH DIRECTION

The increasingly partisan nature of state governments is demonstrated by blue states passing legislation that is more progressive, while red states are implementing policy that is more conservative. How the increase in single-party control impacts bill sponsorship and implementation of public policy in the states is a key question for future research. Given that millions of people live in states that have term limits and few studies have considered how district structure influences of this on legislative bill sponsorship and clearly is a subject that deserves more study.

CONCLUSION

The purpose of this Chapter was to introduce the formative role that faith has played in the shaping of America's public life. The framers of our constitution were deeply concerned about the perils of religious conflict. They recognized that entanglement of religion and government only lead to heightened strife, should the followers of different faiths contend with each other for government endorsement. Their goal was not to suppress religion, but rather to free it from the temptations of secular power. Since there can be no law respecting an establishment of religion, no group can attempt to dominate another, enshrining the tenets of one faith community to the derogation of another. The concerns are not a question of whether or not the state can acknowledge God, but a question of promotion of religion.

The church-state separation and the role of faith in politics within the public sphere in the twenty-first century continue to be debated. In recent years, state legislatures in the United States have undergone great changes in the social identities of their membership within legislatures; however, the consequences of single party control results in declining ideological diversity among members; and the impact of changing social norms.

Each of these factors has increased the political tension because beliefs differences and are reflective in today's political landscape are in conflict and can be attributed to the differential emphasis each placed on these beliefs and exist within each American mainline denomination, and those that embrace and oppose change are at the heart of the culture war. These are broad spectrum differences of social and political issues from abortion, to war, to civil rights. When beliefs are in conflict, there is no balance that is right or wrong. Instead, there is a balance that can gain the strongest national, state or local support. This shows significant variation across states in partisan strength, public opinion, and the content of laws and policies.

Geographical variation in political culture is one factor that helps explain the differences in state laws and politics and is compounded by social changes to the already existing cultural differences that exist by region, and religious ideologies and have become increasingly more political. The resulting cultural wars have been played out within each legislature across the nation. The conflict between red and blue is, at its core, about how both groups interpret religion truth related to family structure.

In conclusion, the separation of church and state does not require banishing moral and religious values from the public square. America's social fabric depends on such values and vision to shape politics. It is possible to express one's faith and convictions about public policy while still respecting the pluralism of American Democracy. Rather than suggesting that we not talk about "God," Democrats should be arguing on moral and religious grounds that all Americans should have economic security, healthcare, and educational opportunity and that true faith results in a compassionate concern for those on the margins (Wallis, 2005). Moving forward, Democrats are wrong to restrict religion to the private sphere- just as Republicans are wrong to define it solely in terms of individual moral choices and sexual ethics. Allowing one side of the political equation to decide what a religious issue is has become both a moral and political tragedy. Not everyone in America has the same religious values, of course. And many moral lessons are open to interpretation. By withdrawing into secularism, Democrats deprive Americans of an important debate. Public reason seeks not to banish religion or its citizens from modern politics but to encourage them to offer rationale claims about basic justice.

REFERENCES

Abrajano, M., & Hajnal, Z. (2015). *White backlash: Immigration, race, and american politics*. Princeton, NJ: Princeton University Press.

Akerlof, G., Yellen, J., & Katz, M. (1996). An analysis of out of wedlock childbearing in the United States. *The Quarterly Journal of Economics*, 277–303.

Barber, M., & McCarty, N. (2013). Causes and consequences of polarization. In *Task force on negotiating agreement in politics*. American Political Science Association. Retrieved from http://www.apsanet.org/portals/54/Files/Task%20 Force%20Reports/Chapter2Mansbridge.pdf

Boston, R. (2003). *Why the religious right is wrong about separation of church & state* (2nd ed.). Amherst, NY: Prometheus Books.

Cahn, R., & Carbone, J. (2010). *Red families v. blue families: legal polarization and the creation of culture*. New York: Oxford University Press.

Carey, J., Niemi, R., & Powell, L. (2000). *Term Limits in the State Legislatures*. Ann Arbor, MI: University of Michigan Press.

Coleman, J., Goldstein, K., & Howell, W. (2011). *Understanding American politics and government*. New York: Longman.

Conlan, T., & Posner, P. (2011). Inflection point? Federalism and the Obama administration. *Publius*, *41*(3), 421–446. doi:10.1093/publius/pjr020

Constitutional Rights Foundation. (1991 Spring). *Bill of Rights in Action*. Retrieved from http://www.crf-usa.org/bill-of-rights-in-action/bria-7-4-b-the-14th-amendment-and-the-second-bill-of-rights

Crane, W., & Watts, M. W. (1968). *State legislative systems*. Englewood Cliffs, NJ: Prentice-Hall, Inc.

Drucker, P. (1956, July). Organized Religion and the American Creed. *The Review of Politics*, 296.

Ehrenhalt, A. (2015, January). Divided we stand. *Governing*. Retrieved from http://www.governing.com/columns/assessments/gov-divided-we-stand.html

Ericson, D., & Green, L. (1999). The Liberal tradition in American politics: Reassessing the legacy of American liberalism. New York: Routledge.

Friedman, L. M., & Schreiber, H. N. (Eds.). (1988). *American law and the constitutional order: Historical perspectives*. Cambridge, MA: Harvard University Press.

Hajnal, Z., & Rivera, M. (2014). Immigration, Latinos, and White partisan politics: The new Democratic defection. *American Journal of Political Science*, *58*(4), 773–789.

Hartz, L. (1955). *The liberal tradition in America: An interpretation of American political thought since the revolution*. New York: Harcourt Brace.

Hunter, J. (1991). *Culture wars: The struggle to define America*. New York: Basic Books.

Jefferson, T. (1802) Jefferson's Letter to the Danbury Baptists. *Library of Congress*. Retrieved from https://www.loc.gov/loc/lcib/9806/danpre.html

Lipset, S. (1997). *American exceptionalism: A double edged sword*. New York: W.W. Norton.

Locke, J. (1689). A Letter Concerning Toleration [Letter to Philip von Limborch]. *Constitution Organization*. Retrieved from http://www.constitution.org/jl/tolerati.html

Longacre, C. S. (2016, May). The "Holy Common Wealth". *Liberty*.

McElroy, W. (2013 December 1). Roger Williams: The Separation of Conscience and State. *The Future Freedom Foundation*. Retrieved from http://www.fff.org/explore-freedom/article/roger-williams-the-separation-of-conscience-and-state

Moncrief, G. F., Squire, P., & Jewell, M. E. (2001). *Who runs for the legislature?* Upper Saddle River, NJ: Prentice Hall.

National Conference of State Legislatures. (2013). *The Term Limited States*. Retrieved from http://www.ncsl.org

Nelson, A. (1991). *Emerging influentials in state legislatures: Women, blacks, and Hispanics*. New York: Praeger.

Norberg, J., & Newton, M. (2015). The effect of term limits on patterns of interest group contributions in state legislatures, 2006–2010. *Interest Groups & Advocacy, 40*(3), 283–296. https://doi.org/10.1057/iga.2015.6

Novak, W. J. (2008). A state of legislatures. *Polity*, *40*(3), 340. doi:10.1057/pol.2008.6

Pallay, G. (2013). Who Runs the States: Part 1: Partisanship of the 50 states between 1992-2013? *Ballotepedia*. Retrieved from https://ballotpedia.org/Ballotpedia:Who_Runs_the_States

Reid, P. (2003). *Constitutional history of the American Revolution: The authority to legislate*. The University of Wisconsin Press.

Rocha, R. (2013, March 21). *Multiple or Malleable Traditions in American Politics? Insights from the Intersection of Immigration, Social Capital, and Welfare Policy*. Retrieved from https://wpsa.research.pdx.edu/papers/docs/Rocha%20WPSA%202013%20March%2021%202013.pdf

Rodgers, D. (1998). Exceptionalism. In A. Molho & G. S. Wood (Eds.), *Imagined Histories: American Historians Interpret the Past*. Princeton University Press.

Shor, B., & McCarty, N. (2011, August). The ideological mapping of American legislatures. *The American Political Science Review*, *105*(03), 530–551. doi:10.1017/S0003055411000153

Stone, D. A. (1997). *Policy paradox: the art of political decision making* (Rev. ed.). New York: Norton.

Storey, T. (2014). Republicans reached historic highs following this year's election. *State Legislature Magazine*. Retrieved from http://www.ncsl.org/research/elections-and-campaigns/scaling-new-heights.aspx

Wuthnow, R. (1988). *The restructuring of American religion*. Princeton, NJ: Princeton University Press.

Yee, A. (2016, January 14). Southern state legislatures: More male, more religious, more racially diverse. *Facing the South*. Retrieved from https://www.facingsouth.org/2016/01/southern-state-legislatures-more-male-more-religion

KEY TERMS AND DEFINITIONS

Culture: Ways of thinking or modes of behavior.

Conservative: For the purposes of this book, it is used to mean political and religious ideologies which seek to preserve the status quo.

Evangelical: Christians who actively seek proselytize and convert others and can be of a variety of political perspectives (includes Pentecostal and charismatic Christians).

Equality: The value that all Americans should be treated the same under the law, be able to influence government, and have an equal opportunity to succeed in life.

Federalism: A form of government that distributes power between national and subnational governments.

Individualism: A belief that all individuals should be able to succeed based on their talents and abilities regardless of group characteristics.

Liberal: For the purpose of this book, a person who favors a political philosophy of progress and the protection of civil liberties.

Liberty: The beliefs that government should allow people the freedom to do as they please with interference from the government.

Nullification: The theory that states have the right to nullify national laws to which they object and believe violate the U.S. Constitution.

Pluralism: Theory that all groups are well represented and single interest controls government decisions.

Polarization: Ideological divisions that create divergence on a range of issues based on a set of beliefs.

Protestant Reformation: Reformation: a religious movement of the 16th century that began as an attempt to reform the Roman Catholic Church and resulted in the creation of Protestant churches.

Religious Freedom: Freedom of religion or Freedom of belief is a principle that supports the freedom of an individual or community, in public or private, to manifest religion or belief in teaching, practice, worship, and observance; the concept is generally recognized also to include the freedom to change religion.

Term Limits: A term limit is a legal restriction that limits the number of terms an officeholder may serve in a particular elected office.

ENDNOTES

1 Commitment to an external, definable and transcendent authority which defines a consistent, unchangeable measure of value, purpose and identity (Hunter, 1991 p. 44).

2 Puritans later became known as Congregationalists.

3 Nebraska is the only state in the nation to have a unicameral (single-chamber) legislature and also the only state to have a nonpartisan legislature that is neither elected nor formally organized along party lines.

4 In 24 states, the legislature is simply called the "Legislature," or the "State Legislature," while in 19 states, the legislature is called the "General Assembly." In Massachusetts and New Hampshire, the legislature is called the "General Court," while North Dakota and Oregon designate the legislature as the "Legislative Assembly" (National Council of State Legislatures, 2013).

APPENDIX

Table 1. States with term limits (National Conference of State Legislatures, 2013)

State	Year Enacted	Limit	Year of Impact
Maine	1993	8	1996
California	1990	12[c]	1996
Colorado	1990	8	1998
Arkansas	1992	6	1998
Michigan	1992	6	1998
Florida	1992	8	2000
Ohio	1992	8	2000
South Dakota	1992	8	2000
Montana	1992	8	2000
Arizona	1992	8	2000
Missouri[a]	1992	8	2002
Oklahoma	1990	12[c]	2004
Louisiana	1995	12	2007
Nevada[b]	1996	12	2010
Nebraska	2000	12	2008

[a] Because of special elections, term limits were effective in 2000 for eight current members of the House and one Senator in 1998.

[b]The Nevada Legislative Council and Attorney General ruled that Nevada's term limits could not be applied to those legislators elected in the same year term limits were passed (1996). They first applied to persons elected in 1998.

[c] In California and Oklahoma, a legislator may serve a total of 12 years in the legislature during his or her lifetime. The total time may be split between the two chambers, or spent in its entirely in a single chamber. Before 2012, California's limits were identical to those in Arkansas: 6 years in the assembly and eight years in the senate.

Chapter 2
Emergence of Faith and Politics at the State Level

ABSTRACT

This chapter describes the ideological forms and beliefs that are considered either evangelical or liberal. The differences between these two types of faith worldviews influence legislative decision making and inform culture. To the extent that gay issues represent a cultural divide between religious traditionalism and progressivism policy outcomes are impacted by these differences.

After giving my life to Christ, I recognized how important it is that people of faith participate in the public square. I have tried to follow the principles of my faith in all aspects of my life, including my involvement in politics ~ Georgia Senator Josh McKoon

INTRODUCTION

Faith disputes over values have a long political history in the United States. From the mid-1800's forward, waves of Catholic immigrants poured into the United States. This phenomenon produced a cultural divide in political loyalties. As the Catholic-Protestant split grew, political issues took on overtones reflecting the religious division. Although such disputes have a highly symbolic edge to them because many morality policies are rarely enforced, Gusfield (1963)

DOI: 10.4018/978-1-5225-2388-8.ch002

argues that these disputes should be seen as attempts to redistribute values, to put the government's stamp of approval on one set of values rather than another. The Temperance movement was an attempt by rural, Protestant, native-born citizens to establish the superiority of their values over those of urban, Catholic immigrants. Accordingly, morality policy is similar to redistributive policy; the main difference being that the redistributed good is not money or government programs, but values. Protestant voters were disproportionately Republican, whereas most Catholics became Democrats. The process resembles that of redistributive politics except groups seek to redistribute values (not income) by having government put its stamp of approval or disapproval on a specified set of values (Gusfield, 1963; Goggin, 1993; Meier, 1994).

This type of redistribution of values continues, protestant fundamentalists by playing a key role in the introduction and passage of bans on same-sex marriage, whether through the legislature or at the ballot box (Barclay & Fisher, 2003; Haider-Markel, 2001). In morality politics, partisanship tends to play an important role. In particular, the Republican Party's focus on traditional family values is strongly associated with less support for gay civil rights and same-sex marriage (Lindaman & Haider-Markel, 2002). Those disputes are over deeply held values, compromise solutions rarely attract any support. Morality politics, like redistributive politics tends to be partisan, seek non-incremental solutions, focus on deeply held values, and flourish in areas with competitive political parties (Ripley & Franklin, 1991; Lowi, 1969). Two examples of this kind of discourse come from legislative hearings in Connecticut and floor debate in Minnesota on same-sex partner recognition:

Marriage is more than a bundle of rights. It also promotes stability in relationships… These couples do not seek to weaken marriage in any way. On the contrary, they want to pledge themselves to adhere to all of its great criteria and ideals. Love, fidelity, intimacy, financial support, health care responsibility, mutuality. Marriage needs more of that kind of commitment, not less. (Connecticut General Assembly, 2002)

We should be encouraging people to make these life-long commitments. We should be proud that people want to do that… I want to defend marriage too. If others want to be married, I like to see commitments like that. That is what we are as human beings: People who have the capacity to love and care for others. (Minnesota Senate, 1997)

Understanding the nature of the rhetoric and the manner in which it is used are crucial in understanding the impacts on the sociopolitical scene. The importance of language and symbols is very real, since the side that control the 'buzzwords' in politics often controls the outcome (Moen, 1992, p. 128). The strategy is to wed a selected set of biblical imperatives with their particular vision of the public good in such a manner that their message may be embraced by ostensibly democratic pluralistic society. These messages are appealing to preferences and predilections which are historically rooted in American culture (Hopson & Smith, 1999). The "taken for granted" presuppositions which underlie language are essential in understanding the effect of such language on public perceptions, preferences and practices. Such concepts as "strong families," "traditional values," "freedom of religion," and "morality," have deep positive resonances within the U.S. body politic (Moen, 1992). Conversely, terms such as "liberal," "humanism," or "homosexual," conjures threatening and repulsive images for many. For traditionally minded legislators, the "liberalization" of social mores and standards provides both a rallying point of opposition as well as sanction for unambiguous, self-definition (absolutism) in opposition to liberalization. The "moral direction" of the nation finds sympathetic constituents across the spectrum of a public constantly exposed to "newsworthy examples of social incoherency" (Postman, 1985). Declaration of fidelity to "morality" sounds like a clarion call for stances that are easily blended with political absolutes.

Cultural outsiders are deemed immoral and contestable issues are divided into morally right or wrong. The language of the Bible resonates throughout American history, so it is not surprising that this language plays an important role in the legislator's development of these ideological constructs in political discourse. Reality is created through talking—through words transmitted over the air or through paper or electronic media. These words, anchored in history, have the power to create community or contest. The methods people actually use to make meanings and provide accounts are "interpretative procedures" (Cicourel, 1970) required by all people to participate in the process of making reality that sustains the presumption of objectivity. Grice (1975) refers to interaction as inevitably involving "conversational implicature," in which participants use, and allow others to use, context as means of constituting the meaning of a word or utterance.

Many legislators base political decisions purely on faith based reasons (Klemp, 2007). Prior research clearly has shown the key role that religious affiliation plays in defining the debate in relation to sexual orientation issues (Barclay & Fisher, 2003). Schroedel's (1999) study of political elites and

Lewis and Roger's (1999) study of Gallup and CNN polls demonstrated the role of religion in influencing an individual's position on gay issues. To the extent that gay issues represent a cultural division between traditionalism and progressivism, this chapter describes the responses of state legislators for and against same-sex marriage.

BACKGROUND

American Protestantism is understood not as a single religious tradition but rather as three distinct traditions – the evangelical Protestant tradition, the mainline Protestant tradition and the historically black Protestant tradition (Pew Research Center, 2015). Each of these traditions is made up of numerous denominations and congregations that share similar beliefs, practices and histories. These denominational families, in turn, are made up of a host of different denominations, all with unique beliefs, practices and histories. Congregations are organizations with core cultural and religious activities that promote their religious vision of society and protect their interests through political activity (Becker, 1999; Chaves, 2004; Ammerman, 2005; Djupe & Gilbert, 2009).

As studies of fundamentalist movements repeatedly made clear, they cannot simply be explained at the level of ideas which can then conveniently be dismissed as irrational (Liebman & Wuthnow, 1983). Fundamentalism arose in the nineteenth century as a reaction against both intellectual and social change (Gill, 1998). Its aim has been to reject modernity and its appeal has been to those either socially marginalized or psychologically discomfited by the pluralism and fragmentation of modern life. It is important to note, too that because fundamentalism has been a broad cultural response to the insecurities of contemporary society, its appeal has not been restricted denominationally to Protestants (King & Nugent, 1979). For the same reason, the attractiveness, viability and significance of such movements have been crucially influenced by their social context. Ammerman (1991) notes that fundamentalism has been the most politically active and culturally visible following periods of major social change. It is a reaction usually based on profound fear and defensiveness against "losing the faith."

According to Smith (1998), the emphasis on the literal nature of the scriptures and on the divinity and return of Jesus Christ found in fundamentalism are often accompanied by a belief in postmillennialism and premillennialism. The belief espoused by postmillennialist doctrines is that Jesus will have a second coming only after the millennial period of peace and harmony on earth. This framework drives believers to attempt to do a great deal of work to establish a moral society in order to prepare for the second coming of Jesus Christ. Premillennialism also is a common belief among fundamentalists. In this view of the millennial period, the second coming of Christ occurs before the thousand-year period of peace, so there is less of a drive to establish of a morally perfect society. To the uninitiated, the intricacies of millennialism sound foreign but these ideas have and continue to influence the thoughts and choices the daily lives of millions of evangelicals.

THE CULTURAL DIVIDE: LIBERAL VS. CONSERVATIVES

Churches within the evangelical tradition tend to share religious beliefs (including the conviction that personal acceptance of Jesus Christ is the only way to salvation), practices (like an emphasis on bringing other people to the faith) and origins (including separatist movements against established religious institutions). Churches in the mainline tradition, by contrast, share other doctrines (such as a less exclusionary view of salvation), practices (such as a strong emphasis on social reform) and origins.

Bellah et al. (1991) argued that the alliance between mainline Protestant denominational authorities and the "liberal democratic welfare state" cost mainline Protestantism its membership as persons developed resentment against "big government" and "big religion." The increasing success of faith driven conservative candidates at the grass roots level (e.g. Municipal and State legislative offices) suggested increased political influence within the Republican Party. An unprecedented 78% of white self-identified "born again Christians" voted Republican in 1994 (Kirkland, 1995). Though many of those self-identified as "born again" do not identify with a religious pressure group, the ideological alliances evident among those groups and the diffusion of their political ideals and rhetoric came together for the election of traditional legislators across the political landscape.

Evangelical goals are to "restore the Christian character of American culture and to provide a Christian solution for social problems of modern society" (Lechner, 1989, p. 56). The concerns arising after "disintegration of American society during the 1960s led to a quest to return to an earlier homogeneity and orthodoxy. Political realignment during the 1970s and 1980s saw the demise of the Democratic stronghold of the South as Southerner' s resonated with the discourse of the Republican party, and religious leaders began to preach the necessity of conservative religious activism in the political sphere (Ammerman, 1991, p. 39). Conservative Protestant groups have experienced significant growth during the past decades, particularly in comparison with older mainline Protestant denominations. While the mainline Protestants' share of the population is significantly smaller today than it was in 2007, the evangelical Protestant share of the population has remained comparatively stable (ticking downward slightly from 26.3% to 25.4% of the population). As a result, evangelicals now constitute a clear majority (55%) of all U.S. Protestants. In 2007, roughly half of Protestants (51%) identified with evangelical churches (Pew Research Center, 2015).

The political views of legislators are linked to an organic moral worldviews; their opinions, values, and convictions are not merely tools that they use, but are a part of a moral worldview out of which arise their religious and political perspectives. By moral worldview, the author means not only the ethical principles of what is right and wrong, but also the "symbolic boundaries by which preferences are molded", values are shaped, and behaviors are managed (Smith 2003). These legislators' moral and political worldviews offer mutual benefits and form a reciprocal bond. The conservative American religious moral worldview supports a strong social conservatism, promotes a traditional family model, opposes same-sex marriage, and advocates against abortion.

This conservative political moral worldview promotes a laissez-faire market economy, lower taxes and the creation of opportunities for entrepreneurs to found new markets, at home and abroad; it favors the spread of democracy abroad for the sake of its political and economic liberty and the religious markets it opens for evangelical proselytizing (Frank 2004; Sharlet 2005). Within the there is a larger evangelical community there holds a set of common cultural characteristics, or what has been called a "civic gospel," that includes the belief that evangelical conversion will address and solve social problems; the government should protect America's religious heritage; the United States was founded as a Christian nation; the promotion of democracy around the world; advocacy for economic, religious, and political liberty (Kellstedt & Green 2003, Wellman 2008); This "civic gospel" has historical roots that have combined a religious vision with a social, economic, and political strategy that is perceived as natural and normal by legislators in their speeches throughout the same-sex marriage. These expressions are neither a superficial ideological instrument nor a passing cultural infatuation, and are suggested by this research to be deeply held moral worldviews (Wellman & Keyes, 2007) and are a key factor in bill sponsorship.

THE CASES

The 1970s and 1980s are marked by several cases[1] in which same-sex couples sought relief for the denial of marriage licenses. The cases took place in several states over the course of two decades, each plaintiff litigating on different constitutional grounds. In keeping with the desire to end discrimination, the first same-sex marriage case began on May 18, 1970. Richard Baker and James McConnell applied for a marriage license in Minneapolis. The clerk denied the request and the couple filed suit. October 15, 1971, the Minnesota Supreme Court in *Baker v. Nelson* (1971) affirmed the trial courts dismal. This was the first appellate decision in the United States on the issue of same-sex marriage. Not another case was brought for 20 years (Eskridge, 1996, p. 48). The Minnesota Supreme Court ruled that a state law limiting marriage to persons of the opposite sex did not violate the U.S. Constitution. The decision was appealed. The United States Supreme Court on October 10, 1972, dismissed the appeal "for want of a substantial federal question" 409 U.S. 810 (1972). Because the case came to the U.S. Supreme Court through mandatory appellate review (not certiorari), the dismissal constituted a decision on the merits and established the decision as precedent[2] (Winnick, 1976).

The case of *Bowers v. Hardwick* (1986) United States Supreme Court decision upheld the constitutionality of a Georgia sodomy law criminalizing oral and anal sex between consenting adults; the issue in Bowers centered on the right of privacy. Since the 1960s, the Court held that a right to privacy was implicit in the due process clause of the Fourteenth Amendment to the United States Constitution. In Bowers, the Court held that this right to privacy did not extend to private, consensual sexual conduct, at least if that conduct involved same-sex sodomy (Eskridge, 1996). The majority opinion in Bowers, written by Justice Byron White, framed the legal question as whether the constitution creates "a fundamental right to engage in homosexual sodomy." Justice White's opinion for the majority answered this question in the negative, stating that "to claim that a right to engage in such conduct is "deeply rooted in this Nation's history and tradition or implicit in the concept of ordered liberty is, at best, facetious" (White, 1986). The concurring opinion by Chief Justice Warren E. Burger emphasized historical negative attitudes toward sodomy, quoting Sir William Blackstone's characterization of sodomy as "a crime not fit to be named." Burger concluded, "To hold that the act of homosexual sodomy is somehow protected as a fundamental right would be to cast aside millennia of moral teaching" (Burger, 1986).

In 1963, the U.S. Supreme Court in *Sherbert v. Verner* (1963), established the Sherbert Test[3], based on the first amendment's free exercise clause. Adell Sherbert was a Seventh Day Adventist who was fired when she would not work on Saturday which was her Sabbath based on her religious beliefs. She was later denied unemployment compensation. The Court ruled that this denial was an unconstitutional burden on her free exercise of religion. The case established the Sherbert Test, as it has come to be known, essentially placing the burden of proof on the government and requiring a demonstration of a compelling interest where a religious person was substantially burdened by a law (*Sherbert v. Verner,* 1963).

Beginning with an Oregon case *Employment Division v. Smith* (1990) the Supreme Court eliminated the *Sherbert Test* because it was too broad when applied to all laws. The ruling meant that government no longer had to justify burdens on the free exercise of religion as long as these burdens were "merely the incidental effect of a generally applicable and otherwise valid provision. Simultaneously, in Hawaii

Baehr v. Anderson (1990) launched the ongoing national discussion over same-sex marriage. These court battles, at the time were seemingly unrelated mobilized religious conservative legislators into action to protect religious freedom and stop the possibility of same-sex marriage.

These legislators, mainly evangelical Protestants mobilized to restrict marriage to heterosexual couples (Green, 2014; Herman, 2000; Soule, 2004). This state-level political conflict promised to have national implications. In subsequent months, as legislators in Massachusetts struggled to comply with the court's ruling; President Bush suggested the possibility of amending the U.S. Constitution to codify marriage as between a man and a woman. In his 2004 State of the Union address, he said: "If judges insist on forcing their arbitrary will upon the people, the only alternative left to the people would be the constitutional process. Our nation must defend the sanctity of marriage."

In 1996, South Carolina Representative Gary Simrill, a Baptist Republican passed House Bill 4502 which prohibited the recognition of same-sex marriages from other states (People for the American Way Foundation, 2000). In the aftermath of the decision, there was a widely-shared sense that free exercise protections had been seriously weakened, if not completely dismantled. The standard of strict scrutiny approach to free exercise suffered a severe blow in the Supreme Court decision in *Oregon Employment Division v. Smith,* overruling the *Sherbet* Test. South Carolina responded to the decision, Republican Senator George "Chip" Campsen, a Deacon at East Cooper Baptist Church sponsored and passed House Bill 3158 "Religious Freedom Act" (RFRA).

Another, South Carolina legislator in 2005, Representative Greg Delleney a Republican church Elder at the evangelical Reformed Presbyterian Church sponsored House Joint Resolution 3133 amending the state constitution as defined as a union between a man and a woman. The bill passed the House by a 96-3 vote and passed the Senate on a voice vote. In 2006, voters ratified the measure.

Followed by Republican Representative Bill Chumley, a deacon at Poplar Baptist Church immediately responded by prefilling in December, 2014, House Bill 3022. The bill had multiple purposes, all designed to prohibit the use of taxpayer funds and payment of government salaries for activities related to the licensing and support of same-sex marriage.

Additional states, including Arizona, Georgia, Kansas, Michigan, South Carolina, and Wyoming, were likely to face strong efforts to pass such legislation. Variants of these types of bills all seek to undermine marriage equality by permitting officials and businesses to refuse to recognize marriages that do not comport with their religious beliefs. With the success of municipal advocacy as an avenue to achieve LGBT equality, it is increasingly likely to see bills limiting the ability of municipalities in a state to pass inclusive non-discrimination ordinances. This type of legislation will likely be introduced in Arkansas, and potentially other states. In 2014, through the federal courts, same-sex marriage was legalized in South Carolina. Responding to this decision in 2015 Republican Senator Lee Bright and a member of the Religious Liberty Commission for the Southern Baptist Convention sponsored Senate Bill 127 to amend the state's RFRA to specify that free exercise may not be restricted during local government proceedings. The amendment language:

No locality, municipality, county, or other instrumentality of this State may restrict the free exercise of speech or religion during the course of any of its proceedings in violation of the First Amendment of the United States or Article I, Section 2 of the Constitution of South Carolina. (Baptist Joint Committee, 2017)

A WORLDVIEW BASED ON FAITH

A worldview is a framework of basic beliefs that an individual holds; whether this fact is realized or not, it shapes a person's view of the world. Everyone, of course, has a worldview. The question is not if people have a worldview, but rather which worldview they have. More pragmatically, everyone brings their worldview to bear on issues of public policy. Faith worldview means not only the ethical principles of what is right and wrong, but also the "symbolic boundaries by which preferences are molded." Values are shaped, and behaviors are managed (Smith, 2003).

Within constructionist thought, a social construct refers to a concept or practice, which appears to be natural and obvious to those who accept it, but is actually an invention or artifact of a particular culture or society (Hacking, 1999). A social constructionist framework reveals the ways that individuals and groups participate in the creation of their social reality. This approach shows how social phenomena are created, institutionalized, and made into tradition by humans. When two or more individuals agree upon the interpretation of an event, a consensus about the event begins to form. One group, however, may have a certain set of agreed-upon or consensual truths, while another group holds a different set of beliefs as consensual truths. Whether the group is small or large, the truth—as seen and agreed upon by a certain set of people—becomes, in effect, the consensus reality (Hacking, 1999). Organized religion is an example of a socially constructed consensus reality with each religion arriving at a certain set of agreed upon truths or doctrines, which may differ from those of other religions.

Conventionally, words like, "religion," "belief" and "faith," are used interchangeably; however, in this chapter these are distinct concepts used by legislators to make decisions. Religion shares a common creed, "denotes a social group...a community of believers" who share "a common status" (Wald, 2003, p. 25). The status of a group may produce shared political preferences that are in the interest of the group, as is the case among legislators. Religion is often viewed as a system of beliefs in a higher power that involves a community of people who share similar beliefs and work together to provide both support and accountability for living up to those beliefs. These beliefs are codified beliefs into sacred texts and–by means of rituals and moral practices that create a philosophy of life, and a world view. The practice of religious beliefs, such as attending church is an example of a religious practice. Evangelicals believe that there is a difference between "belief" and "faith." Faith includes the element of belief, but they are not the same thing. As a dedicated follower of Jesus Christ, "true" faith is evidenced by a change in the way that someone acts (Driskell, 2001). Belief on the other hand can simply be a passive acceptance which may amount to no effects on someone's life. The relationship with God is based on "true" faith where God is revealed in someone's thoughts, actions and priorities. Beliefs are rooted in culture and upbringing.

The research literature finds that morality politics issues are highly salient with little need to acquire any information (technical or otherwise) to participate in the debate. Everyone is an expert on morality. The combination of high salience and low information structures the nature of the politics involved (Gormley, 1986; Lowi, 1969). Citizens, therefore, are active and influential in morality politics with coalitions often mobilized around preexisting religious beliefs. Politicians and political parties find morality issues attractive because the issues offer an easy way to build a political reputation or stereotype one's opponents. Politicians face no information barriers to participate (as in other policy areas such as health insurance reform) and can potentially accrue great benefits from the mobilized electorate. Given the known attempts at coordination between anti-gay-rights social movements and congregations (Smith et al., 2006; Djupe et al., 2007; Camp, 2008), and the expansion of "morality politics" into institutional political tactics (Haider-Markel & Meier, 1996), the concept of a legislator moral worldview helps explain their activity. This is particularly the case with same-sex marriage, and the tension between religious objectors. Because religious groups have explicit moral codes and by extension religious legislators are frequently significant players in morality politics. Religious groups and individuals may influence public policy either indirectly through public opinion or as an elected official who directly sponsoring a bill. The religious organizations likely to have the largest influence are Catholics and Protestant Fundamentalists because their religious doctrines are in conflict with gay behavior (Seltzer, 1993, p. 93).

FAITH DISPUTES AND LEGISLATIVE DECISIONMAKING

The theoretical framework of this chapter is social constructivism and involves an interpretative approach. Blumer (1969) notes two elements involved in the interpretative approach to the study of social phenomena. The first element is exploration, which he defines as an exploratory description, rigorously conducted, of the phenomena under study. The second element of the interpretative method is inspection, which consists of "an intensive focused examination and the empirical content of whatever analytical elements were used for purposes of analysis, and this same kind of examination of the empirical nature of the relations between such elements." Empirical content consists of those phenomena that appear in the area of study, and the analytical elements are those items employed in analyzing the subject matter (Gilsinan, 1989, 1991; Gilsinan & Valentine, 1987). To meet the requirements of the interpretative approach, this exploratory study used a qualitative research design that involved documentation through "thick description." Thick description employs "a multiplicity of complex conceptual structures, many of them superimposed upon or knotted to one another, which are at once strange, irregular, and inexplicit, and which [the researcher] must contrive somehow first to grasp and then to render" (Geertz, 1973). This method enabled the researcher to render an in-depth description of individual legislator actions taken on the same-sex marriage issue.

To begin evangelical and liberal Protestants are bracketed for comparison, these are not the only variations within American Protestantism. For the purposes of this chapter, these groups have relatively homogenous social and symbolic boundaries that comprise their worldview. The research interest of this chapter is in studying the process rather than the outcome, in describing and analyzing the context rather than specific variables, in discovery rather than confirmation (Merriam, 1998). With that goal in mind, the events that occurred in each situation described below provide a rich understanding of the of the legislative decision making.

Interpretation: A Worldview Based on Faith

A worldview based on faith not only shapes and guides values and actions, but they also create organizations and build forms of social and spiritual capital that provide structures of meaning and rewards (Wellman & Keyes, 2007). A worldview is an ordering structure and voices from outside of a particular worldview are unpersuasive because they are perceived as illegitimate and incoherent. Faith positions are not immune to change, but voices of critique must speak in an idiom that makes sense to adherents.

Liberal and evangelical Protestants have a distinct set of ideological and theological characteristics. The 'moral core' is the deepest, most influential layer of an individuals worldview that is a set of faith commitments that tell each group how to live. Each of these carries core convictions that are persistent and durable across time and against challenges (Wellman & Keyes, 2007). The political views of legislators are linked to a faith/moral worldview; their opinions, values, and convictions are not merely tools that they use, but are part of a moral worldview out of which arises their faith and political perspectives. Based on this research, several propositions are described below. These propositions and findings theoretically define and develop how these moral worldviews function at the individual legislator level. The judicial decisions serve as focusing events for legislative action. The Supreme Court[4] has long been a barometer of the nation's culture clashes. Beginning with Judge William Rehnquist's leadership of the Court in 1986, Supreme Court rulings have intensified the debates related to gay rights and religious objectors.

The conclusions offered serve to interconnect the categories and develop a discursive set of theoretical propositions. Given that the research uses a social constructivist perspective to analyze and describe the process of decision making same-sex marriage and religious freedom. Using Wellmans (2008) multilayer approach to describe the nature of evangelical and liberal legislator's worldviews within the states of South Carolina, Georgia and Minnesota legislator's by weaving together the events that occurred within these states a detailed description is constructed. The events were collected from a variety of information sources and then sorted into chronological order before the data was translated into Wellman's (2008) Moral Worldview model.

By describing these phenomena, I hope to contribute to the understanding of the process of constructing social realities and, more specifically, to the understanding how these realities impact legislator's decision-making.

Proposition 1: Moral worldviews are layered structures centered on a moral core in which certain values and opinions are given more weight than others (Wellman & Keyes, 2007). Individual legislators give more weight to values and opinions they perceive to be more directly connected to their moral core.

A visual metaphor for the moral worldview is a concentric circle. The model begins with the deepest layer that represents a person's center or moral core that is persistent and durable across time and challenges (Wellman & Keyes, 2007). Moral worldviews begin at the core and form the moral order of individuals which ultimately shapes their values and actions. Each layer of the circle is interconnected. Those who hold a moral worldview consider deeper layers more central, more important, and less negotiable than outer layers, where comprise is tolerated. This metaphor acknowledges that no two respondents' moral cores and worldviews are exactly the same, particularly in the outer, more negotiable layers. Nevertheless, I noticed in the data a relative consistent homogeneity between the legislators and voters that underlined the social construction of these moral worldviews. The second layer of the model consists of a person's values and beliefs and the third layer of the model contains the economic and political positions of the individual. The final layer of the model is composed an individual's set of culturally conditioned customs and manners, or protocols of social interaction.

Finding 1: The cultural and political views of legislators arise from a core faith worldview with a specific set of moral values.

The conservative cultural and political positions of legislators are neither instrumental nor incidental opinions. Whether on abortion, the death penalty, the Iraq War, or same-sex marriage, these positions are driven by underlying moral structures. Domke (2004), Lakoff (1996), Schudson (2002), Berger (1969), and Smith (1998, 2003) argue similarly that moral worldviews are central features of religious and other ideological movements. Religion (as measured by religious affiliation and attitudes about morality and secularism) has a powerful effect on attitudes towards same-sex marriage (Olsen, Cadge, & Harrison, 2006). Prioritization of moral values above issues is a significant predictor of opposition to same-sex marriage. Thus to assume that opposing gay rights is a key component of the notion of "morality" as a political issue (Olsen, Cadge, & Harrison, 2006); legislators who profess concern about moral values are motivated to sponsor legislation by their opposition to gay rights.

The rulings by Hawaii courts did trigger legislative movements by other states to enact bans on gay marriage. In 1996, following in the footsteps of several other states, Georgia Republican minister, Representative Ron Crews, originally introduced the 1996 legislation that defines marriage as, a union between a man and a woman, stating that he "would like to see the laws of our state conform to God's law" (People of the American Way, 1997). He further referenced *Bowers v. Hardwick* (1986) Supreme Court case that upheld Georgia's sodomy law. He explained that Georgia's courts have never recognized same-sex marriages and that from Bowers, "it follows that Georgia does not recognize same-sex marriages" (Davis, 1996). Georgia Senator Gochenour stated that the law was grounded both in morality and economics. He said that the state is not required to recognize a marriage granted in another state "if it be offensive to the morals and customs of its society, and is contrary to its established public policy" (Davis, 1996).

In March 31, 2004, the Georgia State Legislature passed Senate Resolution 595 states that legal marriages in the State of Georgia are to be limited to those unions between biological men and biological women. When SR 595 passed the state legislature, it also placed a state constitutional amendment on the 2004 election ballot as a referendum, to be voted on by the citizens of the State of Georgia. Legislators and lobbyists alike fought a rather intense battle over this issue while public attention and debate escalated. Politicians also have publicly laid claim to religion as part of their arguments. Georgia State Representative Barbara Bunn, an opponent to same-sex marriages, stated during the House of Representatives debate on March 31, 2004, "We've been called bigots, called full of hate and hate-filled. But the Judeo-Christian values that have held our society together for all these years is not equated to bigotry and hate" (Lee 2004). By stating this, Bunn clearly defines this issue as, for her, one of religious significance. She further stated that the recognition of marriage between persons of the same-sex legislators, said "...the Judeo Christian values that have held our society together for all these years is not equated to bigotry and hate..." (Lee, 2004). Other Republican legislators expressed that what was at "stake is the foundation of our civilization" and "we all know the story of Sodom and Gomorrah" (Lee, 2004). Faith was invoked to preserve the sanctity of marriage.

Whereas, Democrat State Representative Nan Orrock said that,

...this is wrapped in religious rhetoric; we've heard time and time again... volumes of history are full of speeches waiving religious doctrine to embrace segregation and slavery, to justify the Jim Crow laws, to marginalize women... (Wilson, 2004)

The states advertised marriage as a fundamental institution linking it to political citizenship. This argument stated that everyone can get married... any consenting nonrelated couple-except lesbian or gay couples. Republican Georgia State Representative, a Lutheran Sue Burmeister stated that:

Ladies and Gentleman of the House. Gay marriage is not about rights; it is not about hate or bigotry. No one is preventing homosexuals from living together. All homosexuals have a right to get married and to have that marriage sanctioned by the state. They just have to marry someone of the opposite sex. The same right I have, that's what marriage means and has always meant. If society is forced to redefine marriage then we are establishing new and special rights, these rights will not be created in a vacuum without consequences to our society. We will have eroded one of the fundamental supports of our society. Do we in an age of multiculturalism, secularism and tolerance abandon the moral pillars upon which our society is built? Our Christian founding fathers built a system on Judeo Christian roots, which they believed would guarantee not threaten political and religious freedom. They designed a governmental system grounded in the laws of nature, established by the God they believe created them in his image. God's design for marriage is not simply some lofty spiritual ideal. The Bible also outlines a specific plan for human sexuality.

Throughout scripture God's intention for human sexual relationships is clearly limited to the heterosexual union between a man and a woman in marriage. Marriage is not an evolving paradigm. It is deeply rooted in the history, culture and tradition of civil society. It predates our constitution and our nation. Activists also claim that legalizing same sex marriage is the only way these couples may enjoy hospital visitation rights or inherit their deceased partner's estate. This is a smoke screen to distract people from the more serious implications of radically redefining marriage, except when a doctor limits visitation for medical reasons, final authority over who may visit an adult patient rests with that patient with a simple and inexpensive of Power of Attorney or Healthcare Proxy same sex couples have access to hospital visitations. In this case, as in many others, the rights they seek are already available without the redefinition of marriage. The same is true of inheritance rights. Nothing in current law prevents homosexual partners from being joint owners of property such as a home or a car, in which case their survivor would automatically become the owner if the partner dies.

An individual may leave the remainder of his or her estate to whomever he or she wishes without regard to sexual orientation or marital status with a simple Will. Entire estates have been left to trees, and cats and other peculiar survivors.

I am going to leave you with something Stanley Kurtz recently wrote and he wrote, "The difficulties and challenges of homosexuals are special precisely because they do not derive from the "discrimination" of marriage. The real source of the challenges of gay life is the problem of sexual difference. It is terribly difficult to grow up with a different sort of sexuality than most of the world around you. Marriage does not cause this problem and it cannot solve it. (Wilson, 2004)

Also, in 2004, the Georgia Legislature responded to Atlanta enforcing its anti-discrimination ordinance bypassing a law intended to undermine the ability of localities to enforce their duly passed laws. The situation arose when Atlanta Mayor Shirley Franklin ordered the city solicitor to fine the Druid Hills Golf Club for violating the city's anti-discrimination ordinance when it refused to provide spousal benefits to domestic partners. Republican State Representative Earl Erhart sponsored House Bill 67 declaring that, "Any organization or person may elect to, or elect not to, contractually provide to unmarried persons, one or more benefits … that such organization or person …provides to married persons" (Human Rights Campaign, 2004). Thus, any person, employer, club or organization can treat spouses and domestic partners differently and not be in violation of local laws prohibiting discrimination.

Proposition 2: Social groups often share similar moral worldviews, but individual moral worldviews always exhibit some form of differentiation. Differentiation of moral beliefs between individual legislators in a social group will increase as one moves away from the core of the worldview to the outer layers that are perceived as more negotiable (Wellman & Keyes, 2007).

The moral worldviews of layers of legislators are categorized into four analytic strata. For an Evangelical legislator this core or the first layer is the legislator's moral worldview such as a personal relationship with Jesus Christ, based on an act of submission to the authority of their "Lord." This act of allegiance is intimate and intensely subjective. It is intimate in that this submission is not merely intellectual, but is an emotional commitment that is cultivated endlessly through worship, prayer, ritual, and personal piety. It is subjective in that it centers on a personal decision by each individual that engages the core identity of the self (Carpenter & Shenk, 1990). The intimacy and subjective nature of this core is not only continuously nurtured, but also socially constructed. Church leadership molds how these personal decisions should be made and how one should feel about them in the process. Indeed, the transformation of this personal core is central to what many pastors mention as an "authentic" faith. Moreover, this "new self" is the necessary engine of social change. Thus, the transformed self is not only the font of religious salvation; it also is viewed as the cultural and political change within a community as well (Carpenter & Shenk, 1990).

From this core arises a second layer of values considered "moral." This second layer focuses on honesty, integrity, service, traditional sexual morality, devotion to family, and hard work. Liberals embody forms of modernism and personal autonomy, while evangelicals advocate a stringent personal and scriptural traditionalism. Calling for conservative and traditional values around heterosexual marriage over against what is believed to be the political imposition of same-sex marriage by an elite liberal culture. These values are considered unconditionally, absolute. This certainty shields evangelicals against external criticisms and the values of cultural and religious others because voices from outside are unpersuasive because within the bounds of their reality these are illegitimate and incoherent. Thus liberal moral worldviews and critiques that stem from them make no more sense to evangelicals than evangelical critiques do liberals (Wellman 1999, 2002, 2007).

Minnesota, in 1997, the same Legislature passed the "Defense of Marriage Act,'' which restricted marriage to only opposite-sex couples. A year later, Representative Karen Clark introduced a bill to repeal it and allow gay marriage.

It took 16 years, which came two years after the 2011 Legislature -- put an amendment on the statewide ballot asking voters to cement the existing gay marriage ban in the state constitution (Condon, 2013). While on the House floor defending her quest to legalize gay marriage, she was praised from Republicans who opposed the bill. Representative Tony Cornish, from a rural area said…

I don't know of a kinder, gentler woman on this floor that has a bigger heart for the environment, the underprivileged, the downtrodden, the American Indian, especially the women. I admire you. (Condon, 2013)

Economic and political positions are the third layer do not completely coincide with moral positions and mirror the Republican rationales for less government, stronger military, expanding economic markets, and advocacy for democracy. The fourth layer is composed of culturally conditioned customs such as manners, etiquette, and cuisine.

Socially conservative, George Campsen was elected in 1996 to the South Carolina House of Representatives and served until 2003 when he was elected to the State Senate (Cohen et al., 2015). Eighteen years later, as the sponsor of Senate Bill 221 "Student Association Freedom of Religion Act," he is leading the efforts that prohibit any public institution of Higher Learning from enforcing any policy that denies a religious student association any benefit available to any other student association based on the religious student association's requirement that its leaders or members adhere to its sincerely held religious beliefs or standards of conduct (Condon, 2013).

Finding 2: The views of legislators arise from the core of their moral worldview and are a specific set of values. These values are at the heart of fueling the sentiments of individual legislators that comprise the larger traditional values movement.

For legislators, this moral layer calls for conservative and traditional values around heterosexual marriage. From this personal center or core arises a second layer of values or beliefs that legislators consider moral. This type of morality is a descriptive concept broadly constructed to describe a set of moral beliefs.

In June of 2016, deeply Republican South Carolina elected its first openly gay legislator and hailed from the ultra-conservative part of the state that is home to the Christian fundamentalist school Bob Jones University. Republican Representative Jason Elliott, a 46-year-old divorce attorney, said his sexual orientation was not an issue in his campaign and is irrelevant to his job at the Statehouse. He expects his votes to align with his GOP colleagues and said that…

Every South Carolinian has equal rights, not special rights, and I believe each part of the constitution is equally important...in South Carolina, that means respecting other people's viewpoints and protecting religious freedom. (Cope, 2016)

Proposition 3: Moral worldviews are powerful and persuasive to the extent that they achieve perceived coherence, congruency, and integrity. Thus, individuals will abandon previous values and opinions in favor of new ones that seem more congruent with their moral core (Wellman & Keyes, 2007).

The concentric circle suggests that, all else being equal, individuals will adapt the outer layers in such a way that they perceive them to be more congruent with their moral core. I do not believe that legislators and voters employ moral positions instrumentally. Their opinions are not simply "tools" from their toolbox. They spring from a core of personal allegiance which, while socially constructed, they are emotionally and subjectively convincing and legitimized by the conviction that they believe to be morally right.

This proposition addresses how people may reconcile or dismiss potential conflicts between the foundational and more external layers of their moral worldview. Many Christians view of homosexuality (same-sex marriage) is based on Biblical teaching and they regard it as contrary to God's will; suggesting a conflict between traditional Christian morality and social change in Western society. Jim Wallis recalls,

...as an evangelical teenager being told by my church that Christian faith had nothing to do with either racism or war. The evangelical folks I grew up with finally became involved in politics and now insist that faith indeed has real political implications. The issues that drew them in were the cultural breakdown of American society. (Wallis, 1994)

As evidenced by a statement made by Georgia State Representative Douglas Dean, who voted against the constitutional amendment to ban same-sex marriage said: "I was raised just like most people were raised—that was to look down on gays, not because they weren't good people, but because we disagreed with their lifestyles. But I thought we had changed" (Wilson, 2004).

Finding 3: Legislators' and voters' moral worldviews are perceived as absolute and above culture, and thus can withstand criticism (Wellman & Keyes, 2007).

Minnesota legislators responded to the *Baker v. Nelson* (1971) case by introducing bills to Senate File 178 and House File 61 to ensure that marriage was clearly defined as between a man and women. Allan H. Spear was elected to the Minnesota State Senate, the same year that the first same-sex marriage case was decided by the U.S. Supreme Court. Shortly after the 1973 legislative session adjourned, Allan [Spear] wrote a letter on his Senate stationery to Majority Leader Nick Coleman, expressing his appreciation for Coleman's effort to include gay and lesbian people in the state's proposed Human Rights Act. The Minnesota Senate had been the first state legislative body in the country to pass a gay rights bill, but the House didn't follow suit and the bill died. In 1974 Senator Spear came out as the nation's first gay man serving as a legislator. Thereafter, session after session, the Legislature never came closer. Any satisfaction would have to wait another 20 years for fulfillment. Thereafter, session after session, the Legislature never came closer. Any satisfaction would have to wait another 20 years for fulfillment. On March 18, 1993 the debate on Senate File 444 – "The Human Rights Act" began. Senator Spear outlined how the bill would prohibit discrimination based on sexual orientation in housing, employment, public accommodations, public service, access to education and access to credit. He countered the argument that it would offer special privileges to gays and lesbians by saying:

Human rights laws do not give special privileges to anyone; human rights laws merely recognize that in an imperfect society some groups have faced discrimination and some categories have been the basis for unfair discrimination, so we include in our human rights laws those categories around which there have been historic patterns of discrimination — race, religion, gender, nationality. We don't include things like eye color, for example, because we haven't experienced in our society discrimination based on eye color. The question, then, of whether or not a group should be included in our human rights law is whether that group or that category forms the basis of discrimination, and I would argue that historically and still today there is in our society—has been and is — a pattern of discrimination based on sexual orientation….

…. Finally, I'd like to say something on the personal side about this bill and this is not something that comes easily for me — I think those of you who have known me for a while know that I don't talk a lot about my personal life, but I refuse to let other people question the validity of my own life experiences. I've been told by many people that oppose this bill that sexual orientation should not be included in the human rights law because it is a choice, because it is a choice that people make, and if they make a choice, they can change that choice... well, let me tell you, I'm a 55-year old gay man and I'm not just going through a phase!

I can also assure you that my sexual orientation is not something I chose like I would choose to wear a blue shirt and a red tie today... why in the world would I have chosen this? I grew up in the 1950s — everyone I knew was presumably straight, all of my models... homosexuality was only something people whispered about... my first awareness of what I was filled me with absolute panic. I did everything I could to change: I dated girls, I denied my inner feelings, I sought psychiatric care — I didn't make a choice about that... I could do nothing about what I was... I did make a choice, my choice had to do with how I would deal with who I was... I chose, after many years of hiding who I was, to be open, to be who I am, and to live my life without shame or apology, and that's a choice I've never regretted... But I was fortunate — when I came out I was already a tenured college professor, I lived in a tolerant urban community and had supportive friends and family. Not all gay and lesbian people are that fortunate... many today continue to live in fear in hostile communities, in jobs they easily could lose if their sexual orientation was discovered... they're forced to live lives based on lies and deception... Much has been made in the debate that's been waged over this bill about how sexual orientation is determined... most experts agree that it is determined at birth or very early in life — it's not something that is chosen... we are what we are and we are asking only that we have the same rights that others take for granted, nothing special, just the right to a job commensurate with our ability, the right to decent housing, the right to a good education, and that's all this bill does...I've been working on this bill for 20 years — the first time it came before the Minnesota Senate was exactly 20 years ago, when the late senator Nick Coleman asked the Minnesota Senate to pass it, and I think the Senate has considered this bill about eight times over the last 20 years, so it's not exactly a new issue... it's going to be resolved, and the time to resolve it is now... it's time, Minnesota. (Milton, 2010)

The stage was set for House Democrat Representative Karen Clark.[5] She was the chief author of the companion Human Rights bill. Throughout the lobbying efforts for and against the bill, it finally reached the floor of the Senate. The vote count was tight. Two or three votes would make the difference and as it turned out, the fate of the bill would not be decided by a party-line vote. Late in the Senate debate, the Republican minority leader, Dean Johnson, rose to speak. He was widely respected by members of both caucuses, in addition to being elected twice to the House and four times to the Senate; he served as Pastor of Calvary Lutheran Church and as a General in the Minnesota National Guard. He conceded,

...that this was a tough vote, but that men and women throughout American history have been elected because they have good judgment, arguing that even while he didn't understand the gay and lesbian lifestyle, it was prudent to vote as a majority to give rights to the minority...in political history and American history, the arguments are the same...from Abraham Lincoln, when he was chastised in his arguments about slavery, the arguments that Hubert Humphrey used about civil rights, the arguments that were used against the Jews, they are in fact the same...create a great element of fear...and, if we pass this and the House passes it and the Governor signs it, it is the right thing to do. It would be easy to vote against it, more popular with the folks back home, but we were elected to lead, to do what is right and to do what is just, and to seek justice. (Milton, 2010)

Johnson paused, and then shared a story about a colleague of his in the National Guard, Captain Pamela Mindt…

For 12 years, he'd referred men and women to her for mental health counseling, though she was now one of those that the Department of Defense wanted to dismiss as an officer because of her sexual orientation; during those 12 years of association with Captain Mindt it never once occurred to me, never once occurred to me to even ask myself quietly, are you gay or homosexual or heterosexual — it didn't matter, because she did the job, she performed her duties as a commissioned officer in the Minnesota Army National Guard. She's an excellent employee... now, should the Pam Mindts of Minnesota have to live with fear of reprisal? Job loss? Loss of a place to live? So, Madame President, members of the Senate, if you feel stress, if you feel scared, I'm no different than you, but today I'm going to vote — green — yes — in favor of Senate File 444, and extend to a group of people in the State of Minnesota what I consider their civil rights, their human rights, that they too can live with dignity. (Milton, 2010)

Political Views Challenged and Changed

One example of those political views were challenged and changed is the was the speech Representative

Johnson's speech was credited with shifting a few undecided votes to support the bill. When the roll was called, there were 37 ayes and 30 nays, and the bill was passed (Milton, 2010). Five Republicans, including Johnson, voted for it and 13 DFL senators voted against.

Although Minnesota opposed the constitutional amendment to ban same-sex marriage, many districts supported it. While the vote on the amendment was not a perfect indicator of support, or lack thereof, for same-sex marriage, those districts' votes weighed heavy on the minds of lawmakers. Those districts included the district that Republican Senator Brenden Petersen represented. His district voted to define marriage as the union of one man and one woman. He is a co-sponsor of the law that legalized same-sex marriage and was the first legislative Republican to publicly declare his support. In the final debate, he sent this message to his children:

Be bold and be courageous and you will never regret a day in your life… he is more uncertain of his future than he has been, but that he is confident that he was standing on the side of liberty. (Milton, 2010)

Political Views Challenged and Strengthened

In November 2003, the Supreme Judicial Court of Massachusetts ruled in *Goodridge v. Department of Public Health* that the denial of civil marriage rights to gays and lesbians was unconstitutional in that state. Due in large part to this decision, efforts were made to constitutionally ban marriage between same-sex partners and, Republican Michelle Bachman[6] proposed a constitutional amendment that would bar the state from legally recognizing same sex marriage (Brunswick, 2003). These efforts were unsuccessful.

In 2003, Republican Paul Koering, was elected to the Minnesota Senate. In 2004, Bachmann and a coalition of religious leaders announced plans for a "Minnesota for Marriage" rally (Brunswick, 2004). Bachmann's effort to place a marriage amendment on a referendum ballot in 2004 ultimately failed. She resurrected her proposal in March 2005 (Doyle, 2005), but it stalled indefinitely in a senate committee that April (Jones, 2005).

On April 7, 2005, Republican Senator Michele Bachmann made a motion to discharge the measure from committee and to the Senate floor for a second reading. This motion failed by a 36-30 vote. Koering effectively 'outed' himself by breaking from the Republican Party line on a procedural vote in the Minnesota Senate, and a week later explicitly stated his sexual orientation. During his time in office, he voted twice against marriage equality bills arguing that same-sex marriage is a distraction from other more pressing issues (KLKS, 2009). In August 2006, the Minneapolis Star Tribune reported that, in March 2006, Senator Bachmann was on a Minneapolis radio show advocating for a state constitutional amendment to ban same-sex marriage. A caller asked her to explain how he, a heterosexual, would be harmed if his gay neighbors were allowed to marry. Bachmann replied by saying: "Public schools would have to teach that homosexuality and same-sex marriage are normal, natural and that maybe children should try them." The Star Tribune also reported that Bachmann has publicly referred to homosexuality as "sexual dysfunction," "sexual identity disorders", and "personal enslavement" that leads to "sexual anarchy" (KLKS, 2009).

In December 2012, plans were announced to introduce same-sex marriage legislation in 2013 (Budig, 2012). As predicted, in February 28, 2013, HF 1054, officially titled Marriage between two persons was introduced in the Minnesota Legislature to legalize same-sex marriage in the state. The Minnesota House took up the marriage bill that had already been through the Senate Judiciary Committee and the House Civil Law Committee. The bill vote was 75-59 in favor of ending the exclusion of same-sex couples from marriage. Same-sex marriage was legalized on May 14, 2013. The bill allows religious freedom, by allowing those religious leaders who oppose same-sex marriage, the right to decline to wed any homosexual couples.

With all but two Democrats voting for the bill and all but four Republicans voting against it, [19] on May 13, 2013, the Senate passed the bill on a vote of 37-30, with all but three Democrats voting for the bill and all but one Republican voting against (Star Tribune, 2013). Three Democrats – Senators LeRoy Stumpf, Dan Sparks and Lyle Koenen – voted against the bill. One Republican, Sen. Branden Petersen, voted yes. Up until the last moments, some opponents had hoped the bill would fail despite clear indications that it would head to Dayton's desk. Republican Senator Dan Hall, said up until the last minutes, he was praying for a miracle and wanted the Senate to reject the bill. Saying that:

Some people have said that they are concerned about being on the right side of history. I am more concerned about being on the right side of eternity. (Star Tribune, 2013)

Senator Nelson said:

In my heart, I grieve on both sides. Because I know what it's like to be alone and I know what it is like to have somebody close to you and love you. But I grieve inside because I feel we are opening the doors to Sodom and Gomorra. And in the end, God is going to be the judge," said, tears running down her cheeks. (Star Tribune, 2013)

The opponents warn that simply not being forced to "solemnize" same-sex marriages does nothing to protect religious freedom as guaranteed in the First Amendment of the U.S. Constitution and Article I, Section 16 of the Minnesota Constitution. The proposed legislation falls far short of protecting the rights of ministries, non-profits, businesses, and individuals to freely exercise their religious beliefs and abide their consciences.

If marriage is redefined in civil law, individuals and religious organizations - regardless of deeply held beliefs - will be compelled to treat same-sex unions as the equivalent of marriage in their lives, ministries and operations. (Star Tribune, 2013)

RECOMMENDATION

Marriage is a public, relational enactment of sexual orientation identity, and the legalization of marriage equality has created conflicts between same-sex couples and religious objectors. Despite its political appeal, the focus on marriage obscures the relational component of sexual orientation equality and religious objections. Opposition against married same-sex couples, while based rhetorically on marriage, will at its core be based on sexual orientation (NeJaime, 2012). Lesbians and gay men enact their sexual orientation through same-sex relationships, and are at the core of the debate over marriage recognition and religious objections. In fact, the cases cited by religious liberty scholars and advocates underscore the breadth of the conflict and point to the relational component of sexual orientation.

FUTURE RESEARCH DIRECTION

Legislators have moral positions that are immune to change. However, if change is to occur, it must be done in a way that makes sense to legislators and voters. Additional scholarship should explore what causes a change in a person's moral core or their beliefs?

CONCLUSION

America is divided along lines of race, ethnicity, class, gender, religion, region and sex. Ideologies and policies of liberals and conservatives struggle for power among competing interests, instead of searching for the common good. Protestant America split into theological liberals who embraced modernity and traditionalists. These two opposing visions through the geographical heart of the country run a fault line that divides evangelical Christians in America. The politics of Jesus in America from progressive believers, moderate and conservative bents, each claiming they are reacting in his name in the public sphere. The traditionalists or fundamentalists grew out of a series of pamphlets published by conservative Protestants to counter change, history, progress or creeping secularism. These separatists rooted themselves in the certainties of doctrine and behavior yielded by literal readings of the Bible and place substantial importance on evangelism.

The mutual reinforcement of these two worldviews underlines the affinity between the two; each uses the other to expand the reach of their respective moral worldviews either consciously or unconsciously. The common underlying values of freedom self-determination, conservative social norms extend the cultural and political power (Marsden, 2006). This political movement built on the foundation of faith. It is important to understand that one of the most politically relevant tenets is the idea being persecuted by secular society. Sacrifice and martyrdom are essential themes and enables members to claim that minorities are attacking the dominate culture when they seek equality. The theme of persecution mobilizes and enables them to feel comfortable about seeking to deprive others of their civil rights. Politics is the discourse of our public life. Politics can make a great difference, for good and for evil, in the ways that we live together. It is politics that must address the moral human values and do so from all points on the political spectrum.

REFERENCES

Adler, G. (2012). An opening in the congregational closet? Boundary-bridging culture and membership privileges for gays and lesbians in Christian religious congregations. *Social Problems*, *59*(2), 177–206. doi:10.1525/sp.2012.59.2.177

Adler, G., Hoegeman, C., & West, A. (2014). Congregational political activity and same-sex marriage: Social movement theory and evidence for contextual influence. *Sociological Quarterly, 55*(3), 555–586. 10.1111/tsq.12060

America's Changing Religious Landscape. (2015, May 12). Pew Research Center. Retrieved from http://www.pewforum.org/2015/05/12/americas-changing-religious-landscape/

Ammerman, N. (1991). *Fundamentalisms observed.* Chicago: University of Chicago Press.

Ammerman, N. (2005). *Pillars of faith: American congregations and their partners.* Berkeley, CA: University of California Press.

Baker v. Nelson 191 N. W. 2d 185, 186 (Minnesota Supreme Court, 1971), appeal dismissed, 409 (U.S. Supreme Court, 1974).

Baptist Joint Committee. (2017). *State Bill Tracker.* Retrieved from http://bjconline.org/staterfratracker/

Barclay, S., & Fisher, S. (2003). The states and the differing impetus for divergent paths on same sex marriage, 19902001. *Policy Studies Journal: the Journal of the Policy Studies Organization*, *31*(3), 331–352. doi:10.1111/1541-0072.00025

Becker, P. (1999). *Congregations in conflict: Cultural models of local religious life*. Cambridge, UK: Cambridge University Press. doi:10.1017/CBO9780511499319

Berger, P. (1969). *The sacred canopy: Elements of a sociological theory of religion*. Garden City, NY: Doubleday.

Blumer, H. (1969). *Symbolic interactionism: Perspective and method*. Englewood Cliffs, NJ: Prentice-Hall.

Bowers v. Hardwick, 478 U.S. 186 (Georgia, 1986). (n.d.). Retrieved from http://caselaw.lp.findlaw.com/scripts/getcase.pl?court=us&vol=478&invol=186

Brunswick, M. (2003, November 21). Keeping gay marriage outside law: Legislators propose constitutional prohibition. *Star Tribune*.

Brunswick, M. (2004, March 12). Same-sex marriage bill heads to house floor. *Star Tribune*.

Budig, T. W. (2012, December 19). Same-sex marriage supporters want to move quickly on a bill. *Star News*. Retrieved from http://erstarnews.com/2012/12/19/same-sex-marriage-supporters-want-to-move-quickly-on-a-bill/

Burger, C. J. (1986, June 30). *Concurring opinion: Bowers v. Hardwick (No. 85–140) 760 F.2d 1202, reversed*. Retrieved from http://www.law.cornell.edu/supct/html/historics/ USSC_CR_0478_0186_ZC.html

Camp, B. (2008). Mobilizing the base and embarrassing the opposition: Defense of marriage referenda and cross-cutting electoral cleavages. *Sociological Perspectives*, *51*(4), 713–733. doi:10.1525/sop.2008.51.4.713

Carpenter, J. A., & Shenk, W. R. (1990). *Earthen vessels: American evangelicals and foreign missions, 1880–1980*. Grand Rapids, MI: Eerdmans.

Chaves, M. (2004). *Congregations in America*. Cambridge, MA: Harvard University Press.

Cicourel, A. V. (1970). The acquisition of social structure: Toward a development sociology of language and meaning. In J. Douglas (Ed.), *Understanding Everyday life* (pp. 136–138). Chicago: Aldine.

Cohen, R., Barnes, J., Holland, K., Cook, C., Barone, M., Jacobson, L., & Peck, L. (2015). *The almanac of American politics 2016: Members of congress and governors: Their profiles and election results, their states and districts*. Retrieved from http://search.ebscohost.com/login.aspx?direct=true&scope=site&db=nlebk&db=nlabk&AN=1083647

Condon, P. (2013, May 14). Dayton signs same-sex marriage bill at Capitol ceremony. *MPR News*. Retrieved from http://wwww.mprnews.org/story/2013/05/14/politics/dayton-signs-same-sex-marriage-bill

Cope, C. (2016, June 25). SC GOP is changing, says state's first openly gay legislator. *Greenville Online*. Retrieved from http://www.greenvilleonline.com/story/news/politics/2016/06/25/sc-gop-changing-says-states-first-openly-gay-legislator/86375764/

Davis, V. (1996). Marriage generally: Prohibit same-sex marriage. *Georgia State University Law Review*, *13*(1), 137–147.

Djupe, P., & Gilbert, C. (2009). *The political influence of churches*. New York: Cambridge University Press.

Djupe, P., Neiheisel, J., & Sokhey, A. (2007). Clergy and controversy: A study of clergy and gay rights in Columbus, Ohio. In P. Djupe & L. Olson (Eds.), *Religious interests in community conflict: Beyond the culture wars* (pp. 73–102). Waco, TX: Baylor University Press.

Domke, D. (2004). *God willing? Political fundamentalism in the white house, the 'war on terror,' and the echoing press*. London: Pluto Press.

Doyle, P. (2005, March 9). Bill would order vote on ban of same-sex marriage. *Star Tribune*.

Driskell, R. (2001). *What is the difference between faith and belief? A bible study*. Good News Publishers. Retrieved from http://www.whatchristianswanttoknow.com/what-is-the-difference-between-faith-and-belief-a-bible-study/

Eskridge, W. N. (1996). *The case for same sex marriage*. New York, NY: The Free Press.

Frank, T. (2004). *What's the matter with Kansas?* New York: Metropolitan Books.

Geertz, C. (1973). Thick description: Toward an interpretative theory of culture. In C. Geertz (Ed.), *The interpretation of cultures* (pp. 3–30). New York, NY: Basic Books.

Gill, A. (1998). *Rendering unto Caesar: The Catholic Church and the State in Latin America*. Chicago: Univ. Chicago Press.

Gilsinan, J. (1989). They is clowning tough: 911 and the social construction of reality. *Criminology*, *27*(2), 329–343. doi:10.1111/j.1745-9125.1989.tb01035.x

Gilsinan, J. (1991). Public policy and criminology: Historical and philosophical reassessment. *Justice Quarterly*, *18*(2), 201–216. doi:10.1080/07418829100091001

Gilsinan, J., & Valentine, J. (1987). Bending granite: Attempts to change the management perspective of american criminologists and police reformers. *Journal of Police Sciences and Police Administration*, *15*, 196–203.

Goggin, M. (1993). *Understanding the New Politics of Abortion*. Newbury Park, CA: Sage.

Goodridge v. Department of Public Health, 748 N.E. 2d 941 (Mass. App. Ct. 2003). (n.d.). Retrieved from http://www.boston.com/news/daily/18/sjc_gaymarriage_decision.pdf

Gormley, W. T. Jr. (1986). Regulatory Issue Networks in a Federal System. *Polity*, *18*(4), 595–620. doi:10.2307/3234884

Green, M. (2014, April 23). Impeachment hearings against Gov. Nixon underway in Mo. house committee. *St. Louis Public Radio*. Retrieved from http://news.stlpublicradio.org/post/impeachment-hearings-against-gov-nixon-underway-mo-house-committee#stream/0

Grice, H. P. (1975). Logic and conversation. In P. Cole & J. Morgan (Eds.), Syntax and semantics: Vol. 3. *speech acts* (pp. 41–58). New York, NY: Academic Press.

Gusfield, J. R. (1963). *Symbolic crusade: Status politics and the American temperance movement*. Urbana, IL: University of Illinois Press.

Hacking, I. (1999). *The social construction of what?* Cambridge, MA: Harvard University Press.

Haider-Markel, D. (2001). Policy diffusion as a geographical expansion of the scope of political conflict: Same-sex marriage bans in the 1990s. *State Politics & Policy Quarterly*, *1*(1), 5–26. doi:10.1177/153244000100100102

Haider-Markel, D., & Meier, K. (1996). The politics of lesbian and gay rights: Expanding the scope of the conflict. *The Journal of Politics*, *58*(2), 532–349. doi:10.2307/2960229

Herman, D. (2000). The Gay Agenda Is the Devil's Agenda: The Christian Right's Vision and the Role of the State. In C. A. Rimmerman, K. D. Wald, & C. Wilcox (Eds.), *The Politics of Gay Rights*. Chicago, IL: University of Chicago Press.

Hopson, R., & Smith, D. (1999). Changing fortunes: An Analysis of Christian right ascendence within American political discourse. *Journal for the Scientific Study of Religion*, *38*(1), 1–13. doi:10.2307/1387579

Human Rights Campaign. (2004). Equality from state to state: GLBT Americans and state legislation. Washington, DC: Author.

Jones, S. (2005, April 21). Minnesotans rally in defense of marriage. *Cybercast News Services*. Retrieved from https://web.archive.org/web/20070212223013/http://www.cnsnews.com/Culture/archive/200504/CUL20050421a.html

Kellstedt, L., & Green, J. (2003). The politics of the Willow Creek Association pastors. *Journal for the Scientific Study of Religion*, *42*(4), 547–561. doi:10.1046/j.1468-5906.2003.00202.x

King, R., & Nugent, N. (1979). *Respectable rebels: Middle class campaigns in Britain in the 1970s*. London: Hodder and Stoughton.

Kirkland, J. (1995, February). Today's GOP: The party's over for big business. *Fortune*, 50-62.

Klemp, N. J. (2007). Beyond God-talk: The understanding Christian right from the ground up. *Polity*, *39*(4), 522–544. 10.1057/palgrave.polity.2300062

Lakoff, G. (1996). *Moral politics: How liberals and conservatives think* (2nd ed.). Chicago, IL: University of Chicago Press.

Lechner, F. (1989). Cultural aspects of the modern world system. In *Religious Politics in global and comparative perspective*. Westport, CT: Greenwood Press.

Lee, R. (2004, January 30). Gays face defining moment: Anti-gay measures at gold dome prompts call for unprecedented activism. *Southern Voice*. Retrieved from http://www.southernvoice.com

Lewis, G., & Rogers, M. (1999). Does the public support equal employment rights for gays and lesbians? In E. Riggle & B. Tadlock (Eds.), *Gays and lesbians in the democratic process* (pp. 118–145). New York, NY: Columbia University Press.

Liebman, R., & Wuthnow, R. (1983). *The new Christian right*. New York: Aldine Publishing Company.

Lindaman, K., & Haider-Markel, D. (2002). Issue evolution, political parties, and the culture wars. *Political Research Quarterly*, *55*(1), 91–110.

Lowi, T. (1969). *The End of Liberalism*. New York: Norton.

Marsden, G. (2006). The Sword of the Lord: How 'Otherworldly' Fundamentalism Became a Political Power. *Books & Culture: A Christian Review*. Retrieved http://www.booksandculture.com/articles/2006/marapr/3.10.html

Meier, K. (1994). *The politics of sin: Drugs, alcohol and public policy*. Armonk, NY: Shar.

Merriam, S. B. (1998). *Qualitative research and case study applications in education*. San Francisco, CA: Jossey-Bass.

Milton, J. (2010, October 22). 20 years after senate first tried, Minnesota legislature finally gives gays civil rights protection. *MinnPost*. Retrieved from https://www.minnpost.com/politics-policy/2010/10/20-years-after-senate-first-tried-minnesota-legislature-finally-gives-gays-c

Moen, M. (1992). *The transformation of the Christian right*. Tuscaloosa, AL: University of Alabama Press.

NeJaime, D. (2011). Marriage Inequality: Same-Sex Relationships, Religious Exemptions, and the Production of Sexual Orientation Discrimination. *California Law Review*, *100*, 1169–1238. doi:10.15779/Z38MB9R

Oregon Employment Division v. Smith (1990) 494 US 872 (No. 88-1213). (n.d.). Retrieved from https://www.law.cornell.edu/supremecourt/text/494/872

People for the American Way Foundation. (2000). Hostile climate: report on anti-gay activity. Washington, DC: Author.

Pew Research Center. (2015, May 12). *America's Changing Religious Landscape*. Retrieved from http://www.pewforum.org/2015/05/12/americas-changing-religious-landscape/

Postman, N. (1985). *Amusing ourselves to death*. Viking.

Ripley, R., & Franklin, G. (1991). *Congress, the bureaucracy, and public policy* (5th ed.). Pacific Grove, CA: Brooks/Cole Pub. Co.

Schroedel, J. R. (1999). Elite attitudes toward homosexuals. In Gays and lesbians in the democratic process (pp. 89–117). New York, NY: Columbia University Press.

Schudson, M. (2002). *The sociology of news*. New York, NY: W.W. Norton.

Seltzer, R. (1993). AIDS, homosexuality, public opinion, and changing correlates over time. *Journal of Homosexuality*, *26*(1), 85–97. doi:10.1300/J082v26n01_07 PMID:8113607

Sharlet, J. (2005 May). Inside America's Most Powerful Megachurch. *Harper's Magazine*. Retrieved from http://harpers.org/archive/2005/05/inside-americas-most-powerful-megachurch/

Smith, C. (1998). *American evangelicalism: Embattled and thriving*. Chicago, IL: University of Chicago Press.

Smith, C. (2003). *Moral, believing animals: Human personhood and culture*. New York, NY: Oxford University Press. doi:10.1093/acprof:oso/9780195162028.001.0001

Smith, D., DeSantis, M., & Kassel, J. (2006). Same-sex marriage ballot measures and the 2004 presidential election. *State & Local Government Review*, *38*(2), 78–91. doi:10.1177/0160323X0603800202

Soule, S. A. (2004). Going to the chapel? Same-sex marriage bans in the United States, 1973–2000. *Social Problems*, *51*(4), 453–477.

Stolberg, S. (2011a, June 21). Roots of Bachmann's ambition began at home. *The New York Times*. Retrieved from http://www.nytimes.com/2011/06/22/us/politics/22bachmann.html

Stolberg, S. (2011b, July 16). For Bachmann, gay rights stand reflects mix of issues and faith. *The New York Times*. Retrieved from http://www.nytimes.com/2011/07/17/us/politics/17bachmann.html

Wald, K. (2003). *Religion and Politics in the United States*. Lanham, MD: Rowman & Littlefield.

Wallis, J. (1994). The soul of politics: A practical and prophetic vision for change. New York, NY: Orbis Books.

Wellman, J. (2008). *Evangelical vs. liberal: the clash of Christian cultures in the Pacific Northwest*. Oxford, UK: Oxford University Press.

Wellman, J., & Keyes, M. (2007). Portable politics and durable religion: The moral worldviews of american evangelical missionaries. *Sociology of Religion*, *66*(4), 383–406. doi:10.1093/socrel/68.4.383

White, J. (1986, June 30). *Opinion of the court: Bowers v. Hardwick (No. 85–140) 760 F.2d 1202, reversed*. Retrieved from http://www.law.cornell.edu/supct/html/historics/

Wilson, A. (Producer). (2004a, February 16). *Prime Time Lawmakers*. Atlanta: Georgia Public Broadcasting.

Wilson, A. (Producer). (2004b, February 26). *Prime Time Lawmakers*. Atlanta: Georgia Public Broadcasting.

Wilson, A. (Producer). (2004c, March 31). *Prime Time Lawmakers*. Atlanta: Georgia Public Broadcasting.

Winnick, P. (1976). The precedential weight of a dismissal by the supreme court for want of a substantial federal question: Some implications of Hicks v. Miranda. *Columbia Law Review*, *76*(3), 508-511.

KEY TERMS AND DEFINITIONS

Cultural Cleavage: Cleavage separates the voters into advocates and adversaries on a certain issue, or voting for a certain party.

Denominations: Refers to a set of congregations that belong to a single administrative structure characterized by particular doctrines and practices; can be classified as Protestant Fundamentalist were Churches of God, Latter Day Saints, Churches of Christ, Church of the Nazarene, Mennonites, Conservative Baptist Association, Missouri Synod Lutherans, Pentecostal Free Will Baptists, Pentecostal Holiness, the Salvation Army, Seventh- Day Adventists, Southern Baptists, and Wisconsin Synod Lutherans.

Evangelical: Christians who actively seek proselytize and convert others and can be of a variety of political perspectives (includes Pentecostal and charismatic Christians).

Fundamentalism: A literal interpretation of the Bible and the application of that reading to all areas of a person's life and can belong to a variety of denominations.

Ideology: In this book the term applies to ideas and beliefs that have political ramifications.

Morality: concern with the distinction between good and evil or right and wrong; right or good conduct.

Protestantism: the theological system of any of the churches of western Christendom that separated from the Roman Catholic Church during the Reformation.

Post-Millennialism: The view that Jesus Christ will return to earth after believers "rule and reign" for a thousand years.

Pre-Millennialism: The view that Christs return begins the thousand year reign.

Worldview: A concept that attempts to articulate how someone believes, interprets and makes sense of their reality.

ENDNOTES

1. *Baker v. Nelson* (291 Minn. 310; 191 N.W.2d 185; 1971); *Jones v. Hallahan* (501 S.W.2d 588; 1973); *Singer v. Hara* (530 F.2d 247; 1976); *Adams v. Howerton* (673 F.2d 1036; 1982); *De Santo v. Barnsley* (328 Pa. Super. 181; 476 A.2d 952; 1984).
2. A dismissal by the Supreme Court is an adjudication on the merits... a lower federal court must consider itself bound by the dismissal when a similar challenge comes before it.
3. The Sherbert Test, considers: whether the claim involves a sincere religious belief; that the government has a compelling state interest; and, that the government is achieving that goal in the manner least burdensome to religion.
4. The Supreme Court of the United States is the highest judicial body in the United States and leads the federal judiciary. Eras of the Supreme Court are named after the Chief Justice of that time. William Hubbs Rehnquist served on the court beginning in 1972 and was the Chief

Justice of the United States from 1986–2005. The Rehnquist Court was considered conservative (Members of the Supreme Court of the United States, n. d.)

5 Karen Clark was elected in 1980 as the first openly gay person to run and be elected to the Minnesota Legislature.

6 Bachmann's worldview has been attributed to the Christian movement known as Dominionism, citing the influences of theologian Francis Schaeffer as a "profound influence" on her life specifically referring to his film series How Should We Then Live?; and Nancy Pearcey describing the Total Truth: Liberating Christianity from Its Cultural Captivity as a "wonderful" book (Stolberg, 2011a, 2011b). Posner (2011) points to the influence of Christian Reconstructionist Herb Titus and R. J. Rushdoony on Bachmann via the curriculum at O. W. Coburn School of Law. In office, Bachmann's agenda focused on the cultural conservative issues of opposition to abortion and gay marriage.

Section 2

Intersection of Religion and Politics

Explores faith and political culture, and the role that faith plays decisions of state legislators.

Chapter 3
The Use of Faith in Legislative Decision-Making:
Bill Sponsorship

ABSTRACT

In recent decades, same-sex marriage has emerged as a national political issue. As a result, state legislators have sponsored and passed statutes on an array of issues directly related to this topic. This chapter investigates how faith influences an individual legislator's political judgment in the early-stages of decision making related to sponsored bills. At this stage in the legislative process, influences are minimized. The findings indicate that even while legislator's partisanship and ideology largely structure decision-making, legislators as conservative Protestants are more likely to responds when issues involve morality.

Render therefore unto Caesar the things that are Caesar's, and unto God the things which are God's. ~ Matthew 22:21

DOI: 10.4018/978-1-5225-2388-8.ch003

INTRODUCTION

Religion in America has is entwined with politics as the major political parties have become religiously homogenous and polarized over cultural issues (Layman, 1997; Miller & Hoffmann, 1999). Researchers have found strong religious influences that impact the voting behavior of legislators (Yamane & Oldmixon, 2006). Studies show that evangelicals evidence a stronger connection between their religious beliefs and their political attitudes than other religious affiliations do (Wilcox, 1990).

The legal battle over the status of same-sex relationships began with a 1993 Hawaii State Supreme Court decision that publicly suggested discrimination against same-sex couples from marrying might constitute sex discrimination. In response Hawaii and other states moved to enact laws that explicitly limited the legal institution of marriage to heterosexual couples. The US Congress followed with the Defense-of-Marriage Act of 1996 (Pub. L. No. 104-199,110 Stat. 2419), which allowed states to ignore same-sex marriages performed in other states, and defined marriage as "a legal union between one man and one woman." These court cases gave rise to the cultural agenda that fostered legislator differences of an absolutist sort by arousing the passions of those who reject compromise on faith based issues. The US Supreme Court's in the case of *United States v. Obergefell (2015)* decision legalizing same-sex marriage is fueling new momentum to reconsider legislative measures to limit its impact within states.

Legal recognition and sanctioning of same-sex relationships has occurred in various fits and starts across the United States each wave of activity created various responses within the states. Gay issues make their way onto the legislative agenda in the same way that every other policy issue does—legislators introduce policy initiatives in an effort to claim credit, position-take, or engage in symbolic posturing or legislative advocacy (Mayhew,1974). Legislators view gay issues as salient and they draft legislation accordingly.

This chapter will explore how faith influences individual-level legislative decision making to sponsor bills to address the issue of same-sex marriage. Bill sponsorship is an important legislative activity since a policy must be proposed before it is legislatively enacted. To the extent that gay issues represent a cultural cleavage between conservatism and progressivism, there is evidence that legislators' decisions are strongly influenced by phenomena that inform culture. To investigate this possibility, state legislators featured in this chapter were chosen based on court decisions that played a significant role in opposing the intent of the Supreme Court rulings in same-sex marriage decisions. In these instances, state legislators responded by sponsoring legislation. A descriptive content review is included to examine proposed and enacted legislation between 2004 and 2016 that was introduced to mitigate the consequences of these same-same sex court decisions for those religious adherents that had faith objections.

BACKGROUND

Policy decisions in state legislatures may be influenced by any number of sources known to shape human behavior (Patterson, 1983). To pinpoint the factors of influence upon legislative decision-making, researchers have observed the norms governing legislators' behavior, the roles they assume, and the goals and objectives that motivate them (Clausen, 1994). In addition to roll call votes, the legislative process offers members a variety of opportunities to take public positions. Chief among these is a members' ability to sponsor and cosponsor legislation without institutional limit on the type, subject, or number of pieces of legislation (Oleszek, 2007).

In David Mayhew's *Congress: The Electoral Connection* (1974, p. 62), he wrote that "the electoral requirement is not that [a member of Congress] make pleasing things happen, but that he make pleasing judgmental statements. The position itself is the electoral commodity." In later writings, Mayhew was even more blunt in observing that "politicians often get rewarded for taking positions rather than achieving effects" (2001, p. 51). In other words, any activity which offers both a position-taking opportunity and a more substantive role should be promoted in such a way as to enhance or even maximize the amount of electoral benefit the member receives (Lazarus, 2013).

One such activity is bill introduction. When a member introduces a bill, he or she might do so with the intent of having the bill become law and thereby effecting policy change. One of the most well-known aspects of the United States' legislative process is that members sponsor thousands of pieces of legislation every year, but very few are enacted or even receive serious consideration (Krutz, 2015. Most have no real chance of being enacted at all. This implies that sponsorship or co-sponsorship may serve some other purpose besides changing policy. Electorally motivated position taking provides a compelling alternative as does a legislator's faith or religious affiliation which also influences policy preferences and decision-making. While party leaders have the ability and the incentive to whip votes toward the party position, there is very little incentive to exert influence over sponsorship/co-sponsorship decisions—particularly among majority party leaders given that they ultimately control access to the floor. Thus, at a stage in the legislative process not controlled by leadership or influenced by rules and committees, partisanship still emerges as significant. At least in this policy domain, party voting likely indicates affinity toward a set of values on the part of legislators (Snyder & Groseclose, 2000). One of the reasons scholars expect faith to shape political preferences and behaviors, is that religious creeds provide individuals with a set of fundamental values that guide how they should live in the secular realm (Wald, 2003, p. 27). On issues that are relevant to creedal teachings, religion has the potential to influence political preferences and behaviors and animate political engagement (Oldmixon & Hudson, 2008). As is the case of conservative Protestants who on issues of moral absolutes, such as same-sex marriage, the teaching of the church is authoritative. In matters of prudential judgment, church teaching is not authoritative (Oldmixon & Hudson, 2008). Therefore, individuals and legislators are free to apply their own reasoned and morally informed judgment. To the extent that the church adopts policy positions, legislators support that position. To the extent that gay issues represent a cultural cleavage between faith traditionalism and progressivism, one would expect a legislator's decision making to be strongly influenced by phenomena that inform culture. To investigate this possibility, this chapter describes the legislative reactions to court decisions*: Employment Division v. Smith*, (1990); *Baehr v. Anderson*, (1990-1999); and *Church of Lukuni Babalu Ayer v. City of Hialeah*, (1993). These decisions establish the connection between religious freedom and bill sponsorship towards the legalization of same-sex marriage.

CLEAVAGES OF CULTURE

By "culture" this chapter refers to a "moral order" (Wuthnow, 1988)—a shared sense of how people ought to live. As a consequence of cultural disagreement, there "has been an upsurge in demands and political causes linked less to economics and class than to the lifestyle and social 'identity' in which different groups seek to legitimize the cultural values they hold dear" (Smith & Tatalovich, 2003, p.50).

Therefore, cultures compete for status and legitimacy in the public sphere (Smith & Tatalovich, 2003, p.17). As competing cultural groups demand that government institutionalize their values and preferred social relationships, cultural conflicts become political conflicts (Wildavsky, 1987). As cultural encounters unfold, one group generally presses for recognition of its status, while another group rallies to uphold the status quo (Smith & Tatalovich, 2003, p.25). The battle over gay rights clearly fits this pattern. Beginning in earnest after the 1969 Stonewall Riots, gays and lesbians continually engage the political system in increasing numbers to legitimize their status, and they meet firm resistance. The clashes over gay rights represents what is arguably one of the dominant cultural cleavages of the post material era in the United States (Inglehart, 1990)—the fight between religious traditionalism and progressivism (Layman & Carmines, 1997).

Gay issues represent one of the most salient political cleavages of the post materialist era—the cleavage between religious traditionalism and progressive sexuality. Therefore, the analysis proceeded on the assumption that on gay issues, legislators are driven by a desire to legitimize a culture, a set of values, in law. Sponsorship and co-sponsorship is a position-taking opportunity. Vulnerable members can demonstrate aggressive legislative activity, and minority members can advocate for policy when they are denied access to the floor (Kroger, 2003). Theoretically, the stakes of roll call voting are higher because policy is made at this stage of the legislative process. Generally speaking, the stark polarization of legislators on gay issues and cultural issues likely augments the historical cleavages between members along the moral policy dimension. This environment can only intensify the level of division within institutions. Still, these cultural cleavages emerge throughout.

Religious Freedom Restoration Act

The federal Religious Freedom Response Act (RFRA) has its origins in Oregon. Prior to 1990, U.S. Supreme Court decisions established a high standard for justifying the imposition of a substantial burden on the rights of someone to freely exercise their religion. "Strict scrutiny" was required. The government had to show it had a "compelling interest" and the burden imposed couldn't be achieved by less restrictive measures. That requirement changed in a 1990 ruling when the court upheld an Oregon Employment Division decision to deny unemployment benefits to two Native American rehab center employees fired because they had ingested peyote in a religious ritual. This decision in *Employment Division v. Smith* (1990), where the Supreme Court eliminated the *Sherbert Test* because it was too broad when applied to all laws. The ruling meant that government no longer had to justify burdens on the free exercise of religion as long as these burdens were "merely the incidental effect of a generally applicable and otherwise valid provision" (*Employment Division v. Smith,* 1990). In short, the government no longer had to prove it had a "compelling interest," merely a "legitimate" interest; the majority opinion was delivered by Justice Antonin Scalia,

The First Amendment forbids government from prohibiting the "free exercise" of religion. This means that government may not regulate beliefs as such, either by compelling certain beliefs or forbidding them. Religious belief frequently entails the performance of physical acts—assembling for worship, consumption of bread and wine, abstaining from certain foods or behaviors. Government could no more ban the performance of these physical acts when engaged in for religious reasons than it could ban the religious beliefs that compel those actions in the first place. It would doubtless be unconstitutional, for example, to ban the casting of statues that are to be used for worship purposes or to prohibit bowing down before a golden calf. (Employment Division v. Smith, 1990)

Oregon's ban on the possession of peyote was not a law specifically aimed at a physical act engaged in for a religious reason. Rather, it is a law that applies to everyone who might possess peyote, for whatever reason—a "neutral law of general applicability" (*Employment Division v. Smith,* 1990). Scalia characterized the employees' argument as an attempt to use their religious motivation to use peyote in order to place themselves beyond the reach of Oregon's neutral, generally applicable ban on the possession of peyote. The Court held that the First Amendment's protection of the "free exercise" of religion does not allow a person to use a religious motivation as a reason not to obey such generally applicable laws (*Employment Division v. Smith,* 1990). In this case, the Court held that religious beliefs did not excuse people from complying with laws, as opposed to interpreting the First Amendment to require an exemption. Requiring claims for religious exemptions to be vetted through the legislative process could put less popular religions at a disadvantage, but the Court held that this situation was preferable to the relative anarchy that would result from "a system in which each conscience is a law unto itself" (*Employment Division v. Smith,* 1990).

In response to the *Smith* decision, President Bill Clinton and the US Congress passed the Religious Freedom Restoration Act (RFRA), requiring strict scrutiny when a neutral law of general applicability "substantially burden[s] a person's exercise of religion" (Liptak, 2014). RFRA provided a strict scrutiny standard, required a narrowly tailored regulation serving a compelling government interest in any case that substantially burdens the free exercise of religion, regardless of the intent and general applicability of the law (Williamson, 1997). This legislation was bipartisan aiming to restore and codify Americans' religious freedom rights by requiring that even laws of general applicability must be narrowly tailored to meet a compelling government interest in instances where free exercise of religion is affected. A unanimous U.S. House and a nearly unanimous U.S. Senate passed the bill, and President Bill Clinton signed it into law. The bill sought to undo the 1990 Supreme Court *Smith* decision, and it reestablished the *Sherbert* Test (strict scrutiny).

The act was considered applicable to both states and the federal government until 1997, when the Supreme Court ruled in the Texas case of City *of Boerne v. Flores* (1997) the decision by the US overturned the Texas case of *City of Boerne v. Flores* (1997) held Religious Freedom Restoration Act unconstitutional by the United States Supreme Court, as applied to the states ruling that RFRA is not a proper exercise of Congress's enforcement power. The Court, in an opinion by Justice Anthony Kennedy, struck down RFRA as it applied to the states as an unconstitutional use of Congress's enforcement powers *(City of Boerne v. Flores*, 1997).

In the *Church of Lukumi Babalu Aye, Inc. v. City of Hialeah* (1993), its first free exercise case after *Smith*, the Supreme Court invalidated a Florida city ordinance prohibiting animal sacrifices performed as part of religious rituals. The Church of the Lukumi-Babalu Aye, Inc. was a Florida not-for-profit organization that practiced the Santeria religion. After the church leased land in response the city and announced plans to establish a house of worship and other facilities there, the city council held an emergency public session and passed ordinances to prevent the practice. The Court held that the purpose of the laws was to suppress the Santeria religion. The only conduct subject to the ordinances was animal sacrifice, the central element of the Santeria worship services, and they were therefore not neutral. The Court also held that the ordinances were not of general applicability, but selectively targeted to conduct motivated by religious belief (Wallsten, 1997).

Defense of Marriage Act

Congress passed in response to the pending outcome in Hawaii passed the Defense of Marriage Act Defense of Marriage Act (DOMA), Pub. L. No. 104-199, 110Stat. 2419 & 2420 (1996) in response to concerns that Hawaii would start recognizing marriage equality, and other states then would have to recognize same-sex marriages entered into in Hawaii. Then, in 1998, Hawaii amended its constitution to give the legislature the right to define marriage as limited to a man and a woman (National Conference of State Legislatures, 2013). Since the Defense of Marriage Act, the issue of same-sex marriage has dominated the political discourse of lesbian, gay, bisexual, and transgender politics. Scholars claim that the litigation in Hawaii that took place in the 1990s was responsible for the subsequent political activity surrounding same-sex marriage in the United States, including the Defense of Marriage Act.

State Reactions

A number of states passed state RFRAs, applying the rule to the laws of their own state, but the *Smith* case remains the authority in these matters in many states (Rutten, 2014). The interconnection between cases involving religious freedom and same sex marriage was beginning to become apparent. By the end of 2004 seven state legislatures passed constitutional amendments and referred them to the voters. All of these amendments were approved. The margins of approval ranged from a low of 57 percent in Oregon to a high of 86 percent in Mississippi. In addition to these legislative referrals, six citizen-initiated attempts to amend state constitutions to prohibit marriage for same-sex couples were also approved by voters (Arkansas, Michigan, Montana, North Dakota, Ohio, and Oregon) (Evans, 2004).

On December 17, 1990, three couples –applied for marriage licenses with Hawaii's Department of Health. Hawaii's marriage statute contains certain prerequisites that a couple must meet in order to enter into a valid marriage contract. These requirements, among others, include a minimum age, a barring of certain marriage contracts based on relation, and a confirmation that each person is not lawfully married to another at the time of application (Hawaii Revised Statutes §572-1). While there are gendered terms throughout the text implying that individuals seeking a license should be of the opposite sex, no statute specified that the couple entering marriage must be composed of individuals of the opposite sex.

On April 12, 1991, the three couples were all denied marriage licenses, since the Department of Health interpreted the statute's gendered terms to indicate that same sex couples did not have the right to marry. The couples filed a complaint for injunctive and declaratory relief with Hawaii's First Circuit Court, arguing that their right to privacy had been violated and that the couples were not afforded equal protection and due process of the law, which are explicitly written into the Hawaii State Constitution. In early October 1991, after several motions from both sides, the First Circuit Court dismissed the plaintiffs' complaints, claiming no legitimate claim on which they could be granted relief (*Baehr v. Lewin*, 1993).

In 1993, in a case called *Baehr v. Lewin*, Hawaii's Supreme Court held that the state's marriage laws discriminated against same-sex couples because it violated that state's constitution by denying them marriage licenses—the first U.S. court ever to make such a ruling. This decision marked the first time that any jurisdiction attempted to legalize same-sex marriage. Although the battle in Hawaii began in the court, it ended up in the state legislature where it would the this battle would be waged across the nation. Legislators responded to the promotion of same-sex marriage by sponsoring bills claiming that it contravenes their religious principles. At the time, it looked like Hawaii was on the road to marriage equality, but backlash from legislators soon blocked the way.

Responding to the Hawaii Supreme Court's decision in *Baehr v. Lewin* (1993), the Hawaii legislature held numerous public hearings on the issue of same-sex marriage in the fall of 1993 (H.R. 3396, 1996). Public opinion polls in Hawaii demonstrated that the majority of Hawaii residents were opposed to the recognition of same-sex marriages with numbers hovering around 70% (Yuen, 1998; Brewer & Wilcox, 2005). In response to the public's concern, the legislature passed Act 217, which revised the Hawaii statute §572- 1 to include a clause that explicitly reserved the contract of marriage to a man and a woman and set up a commission to research same-sex marriage and the distribution of marriage benefits to same-sex couples. A series of bills to prohibit same-sex marriage were introduced in the Hawaii House of representatives in 1996, all in anticipation of a state Supreme Court ruling on the subject. House Bill 2367 would have amended the state Constitution so that marriage would be exclusively reserved for the union of a man and a woman (People of the American Way, 1999), but it died in the House Committee on Judiciary. Two other bills HB 2524 and HB 3347 which attempted to establish licensure and regulatory control over the union of a man and a woman, died in Conference Committee (Star Bulletin, 1997).

The reverberation of the case by the end of 1996, 16 states had enacted legislation that would preempt them from having to recognize same-sex marriages performed in other states, 15 of which took place in 1996 alone (Barclay, 2010). Before the case was heard by the circuit court, a flurry of activity was also taking place in Congress that would quickly nationalize the issue of same-sex marriage to an unprecedented place on the national and state governments' agendas.

In December, 1996 a Hawaii judge ruled that gays and lesbians should not be prohibited from marrying their partners, prompting a political backlash in many parts of the country. Republican House, Speaker Daniel Webster, a fundamentalist Christian with ties to a Chicago group who wants to put the values of the Bible back into government for the first time in 122 years, the Republican Party controlled both chambers of the Legislature. A Baptist, Webster is quoted in the House Clerk's manual as saying that" any accomplishments that I may have achieved come only from the investment that God and others have made in my life" (Wallsten, 1997).Webster promised his personal religious beliefs would not dictate the Legislature's agenda by stating that,

Through the majority office, there will be a Republican agenda and it will deal with what we believe to be the most important issues of the session ... promote free and open debate on a variety of issues in the House... formed policy councils that will screen every bill filed to determine whether it should be heard on the floor. Does the bill promote, defend, advantage and empower constructive familial relationships? (Wallsten, 1997)

Even though the decision is under appeal but, if it is upheld, some Florida lawmakers fear gays would flock to Hawaii to get married and then move back to the Sunshine State, where the law recognizes marriages endorsed by other states. That's why Republicans Senators John Grant and Representative Johnnie Byrd are sponsoring the "Florida Defense of Marriage Act." The measure in the Senate had the signatures of 21 senators, Democrats and Republicans. That guarantees it will get the support of a majority in the 40-seat chamber. In the House, 30 of the chamber's 120 members have signed on. State Representative Johnnie Byrd said:

I'm a conservative Christian, certainly marriage is the basic building block of our society. That's one thing that has served us well. We need to stand by the traditional definition of marriage. (Wallsten, 1997)

State Senator John Grant said:

...from a moral standpoint, for 600 years the concept of marriage has meant one man and one woman... does not want gay people to enjoy the tax benefits and entitlements that married people get, such as corporate health insurance. If a marriage exists, that raises a whole lot of other rights and privileges... who knows how many homosexual marriages there would be? (Wallsten, 1997)

Speaker Webster, supports the ban on same-sex marriages legislation, and explains how the measure stacks up against his five guiding principles of less government and more personal freedom.

That's less government...we don't want the state of Hawaii dictating what we do in the state of Florida. On the foundation of our state is based on the legitimacy of the family, and gay marriages would disrupt that legitimacy. (A ban on gay marriages) is allowing for what the traditional family is supposed to do... (Wallsten, 1997)

Meanwhile openly gay Oregon Republican State Representative Chuck Carpenter recalls the events of the 1997 legislature trying to pass non-discrimination in employment bill:

It was April 15th and I made a motion on the House floor to withdraw the bill from its committee, and at that point everything came to a screeching halt. A lot of the Republicans, as I recall, fled the building because they were afraid they would actually have to face the issue. The Democrats just held with me and Jim, and I negotiated with the Speaker, and after about two or three days of this the Speaker finally agreed the bill would be re-drafted and assigned to the Commerce Committee, and that we would have a public hearing, and within a week, a vote. We had the public hearing and a work session one evening and we passed it out of committee with only one "no." That was the frustration of the thing – we knew we had the votes – and it was just people playing games with us; lying and being deceitful. Then we passed it on the House floor a couple of days later 40-20. A very large margin – we were surprised with the bipartisan support. Then it went over to the Senate where we did not have the leverage that we had in the House, and that was it. It was one vote short in the Republican caucus and it never went forward. It's just the way politics tends to be. That's the way it goes. But we were exhilarated. I was exhilarated that we could make a difference, that we raised these issues very successfully in the House and that we passed it. I felt great about that – and I was terribly disappointed that we weren't able to pass it in the Senate. (Out and Elected, 1994)

On April 29, 1997, both houses of the Hawaii legislature passed, House Bill No. 117 proposing an amendment to the Hawaii Constitution (the marriage amendment). The marriage amendment was ratified by the electorate in November 1998 (Yuen, 1998).

In 1991 Kate Brown was appointed to the Oregon House of Representatives, filling a vacancy left by a predecessor who took an executive appointment (Schwarz, 2015). She was elected to a second term before being elected to the Oregon State Senate in 1996. Two years later, she was elected Senate Democratic Leader. In 2004, senators made her the first woman to serve as Oregon's Senate Majority Leader. Unexpectedly, on March 3, 2004, Multnomah County began issuing licenses to same-sex couples after its attorney issued a legal opinion that such marriages are lawful (Callimachi, 2004). Legal challenges ensued and a Judge ordered the county to stop issuing same-sex marriage licenses, and ordered the state to recognize the 3,022 same-sex marriage licenses already issued. The Oregon state registrar had been holding the completed licenses pending a court decision as to their validity, rather than entering them into the state's records system. The Defense of Marriage Coalition was formed in reaction to same-sex marriages performed in Multnomah County. On May 21, 2004, the group received approval for the language of a proposed initiative to prohibit same-sex marriage. On November 2, 2004, voters approved Oregon Ballot Measure 36 by a margin of 57% to 43% Ballot Measure 36, a constitutional amendment defining the marriage of a man and a woman as the only one recognized by the state.

On July 8, 2005, Oregon State Senators Kate Brown, Ben Westlund, Frank Morse and Alan Bates sponsored Senate Bill 1000 to create civil unions and prohibit discrimination based on sexual orientation in housing, employment, public accommodations and public services. The vote at the Oregon State Capitol in Salem was 19-10 in favor of the measure (Prengaman, 2003). In the Republican-controlled House of Representatives where the bill had to meet approval House Speaker Karen Minnis, announced that she would not let the bill be passed (Prengaman, 2003). On July 21, the House performed a series of moves where the bill was amended, removing most of its language and replacing it with different text, effectively killing the bill. A shift in power in the house changed the fate of the bill after the November 2006 mid-term elections, Democrats won a majority of the formerly Republican-controlled

House. In early 2007, Democrats re-introduced a bill in the House similar to the 2005 legislation. The bill adopted the term "domestic partnership" to describe these unions; the terms "marriage" or "civil union" were absent (Prengaman, 2003).

This bill passed easily through the legislature on April 17, 2007 (House vote of 34-26) and on May 2, 2007 (Senate vote of 21-9), Governor Kulongoski signed the "Oregon Family Fairness Act" on May 9, 2007. In 2009, paperwork issues were problematic when couples entering domestic partnerships wanted to change or hyphenate their names had to follow a different paperwork trail than those entering traditional marriages. Democrat Representative Tina Kotek sponsored House Bill 2839 that created a similar process for couples seeking to change their names after entering into domestic partnerships. Without the change, she said "it was confusing and problematic not only for the couples, but also for the agencies involved" (Cole, 2009). Only one House member spoke against the bill. Republican Representative Dennis Richardson said that "This bill may be a technical fix, but it is a technical fix on a bill contrary to the will of the people" (Cole, 2009).

In 2009, Senate Bill 786 Oregon Workplace Religious Freedom Act passed by a vote of 38-21. Originally the measure started in the House as HB 3539 during the 2007 legislative session, and was reintroduced in 2009 as Senate Bill 786 (Religious Liberty, 2009). Speaker Hunt also passed the anti-discrimination law to protect LGBT Oregonians and domestic partnerships (Biography, 2010). On February 13, 2015, Governor John Kitzhaber announced his pending resignation amid a public corruption scandal. Kate Brown succeeded him on February 18, 2015, since the Oregon Constitution identified the secretary of state as the successor when the Governor leaves office prematurely (Willamette Week, 2015). Her win in the 2016 governor's race made her the first openly bisexual person elected as a United States governor (and the first openly LGBT person elected) (Horton, 2016).

In 2011, civil union legislation, Senate Bill 232, sailed through the Senate and House and was signed by Hawaii Governor Abercrombie. In the 2011 legislation session, the civil union bill was approved 31-19 by the House, and 19-6 by the Senate House Majority Leader Blake Oshiro, who is gay and led the effort, was chosen by Governor Abercrombie to become a member of his staff. Also, in 2011 Hawaii State Representative Georgette "Jo" Jordan (D) who is openly a lesbian was appointed by Governor Abercrombie (Lee, 2013)

While public and legislative support in favor of civil unions was apparently on the rise, the ultimate goal of marriage equality for gays and lesbians did not die down. In the case of *United States v. Windsor(2013)* the Supreme

Court struck down a section of the Defense of Marriage Act that restricted marriage to a union between a man and a woman. In September of that year, Governor Abercrombie called Senate and House members into special session. Democrat Senator Brickwood Galuteria introduced Senate Bill1 to enact same-sex marriage after a 12-hour hearing in the Senate and more than 55 hours of public testimony in the House. It passed and Democrat Representative Georgette "Jo" Jordan (D) who is openly gay and Republican Representative Bob McDermott both voted against Senate Bill 1. Representative McDermott filed a lawsuit claiming that same-sex marriage cannot be legalized until the court further defines the existing amendment (Karlamangla, 2013). Representative Jordan said she was guided by one question:

[A]re we creating a measure that meets the needs of all? really... not happy with the exemptions. Too narrow. I'm not here to protect the big churches or the little churches, I'm saying we can't erode what's currently out there. We don't want to scratch at the religious protections at all. (Lee, 2013)

INVESTIGATING BILL SPONSORSHIP

Data Collection

In order to investigate how faith may have influenced an individual legislators decision to sponsor legislation.

This section of the chapter seeks to develop a descriptive content review for bills religious freedom bills introduced to quantitatively describe the proposed and enacted legislation in all 50 states between 2004 and 2016. The information was obtained through unobtrusive techniques, either using public sources or relying on informed observers. Using LexisNexis (StateNet) legislative tracking service, a systematic and structured keyword search examined state-level bills that were introduced and failed, and those that were introduced and ultimately became law. From the initial list of bills that related to religious freedom bills a refined search was conducted that narrowed the criteria to only include those bills that mentioned "balancing test between burdens on an individual" verses "compelling government interest." While this method offers a broad view of religious freedom related measures, some relevant legislation may not be documented and information gaps may exist between the various sources. The research was compiled from data gathered from the following sources is listed in Appendix 1.

In addition to using LexisNexis other data sources were used to address the questions of bill sponsorship (i.e. party affiliation, religious affiliation and ideology); data was gathered from archival sources including Project Vote Smart ("Project Vote Smart - The Voter's Self Defense System," n.d.). This organization provides information on candidates and elected officials and is funded exclusively through contributions from private citizens. The database contains voting records; biographical information; issue positions; interest group ratings; public statements; and campaign finances.

Guth & Kellstedt, (2001) adopted an "unobtrusive" approach, using internet sources to garner information about legislator religious involvement beyond affiliation. Religious affiliation was in some instances reported on the official member legislative website further attempts were made to include all the data that could be acquired about that bill sponsors religious affiliation, behavior and beliefs; to assess if the bill's sponsor was motived by faith in sponsoring a religious freedom bill. This approach was used to review of the legislator's specific congregation web site assisted in categorizing opposition to same-sex marriage, data on congregations' internal attitudes toward sexuality and marriage. Legislators often list much more specific on their campaign websites. Many name their local house of worship, and some detail personal activity, such as holding leadership positions, serving on committees, teaching Sunday school. Some claim to be "regular attendees" or otherwise indicate the extent of their religious involvement. Those assertions were taken at face value as indicators of religious commitment – unless evidence was found to the contrary.

Given that denominational identification is a central component of an individual's religious identity and it "remains a strong source of political attitudes and orientations" (Wilcox, Jelen, & Leege, 1993, p. 89). A congregation's religious tradition, then, was used as a proxy for directionality of organizational stance on same-sex marriage, with White Mainline Protestant congregations being supportive and White Evangelical Protestant being opposed. The following denominations were coded as evangelical: all Baptists, Assemblies of God, and Brethren in Christ, Christian Missionary Alliance, Christian Reformed Church, Church of God, Church of Christ, Nazarenes, Adventists, Christian Scientists, Lutheran-Missouri Synod, and self-identified evangelical legislators.

The inclusion of a salience measure allows us to move beyond discrete denominational classifications, and measure the extent to which religious commitment, in addition to identification, affects decision-making. Reliable measures of religious salience are difficult to attain. While some have attempted to measure salience using interviews (Benson &Williams, 1982; Yamane & Oldmixon, 2006). As indicated in Table 1 legislators who mentioned religious involvement or their religious identification in their biographies were noted that being said, this was used as a blunt measurement instrument. It may be a measure of salience, but it may also capture the desire to project religious salience to constituents.

Bill Identification and Coding

The full text of identified bills were collected and scanned, resulting initially, in a total of 1235 bills. After a refined search was completed this resulted in two hundred and twenty-nine bills, a further review resulted in 130 religious freedom bills for inclusion. Bills were omitted on a second read, if the bill did not clearly relate to religious freedom. A coding tool was developed that included general bill information (e.g. bill status, sponsor, party affiliation, year introduced, originating chamber, co-sponsors, and level of bill partisanship). The data set was compared with other publicly available collection of state religious freedom bills listed in Appendix 1. If a discrepancy was noted, further research was conducted to examine the text of the bill to see if it related or was beyond the scope of the study. The bill was then coded as falling under a specific topic area if the language of the bill indicated a presence of that characterization. Data was collected from various organizational sources listed

Table 1. Top RFRA states bill introduction from 2005-2016

Region	State	Number of Bills (n=568)
South	WV	13
South	TX	9
South	GA	8
Midwest	OK	8
West	HI	8
Midwest	IN	5
Midwest	MO	5

in Appendix 2 and classified into six categories. Of the six classifications listed in Appendix 2 the focus is limited to religious freedom and anti-same-sex marriage or marriage refusal initiatives.

Analysis and Discussion

Descriptive statistics were used to describe the basic features of the data, on the topic of same-sex marriage and religious tradition differences are clear. In a recent analysis of Christian congregations, Adler (2012) reported that White Evangelical Protestant congregations are less likely than other religious traditions to be open to gay and lesbian members. Clergy discussion of homosexuality/gay rights occurs with greater frequency within denominations in the Evangelical Protestant religious tradition (Guth et al. 1997; Djupe & Gilbert, 2002, 2009). Denominational identification provides individuals with a group identity that is attached to "broader cultural traditions," and it is politically important for that reason (Kellstedt & Green, 1993, p. 65).

Opponents of gay rights often see progressive sexuality as a threat to traditionalism and "proper" social values (Wilcox, 2000). They are guided by a moral vision that considers traditional families and sexual relations as preferred by God and, therefore, correct and worthy of honor. These people are often affiliated with religious denominations that espouse high levels of theological and social conservatism (Button, Rienzo, & Wald, 1997). As shown in Table 2 between 2005 and 2016 shows the total numbers of bills introduced and are classified by category; through the period shows the number of anti-same sex marriage bills introduced was 4 times greater than the number of RFRA bills. Table 3 examines the time trend in the RFRA types of bills introduced between 2005 and 2016, and the averaged 11 bills/

Table 2. Total number of anti-gay bills from 2005-2016

Category	Number of Bills	Percent of Total Bills (n= 1235)
RFRA	133	11.1
Marriage	568	47.3
Parenting	82	6.8
Healthcare	62	5.2
Student	275	22.9
Government Services	63	5.2
Other	53	4.4

Table 3. Number of anti-gay bills introduced from 2005-2016

Issue	2016	2015	2014	2013	2012	2011	2010	2009	2008	2007	2006	2005	Overall Mean
RFRA	21	39	19	20	5	19	7	1	1	1	0	0	11.1
Marriage	62	77	37	27	16	45	40	39	20	43	70	92	47.3
Total	116	226	96	87	58	127	72	97	33	66	123	120	102.9
Average per Year	17	32	14	12	8	17	11	138	4.8	9.6	17.6		

year beginning in 2010; as compared to the number of anti-same-sex marriage bills introduce roughly 4 times as many were introduced.

Morality politics often invoke strong ideological divisions, with conservatives defending traditional values and norms, while liberals argue for tolerance and an acceptance of nontraditional lifestyles (Buchanan & Ohsfeldt, 1993). Additional factors party affiliation, member ideology as reflected in expressed opposition to same-sex marriage (e.g. sponsored a bill, voted in opposition or indicated publically). Throughout the period as illustrated in Table 4 the number of anti-same sex marriage bills was introduced peaked at 16.2% in 2005, compared to the number of RFRA bills at 29.3% in 2015. This substantial rise and subsequent fall in the number of bills observed suggests that as same-sex marriage was legalized either thru court decisions or statute, other legislative measures were being introduced.

Legislators have strong feelings about morality and how it relates to social life in general, and to social institutions such as marriage in particular (Becker, 1999; Ammerman, 2005; Edgell, 2006). Table 5 provides the summary details of the bill coding variables from 2005-2016; of the total number of 130 bills were introduced in the house 59.2% than in the senate 40.8%; 65.9% the bill sponsors were Republicans as compared to 19.2% that were Democrats and 6.9% was introduced by committee; a greater percentage of bills were sponsored by a single party (70.1%) verses bills with bipartisan sponsors (29.2%). Of the seven bills that were passed these were slightly bipartisan

Table 4. Proportion of yearly trends of bills analyzed by topic: State legislative approaches to addressing gay issues, 2005-2016

Issue	2016	2015	2014	2013	2012	2011	2010	2009	2008	2007	2006	2005
RFRA, %	15.8	29.3	14.3	15	3.8	14.3	5.3	0	0	0	0	0
Marriage, %	10.9	13.6	6.5	4.8	2.8	7.9	7	6.9	3.5	7.6	12.3	16.2

Table 5. Bill coding variables: state legislator approaches to religious freedom 2010-2016

Variable	Introduced, Number	(%) Introduced	(%) Enacted
Originating Chamber			
House	77	59.2	
Senate	53	40.4	
Legislative			
Total	130		
Year Introduced			
2010	7	5.4	1
2011	19	14.6	1
2012	5	3.9	0
2013	20	15.4	2
2014	19	14.6	1
2015	39	30	2
2016	21	16.2	1
Total	130		
Primary Sponsor Party			
Democrat	25	19.2	
Republican	105	65.9	
Both Republican and Democrat	37	29.2	
Committee	9	6.9	
Co-Sponsor Party			
Bipartisan	37	29.2	
Single Party	93	70.1	
Primary Sponsor Religious Affiliation			
Baptist	33	25.6	
Catholic	12	8.5	
Christian	11	12.2	
Evangelical	31	30.5	
Lutheran Evangelical	5	3.8	
Methodist	5	3.8	
Mormon	11	8.5	
Non-denominational	4	1.3	
Pentecostal	4	1.3	
Unknown	8	7.3	

with the primary sponsor as a Republican (and had at least one Democrat co-sponsor); only 1 bill that passed where the lead sponsor was a Democrat. All of the legislatures that passed RFRA bills were controlled single party Republicans (The outcome of interest was bill sponsorship not enactment). Seventy-five percent of those bill were sponsored by males, 2% were female; <1% were sponsored by minorities; 25.4% of the bills were sponsored by women; 5.4% or 7 bills were passed into law; including the vetoed bills increases the passage rate to 8.5%.).

The cultural threat perceived by legislators with the legalization of same-sex marriage has created a backlash against this social change. This counter mobilization has been demonstrated by the increase in the number of anti-gay bills introduced across nation in recent years. Table 6 ranks the number of RFRA bills sponsored per region. The south region introduced the highest percentage of RFRA related bills (47%); 5 times higher than the Northeast (9.1%); is the only region in the US where the percentage of evangelicals has increased by 8%; the Midwest increase of 62.5% of unaffiliated, followed by West with 52% and the Northeast with 28% (Pew Research, 2015).

Allowing the ideological part of Christianity to flourish under the banner of religious freedom weakens the spiritual part of the religion itself and makes things more complicated. Politics dominates our lives and there is always a temptation to make a religion out of politics. Those obsessed with a political mission are fearless and resourceful. Relieved of the need to exercise individual moral judgment, they become ruthless, talented strategists and remorseless legislators. Table 6 emphasizes that 72% of the number of anti-same sex marriage bills during that period originated from the states of (NJ, MN,MD); as compared to 13% of the southern states bills that were initiated in (MD, OK, WV). Bills were introduced from thirty-six states during 2005-2016 time

Table 6. Top anti-same sex marriage bill introduction from 2005-2016

Region	State	Number of Bills (n=568)
Northeast	NJ	35
South	MN	33
South	MD	26
Midwest	OK	26
South	WV	23
West	NM	21

periods no bills were identified in 14 States: Connecticut, Massachusetts, New Jersey, Rhode Island, Vermont, Illinois, Minnesota, Nebraska, North Dakota, Alaska, Washington, Alabama, Delaware, and Maryland. Of the 130 analyzed bills, 7 bills were passed into law (5.4%). States that introduced at least 1 Religious Freedom bill during the study period varied in geography.

Without a doubt, U.S. religious heritage affects how legislators and citizens understand politics, even in situations where political positions are exempt from obvious ties to an obvious religious belief. Other studies indicate a correlation between denominational membership and votes on many same-sex marriage and abortion issues. Twenty-five percent of the bill sponsors self-identified as Baptist combined with the number of evangelicals (56%) of the sponsored RFRA legislation. Additionally, 25% of the legislators self-disclosed that they were active members of their church (e.g. Pastor, deacon, elder, Sunday school teacher, etc.). Indeed, denominational identification encapsulates "differences in belief, practice, and commitment, even for individuals with minimal religiosity. Many legislators base political decisions on faith reasons (Klemp, 2007). Prior research clearly has shown the key role that religious affiliation plays in defining the debate in relation to sexual orientation issues (Barclay & Fisher, 2003).

Schroedel's (1999) study of political elites and Lewis and Roger's (1999) study of Gallup and CNN polls demonstrated the role of religion in influencing an individual's position on gay issues. Table 6 and 7 provide an overview by geographic region most bills were introduced in the south and the fewest bills introduced in the Midwest. There was geographic variation in the number of bills introduced between 2005 and 2016. The average number of RFRA bills introduced per state was11.1; West Virginia introduced the most RFRA bills compared to New Jersey that introduced the most anti-same same marriage bills Four Southern States accounted for 29% of the RFRA bills sponsored (WV, TX, GA, OK); followed by the Midwestern States of (IN, MO) with 7.7%. When comparing the number of bills sponsored per region with the percent of evangelicals, the south is the only region that has increased the number of evangelical by 8% from 2007.Where the other regions increasing are found in the number of unaffiliated.

This chapter identified areas in which state policy makers focus legislative efforts towards addressing their concerns about same sex marriage through the introduction of bills that would expand religious freedom protections for objectors. The correlation between a legislator's moral worldview and bill sponsorship does not prove causality, but it does show the ideological parallels of this relationship. The states that passed a RFRA bill only 1 state has term limits (Arkansas); enacting states were governed by a single party; only two states (VA, KY) had split chambers.

SOLUTIONS AND RECOMMENDATIONS

Although this chapter contribute the body of literature on state legislation and the use of faith in bill sponsorship. Future research should continue to monitor the number and types of bills with more focus on individual legislators with regard to their particular faith. Some legislators only describe themselves as Christians and that dilutes the substantive nature of their faith in action. When a legislator disclose what church they attend that at the very least provides a starting point to ascertain salience. More attention is required to discover and understand the religious factor in legislative behavior.

CONCLUSION

The contemporary republican revival occurs at a time of heightened political fragmentation. In this context, the problem of unshared religious norms poses just one of the many areas of difference. The manifestation of this shift in vision from secular constitutionalism to the dominance of sectarian religious values in political policy is nowhere more apparent than within the state legislatures across the U.S. The accompanying dangers to democracy are also nowhere more palpable. The call for engagement is prevalent in the religious sector and has been answered by state legislative bill sponsorship. In one sense, conceiving an active role for faith in politics implies a restoration or a return to an established church that sanctions and provides authority for law and its exercise of coercive power. But the conception of an active role for faith in politics is incompatible with both the contemporary revival and classical republican theory. This reasoning applies to legislators and how they decide to sponsor bills. Legislator's fundamental beliefs will influence decision-making will have some influence on judgment.

REFERENCES

Adler, G. (2012). An Opening in the Congregational Closet? Boundary-Bridging Culture and Membership Privileges for Gays and Lesbians in Christian Religious Congregations. *Social Problems*, *59*, 177–206.

Ammerman, N. (2005). *Pillars of faith: American congregations and their partners*. Berkeley, CA: University of California Press.

Baehr v. Lewin (74Haw. 530; 852 P.2d 44; 1993)

Becker, P. (1999). *Congregations in Conflict: Cultural Models of Local Religious Life*. Cambridge, UK: Cambridge University Press. doi:10.1017/CBO9780511499319

Benson, P. L., & Williams, D. L. (1982). *Religion on Capitol Hill: Myths and Realities*. San Francisco: Harper and Row.

Biography. (2010). *Representative Dave Hunt*. Oregon House of Representatives. Retrieved from https://web.archive.org/web/20101206133356/http://www.leg.state.or.us/hunt/bio.htm

Brewer, P., & Wilcox, C. (2005). Same-Sex Marriage and Civil Unions. *Public Opinion Quarterly*, *69*(4), 599-616. DOI: https://doi.org/10.1093/poq/nfi052

Buchanan, R. J., & Ohsfeldt, R. L. (1993). The attitudes of state legislators and state medicaid policies related to AIDS. *Policy Studies Journal: the Journal of the Policy Studies Organization*, *21*(4), 651–671. doi:10.1111/j.1541-0072.1993.tb02164.x

Button, J., Rienzo, B., & Wald, K. (1997). *Private Lives, Public Controversies: Battles Over Gay Rights in American Communities*. Washington, DC: CQ Press.

Callimachi, R. (2004 March 2). *Multnomah county authorizes same-sex marriages starting Wednesday*. Associated Press. Retrieved from http://web.archive.org/web/20040404020900/http://www.sfgate.com/cgi-bin/article.cgi?f=/news/archive/2004/03/02/state2223EST7030.DTL

City of Boerne v. Flores, 521 U.S. 507 (1997)

Clausen, A. R. (1994). *How congressmen decide*. New York, NY: St. Martin's.

Cole, M. (2009, April 27). House tweaks domestic partnership law for same-sex couples. *Oregon Live*. Retrieved from http://www.oregonlive.com/news/index.ssf/2009/04/house_tweaks_domestic_partners.html

Defense of Marriage Act, Pub. L. No. 104–199, 110 Stat. 2419 (1996).

Djupe, P., & Gilbert, C. (2002). *The political influence of churches*. New York: Cambridge University Press.

Djupe, P., & Gilbert, C. (2009). *The political influence of churches*. New York: Cambridge University Press.

Edgell, P. (2006). *Religion and family in a changing society*. Princeton, NJ: Princeton University Press.

Evans, C. (2004, December). *Equality from State to State: Gay, Lesbian, Bisexual and Transgender Americans and State Legislation*. Human Rights Campaign Foundation. Retrieved from http://s3.amazonaws.com/hrc-assets//files/assets/resources/2004statetostate.pdf

Guth, J. L., Green, J. C., Kellstedt, L. A., Smidt, C. E., & Poloma, M. M. (1997). *The Bully Pulpit: The Politics of Protestant Clergy*. Lawrence, KS: University Press of Kansas.

Guth, J. L., & Kellstedt, L. A. (2001). Religion and Congress. In C. E. Smidt (Ed.), *In God We Trust: Religion and American Political Life* (pp. 213–233). Grand Rapids, MI: Baker Academic.

Horton, H. (2016 September 9). People are celebrating women who made history on US Election night in response to Donald Trump win. *The Daily Telegraph*. Retrieved from http://www.telegraph.co.uk/news/2016/11/09/people-are-celebrating-women-who-made-history-on-us-election-nig/

Karlamangla, S. (2013 November 14). Hawaii is 15th state to OK gay marriage; The governor makes it official. Opponents promise a fight. *Los Angeles Times*. Retrieved from http://search.proquest.com.lib.kaplan.edu/newsstand/docview/1457749097/fulltext/BF27706CF98343D0PQ/10?accountid=34544

Kellstedt, L., & Green, J. (1993). Knowing God's Many People: Denominational Preference and Political Behavior. In Rediscovering the Religious Factor in American Politics. Sharpe.

Kroger, G. (2003). Position taking and cosponsorship in the U.S. House. *Legislative Studies Quarterly*, *28*(2), 225–246. doi:10.3162/036298003X200872

Layman, G., & Carmines, E. (1997). Cultural conflict in american politics: Religious traditionalism, postmaterialism, and U.S. political behavior. *The Journal of Politics*, *59*(3), 751–777. doi:10.2307/2998636

Lazarus, J. (2013). Issue salience and bill introduction in the house and senate. *Congress & the Presidency, 40*(3), 215–229. <ALIGNMENT.qj></ALIGNMENT>10.1080/07343469.2013.822944

Lee, D. (2013, November). Why Rep. Jo Jordan Voted Against Marriage Equality. *Honolulu Magazine*. Retrieved from http://www.honolulumagazine.com/Honolulu- Magazine/November-2013/Exclusive-Why-Rep-Jo-Jordan-voted-against- Marriage-Equality/

Lewis, G. B., & Rogers, M. A. (1999). Does the public support equal employment rights for gays and lesbians? In E. D. B. Riggle & B. L. Tadlock (Eds.), *Gays and lesbians in the democratic process* (pp. 118–145). New York, NY: Columbia University Press.

Liptak, A. (2014, March 24). Ruling Could Have Reach Beyond Issue of Contraception. *The New York Times*.

Mayhew, D. (1974). *Congress: The Electoral Connection*. New Haven, CT: Yale University Press.

Oldmixon, E., & Hudson, W. (2008). When church teachings and policy commitments collide: Perspectives on catholics in the U.S. house of representatives. *Politics and Religion, 1*(1), 113–135. <ALIGNMENT.qj></ALIGNMENT>10.1017/S1755048308000060

Out and Elected in the USA 1974-2004. (1994). Retrieved from http://outhistory.org/exhibits/show/out-and-elected/1994/chuck-carpenter

Patterson, S. C. (1983). Legislators and legislatures in the American States. In H. Jacob & K. N. Vines (Eds.), *Politics in the American States: A comparative analysis*. Boston, MA: Little Brown.

Prengaman, P. (2003, June 29). Minnis duo stands apart in Oregon Legislature. *The Register-Guard.* Retrieved from https://news.google.com/newspapers?nid=1310&dat=20030629&id=KFoUAAAAIBAJ&sjid=l-sDAAAAIBAJ&pg=3484,6635829

Religious Freedom Restoration Act of 1993, Pub. L. No. 103-141, 107 Stat. 1488 (November 16, 1993), codified at 42 U.S.C. § 2000bb through 42 U.S.C. § 2000bb-4

Religious Liberty. (2009, July 21). *Governor signs Oregon workplace religious freedom act*. Retrieved from http://religiousliberty.tv/governor-quietly-signs-oregon-workplace-religious-freedom-act.html

Schroedel, J. R. (1999). Elite attitudes toward homosexuals. In E.D.B. Riggle & B.L. Tadlock (Eds.), Gays and lesbians in the democratic process (pp. 89–117). New York, NY: Columbia University Press.

Smith, T., & Tatalovich, R. (2003). *Cultures at War: Moral Conflicts in Western Democracies*. Orchard Park, NY: Broadview Press.

Snyder, J., & Groseclose, T. (2000). Estimating party influence in congressional roll-call voting. *American Journal of Political Science*, *44*(2), 187–205. doi:10.2307/2669305

United States v. Windsor, 570 U.S. ___ (2013) (Docket No. 12-307)

Wald, K. (2003). *Religion and Politics in the United States*. Lanham, MD: Rowman & Littlefield.

Wallsten, P. (1997 February). Church meets state series: For a better Florida: Social issues. *St. Petersburg Times*. Retrieved from http://search.proquest.com.lib.kaplan.edu/newsstand/docview/263220057/fulltext/BF27706CF98343D0PQ/54?accountid=34544

Wilcox, C. (2000). *Onward Christian soldiers? The religious right in American politics* (2nd ed.). Boulder, CO: Westview Press.

Wilcox, C., Jelen, T., & Leege, D. (1993). Religious group identifications: Toward a cognitive theory of religious mobilization. *Rediscovering the Religious Factor in American Politics*, 72-99.

Wildavsky, A. (1987). Choosing preferences by constructing institutions: A cultural theory of preference formation. *The American Political Science Review*, *81*, 3–44.

Willamette Week. (2015, February 13). *Gov. John Kitzhaber announces his resignation*. Retrieved from http://www.wweek.com/portland/blog-32833-gov-john-kitzhaber-announces-his-resignation.html

Williamson, E. C. (1997). City of Boerne v. Flores and the Religious Freedom Restoration Act: The Delicate Balance Between Religious Freedom and Historic Preservation. *Journal of Land Use and Environmental Law*, *13*(1), 107–159.

Wuthnow, R. (1988). *The Restructuring of American Religion: Society and Faith since World War II*. Princeton University Press.

Yamane, D., & Oldmixon, E. (2006). Religion in the legislative arena: Affiliation, salience, advocacy, and public policymaking. *Legislative Studies Quarterly, 31*(3), 433–460. <ALIGNMENT.qj></ALIGNMENT>10.3162/036298006X201878

Yuen, M. (1998, December 24). State: Same-sex marriage OK must be overturned: The court is told lawmakers now have the power to limit marriage to opposite-sex pairs. *Honolulu Star – Bulletin*. Retrieved from http://search.proquest.com.lib.kaplan.edu/newsstand/docview/412257756/BF27706CF98343D0PQ/29?accountid=34544

KEY TERMS AND DEFINITIONS

Cultural Cleavage: Cleavage separates the voters into advocates and adversaries on a certain issue, or voting for a certain party.

Moral Worldview: A worldview is based on the infallible Word of God.

Roll Call Vote: A recorded vote is a vote in which the names of those voting for and against a motion may be recorded. In many deliberative bodies, questions may be decided by voice vote, but the voice vote does not allow one to determine at a later date which members voted for and against the motion.

Traditionalism: The theory that all moral truth comes from divine revelation passed on by tradition.

Whip: an official of a political party appointed to maintain discipline among its members in Congress or Parliament, especially so as to ensure attendance and voting in debates.

APPENDIX 1: DATA COLLECTION SOURCES

- Project VoteSmart
- The Pew Research Center's 2015 U.S. Religious Landscape Study
- Legislators' personal websites
- Membership lists from the National Black Caucus of State Legislators, the National Hispanic Caucus of State Legislators and the Asian Pacific Islander Legislative Caucus
- Key state legislative staff offices
- American Civil Liberties Union (2017). Past Anti-LGBT Religious Exemption Legislation across the country. Retrieved from https://www.aclu.org/other/past-anti-lgbt-religious-exemption-legislation-across-country?redirect=anti-lgbt-religious-refusals-legislation-across-country
- Baptist Joint Committee for Religious Liberty. (2017)State RFRA bill tracker. Retrieved from http://bjconline.org/staterfratracker/
- Hamilton, M. (2016). Development of State RFRA Statutes. RFRA Perils. Retrieved from http://rfraperils.com/states/
- Human Rights Campaign. (2017). Equality from State to State & State Equality Index Archives. Retrieved from http://www.hrc.org/resources/equality-from-state-to-state
- Law Librarians Society of Washington, DC. (2016 November 30). State Legislatures, State Laws, and State Regulations: Website Links and Telephone Numbers. Retrieved from http://www.llsdc.org/state-legislation#OT
- National Conference of State Legislatures. (2016 December 31). 2016 State Religious Freedom Restoration Act Legislation. Retrieved from http://www.ncsl.org/research/civil-and-criminal-justice/2016-state-religious-freedom-restoration-act-legislation.aspx
- National Conference of State Legislatures (2015 October 15). State Religious Freedom Restoration Acts. Retrieved from http://www.ncsl.org/research/civil-and-criminal-justice/state-rfra-statutes.aspx
- National Conference of State Legislatures. (2015 June 26) Same-sex Marriage Laws. Retrieved from http://www.ncsl.org/research/human-services/same-sex-marriage-laws.aspx

- National Conference of State Legislatures (2016 August 4). Marriage Solemnization: Religious Exemption Statutes. Retrieved from http://www.ncsl.org/research/human-services/same-sex-marriage-religious-exemptions-statutes.aspx#resources
- Protect thy Neighbor. (2017). Legislation Tracker. Retrieved from http://www.protectthyneighbor.org/legislation/

APPENDIX 2

Table 7. Classification of legislation

Classification of Legislation	Description
Religious Freedom Restoration Acts	Allow lawsuits against any governmental policy, such as nondiscrimination laws, that substantially burdens someone's religious beliefs. The government must prove that enforcing the policy is the least restrictive way of furthering a compelling governmental interest.
Marriage Refusals	These bills allow different kinds of refusals regarding marriage. They vary from state to state, but in general, do one or more of the following: Allow certain people authorized by the state, such as magistrates, judges, clerks and/or clergy, to refuse to perform marriages and/or issue marriage licenses. Other bills attempt to override the federal courts' constitutional decisions on marriage for same-sex couples. Other bills allow individuals, businesses and/or religious organizations to refuse to provide goods and services relating to marriage, and/or refuse to treat marriages as valid based on their religious beliefs. Some of these bills target same sex couples; others would allow a refusal to act as to any kind of marriage.
Adoption & Foster Care	Adoption and foster care agencies could refuse to provide any adoption services that would conflict with the sincerely held religious beliefs of the agency, regardless of the best interests of the children in their care.
Access to Health Services	Legislation would allow those with religious objections to undermine professional standards that apply equally to everyone. For instance, a high school guidance counselor could refuse to counsel a gay teenager, citing their sincerely held religious beliefs.
Colleges & University Student Groups	Requires public colleges and universities to give benefits, including access to funding and the use of facilities, to student organizations even if the organization discriminates based on their religious beliefs.
Other Anti-LGBT Backlash Legislation	Other laws include laws allowing businesses to discriminate, a proposal to eliminate marriage licenses altogether, and laws that would ban local nondiscrimination ordinances.

Chapter 4
The Holy Wars of Marriage

ABSTRACT

This chapter will focus on the biggest moral issue in recent history-the debate over same-sex marriage. This unprecedented case began in 1990 when three same-sex couples applied for marriage licenses from the State of Hawaii. They were refused and challenged the state's decision. In May 1993, the Hawaiian Supreme Court ruled the state needed to show compelling reasons why the same-sex couples should not be allowed to marry. Although the battle in Hawaii began in the court, it ended up in the state legislature where it spread rapidly across the nation. Legislators have responded to the promotion of same-sex marriage by sponsoring and passing bills claiming that it contravenes their faith based principles.

Thou shalt not lie with mankind, as with womankind: it is an abomination ~ Leviticus 18:22

INTRODUCTION

Marriage is a word applied to both ceremonial events and to legal contracts. The nature and form of both have changed through the centuries. Historically, Christian marriage could be a brutal institution, disposed to treat women and children as commodities. Governments took an interest in marriage in order to deal with points of law such as inheritance rights. In the United States

DOI: 10.4018/978-1-5225-2388-8.ch004

today, each state governs its own marriage laws. Legal provisions related to marriage number into the hundreds in each state, and more than a thousand on the federal level. The legal issues surrounding same-sex marriage in the United States are complicated by the nation's federal system of government. In other words, any marriage recognized by a state was recognized by the federal government, even if that marriage was not recognized by one or more other states (as was the case with interracial marriage before 1967).

Throughout U.S. history, the laws of each state have defined marriage. At no time has marriage been defined by federal law. Without exception, since the founding of the Republic, marriage has been a matter of state concern and control. However, on September 21, 1996, Democratic President Bill Clinton signed into law the "Defense of Marriage Act" (DOMA), this legislation authorized states not to give "full faith and credit" to same-sex marriage. Further, it defined marriage for the purpose of federal law as "only a legal union between one man and one woman as husband and wife. The word "spouse," it asserted, only referred "to a person of the opposite sex who is a husband or wife" (People for the American Way, 1997).. Thus, DOMA banned the possibility of federal government recognition of same-sex couples, should individual states allow their marriage. DOMA did not preclude states from choosing to perform or recognize same-sex marriages; instead it focused on the recognition conditions of marriages performed in other jurisdictions. As Table 2 (see Appendix) indicates, states varied in their response to regulate same-sex marriage suggesting that DOMA was not a definitive statement impacting the sentiments of individual states.

The passage of this bill during an era of Republican ascendancy is unsurprising. In 1996, Republicans had solid majorities in both the House and Senate, and the Democratic president had won with only 43 percent of the vote. Since the mid-1960s, Republicans have opposed extending civil rights to disadvantaged groups at least partly because, as Hillygus and Shields (2008) note, much of the Grand

Old Party (GOP)'s southern strategy was predicated on making race-based appeals to recruit Democratic white southern voters to the GOP as Republicans stonewalled advances in civil rights by propounding "states' rights" arguments that asserted that these decisions should be left to the individual states (Karol, 2009). States' rights are a critical component of the U.S. system, and the argument is against overreaching federal powers. What was a surprise was the opposition of leading Democrats to same-sex marriage. Democrats had been the party for the extension of civil rights to virtually all disenfranchised groups whether based on race, ethnicity, gender, or age. On issues of gay rights; however, many Democrats embraced the states' rights arguments advanced by Republicans to deny civil rights to one of their party's staunchest allies, the lesbian, gay, bisexual, and transgender (LGBT) community. State legislatures have been deeply involved in the debates about how to define marriage and whether the official recognition of "marriage" should be limited to relationships involving one man and one woman or that same-sex couples should also be entitled to "marriage." State legislatures have gone both ways in this debate: either enacting "defense of marriage" laws and constitutional provisions in opposition, or going instead in the opposite direction, adopting laws allowing same sex marriage. As demonstrated in Table 1 (see Appendix) State laws and/or constitutional provisions that limit marriage to relationships between a man and a woman were passed by 30 states with constitutional provisions, and by 41 statutory provisions.

This chapter will present an overview of Federal and State court cases that triggered national outrage which manifested in state legislative action across the country to pass statutes and constitutional amendments banning same-marriage. Debates within state legislatures are frequently sparked by concerns about judicial activism, as indicated the examination of court rulings related to same-sex marriage. Often lost in the wave of state legislative prohibitions is that the highest courts, when confronted, rule in the same direction as the most recently expressed legislative preference (Barclay, 2010). Even where the courts appeared to act in contradiction of the expressed preferences of the elected branches both (Graber, 1993; Lovell, 2003) propose that legislatures actually encourage the judiciary to take the primary role in those policy area that have the potential to threaten policy coalitions.

BACKGROUND

A review of the history of marriage shows that the institution has been a fluid paradigm, changing with culture and societal norms of the time. Originally, polygamy (having more than one wife at a time) was common in ancient civilizations in the Middle East. In the Bible, for example, marriage was traditionally polygamous. Abraham was married to both Sarah and Hagar and had children with both (29 Genesis 11:23 King James Version). Solomon was said to have had more than one thousand wives (1 Kings). Polygamy was, and still is, common in Islamic cultures. The Quran permits a man to have up to four wives (Quran, 4:3). Even today, polygamy is found throughout the Middle East.

The Catholic Church was not formally involved in marriage ceremonies until the Middle Ages. Up until the twelfth century, if a priest were present at a marriage, he performed blessings and prayers during the ceremony. The couple would also offer their own prayers. The priest would then asked the couple to agree to be committed to each other in the presence of all attendees (Glavich, 2000). From the fifth to approximately the fourteenth century, the Roman Catholic Church conducted special ceremonies to bless same-sex unions, which were considered spiritual, though not sexual unions (Boswell, 1994). In 1563, the Council of Trent defined Catholic marriage as a ceremony celebrated by a priest in a Catholic church before two witnesses. By the seventeenth century, the wedding ceremony was a religious event in all of the countries in Europe. In England, weddings in the thirteenth century among the upper class became a religious event. Even then, the church only blessed the marriage and did not require the parties to make a civil, binding commitment to each other (Batchelor, 2003). Marriage law, as it operated in England from the fourteenth to nineteenth centuries was a mess. The church asserted that mere verbal consent, freely given and duly witnessed, constituted a binding marriage. But common law denied the effect of the transmission of property of these private contracts.

In 1753, England passed the Marriage Act. This statutory legislation was the first to require a formal ceremony taking the control of marriage from individuals and the church and turning it over to the state as a legal entity (Probert, 2009). From that point on, marriages that had not taken place in the Church of England or in a synagogue were rendered invalid; although church law had regularized the ceremony of marriage by insisting that bans were read and license fees paid. Prior to 1753, the civil law required only that a marriage could be proved to have taken place. Since the Marriage Act, the only legally recognized marriages were those performed by the Church of England, Jews and Quakers. This meant that Roman Catholics and members of other Christian congregations, as well as atheists, Muslims, Hindus or members of any other religious body, had to be married according to (the Anglican) rites and ceremonies which they did not support, and by a priest who they believed had no authority. If they did not do so, they had no legal rights as married people. Then in 1836, a second Marriage Act was passed. This act reflected the cultural views of the time. Accordingly, marriage was a civil action effected by mutual consent and did not require a religious ceremony (Batchelor, 2003).

During Colonial times, Americans followed the customs of England. Thus, a religious ceremony was secondary to a civil ceremony in many colonies. In some colonies, civil magistrates were given authority to perform marriage ceremonies without any religious requirements. Some colonies, however, required that the customs of the church prevail and did not permit a civil marriage ceremony. In the seventeenth and eighteenth centuries, marriage in America evolved into the monogamous one- man, one-woman model of today.

The institution of marriage and marriage equality laws have been in a consistent state of change ever since the original formation of the United States. In order to understand the national debate about marriage equality it's important to understand its historical context (Cherlin, 2004; Coontz, 2005). For most of Western history, marriage was an institution for securing wealth, property rights, and power. Only in the 19th century did it come to be defined as an institution based on love. In the mid-20th century, the dominant model of marriage in the United States was centered on emotional intimacy (husbands and wives were lovers, friends, and companions to each other) with clear gender defined roles (with a male breadwinner father and a female homemaker mother).

By the 1960s, however, cultural shifts threw this "Ozzie and Harriet" model into upheaval. Increasing labor force participation by women and the rise of a feminist movement led to challenges to longstanding gender roles, including those at the core of traditional marriage (Herek, 2006). Improved birth control technologies and a revolution in sexual mores facilitated the separation of sexual behavior from reproduction along with increased acceptance of non-marital sex. With the rise of the human potential movement, self-fulfillment and the development of personal identity, individuals were accorded greater freedom in making life decisions, including whether to marry or remain married. In the face of these changes, people increasingly evaluated marriage according to an individualistic criterion, with marital satisfaction defined more in terms of self-fulfillment than by the performance of culturally prescribed spousal roles (Cherlin, 2004; Coontz, 2005). Around the same time, lesbian and gay (and, later, bisexual and transgender, forming the LGBT community) people began to publicly affirm their sexual orientation, creating visible communities that worked towards ending discrimination based on sexuality (D'Emilio, 1983).

As early as the 1970s, the LGBT community declared that their unions met contemporary criteria for civil marriage and argued with growing insistence that the institution's social and legal benefits should be extended to them (Chauncey, 2004; Lewin, 1998). Meanwhile, political and religious conservatives called for the restoration of marriage as an institution for defining the boundaries for sexuality, child rearing, and gender roles. Many of those same conservatives had consistently fought the gay community's efforts to eliminate inequalities between heterosexuals and sexual minorities in other areas, such as employment and housing. The marriage issue provided yet another arena for battle (Chauncey, 2004; Herman, 1998).

SAME SEX MARRIAGE AND THE PUBLIC AGENDA

In April of 2001, just such a crisis event appeared drawing sustained media attention. A Massachusetts marriage case sparked national debate when same-sex couples sued for legal marriage in what became known as *Goodridge v. Department of Public Health* (2003). On November 18, 2003, the Massachusetts Supreme Court ruled that same-sex couples are legally entitled to civil marriage under the Massachusetts Constitution. The 4–3 ruling did not order licenses to be issued to the couples who challenged the law; instead the court ordered the Legislature to change the civil marriage statutes within 180 days. On May 17, 2004, Massachusetts became the first state in America to offer legal same-sex marriage. Starting in 2003, Pew began asking a question about same-sex marriage as part of its News Interest Index. In June of that year, the U.S. Supreme Court's ruling in the case of *Lawrence v. Texas* (2003) not only threw out existing sodomy laws but also provoked further debate over same-sex marriage. In Pew's poll three months later, about half of the respondents said that they were following "the issue of gay and lesbian marriage" very or fairly closely (Brewer & Wilcox, 2005).

Just as that poll was in the field, San Francisco Mayor Gavin Newsome directed city officials to begin granting marriage licenses to same-sex couples, a decision that was followed by similar efforts on the part of elected officials in various other localities. In the interim, local government officials in several other jurisdictions around the country briefly issued marriage licenses to same-sex partners until they were stopped by state courts or officials. Licenses were issued to 4,037 couples in San Francisco in February and March 2004 (Murphy, 2004), to 3,022 couples in Multnomah County, Oregon, in March and April 2004 ("Gay Weddings Halted, but Marriages Stand," 2004), and to 68 couples in Sandoval County, New Mexico, in February 2004 (Pinello, 2006).

Because legislators already believed that American family values were in a state of moral collapse, these court decisions served as "focusing events" and were perceived as creating a significant moral crisis across the nation. There is no question that the national debate regarding same-sex marriage had a profound impact on the 2004 state legislative sessions. The crisis in Massachusetts and the concern that same-sex marriage could be legalized triggered immediate legislative action as evidenced by Table 1 (see Appendix), where thirteen states responded to events in Massachusetts and initiated state constitutional amendments banning same sex marriages[1]. As Table 2 (see Appendix) indicates from 1996 to 2014, thirty-seven states in 2004 had statutes defining marriage as "between one man and one woman" and four had state constitutional amendments. While the proliferation of state Defense of Marriage Acts in 1996 contributed to the nationalization of the same-sex marriage debate, these state mini DOMAs in early 1996 created substantial issue salience over same-sex marriage, which had not previously existed.

Haider-Markel's (2001) study of policy diffusion of same-sex marriage examines the influence of conservative religious groups at the state level and finds that all of the states that introduced legislation banning same-sex marriage had conservative groups lobbying for the bill. Twenty-five states had these groups help draft the bill, and 39 states had established connections between the sponsor of the bill and a conservative religious group (Haider-Markel, 2001). Some scholars argue that the states were a more favorable battleground for those opposed to same-sex marriages and that the diffusion of policy from one state to another was a coordinated effort by opposition interest groups to increase the salience of the issue of same-sex marriage and geographically expand the arena of conflict with the ultimate goal of putting it on the national agenda (Haider-Markel, 2000, 2001; Blomquist, 2007). State legislators who were opposed to the legalization of same-sex marriage responded to the imminent threat of same-sex marriage with the looming decision in *Baehr v. Miike* (1996 WL 694235, Hawaii Cir.Ct.) by passing legislation. These individuals purposefully introduced the issue of same-sex marriage to both the systemic and formal agenda. Those individuals that sponsored the bills to oppose same-sex marriage did so because of moral concerns and furthered the perception of "moral" crisis that same-sex marriage would be legalized. In Georgia lead sponsor of Senate Bill 595, a constitutional amendment to ban same sex marriage in the House, Republican State Representative Bill Hembree, stated:

We're reacting to what's happening around the country. We're reacting to what happened in Massachusetts when their Supreme Court said that "same sex marriages could happen." We're reacting to what happened in San Francisco when their Mayor said: "Yeah, I'll sign that marriage certificate, it's okay." The Mayor of Chicago, Mayor Daly, has also indicated that he too would do the same thing as the mayor of San Francisco, so we are reacting to the institution of marriage and trying to make sure that if people come to the State of Georgia that our institution, that our definition of marriage, between a man and a woman, stands. And so basically we're defending our State Constitution about what's happening around the country and so that's the effort behind this, that's it. (Wilson, 2004)

These legislators introduced bills that intensified the issue and its importance thus, increasing the chances that same-sex marriage would make it onto the other states formal agendas.

Court Cases and Legislative Battles

The intersection of the faithful and the gay rights movement is in the states. The idea of extending marriage rights to same-sex couples became a political issue in the United States in the 1990s, when the Hawaii State Supreme Court ruled in *Baehr v. Lewin* (1993) that refusing to grant marriage licenses to same-sex couples was sex-discrimination under the State's constitution. However, the court did not immediately order the state to begin issuing marriage licenses to same-sex couples; rather, it stayed its ruling and ordered the State to justify its discrimination. This ruling galvanized opposition to same-sex marriage around the country and led to the very first "defense of marriage" amendment to a state constitution (Eskridge, 1999). Many state legislators in the United States scrambled to enact laws that prevented recognition out-of-state marriages licenses held by same-sex couples. As marriage is governed by state law, its provisions vary from state to state. For instance, states variously restrict the legal age at which one can marry, as well as closeness of kinship. The United States Constitution makes clear under the "Full Faith and Credit" clause that legal contracts, such as marriages, made in one state are to be honored by all other states. This precluded a marriage in one state from suddenly becoming illegal when a couple crosses a state line.

The biggest headlines of 1996 came from the U.S. Supreme Court decision in *Romer v. Evans* ruling overturning Colorado's Amendment 2, which prohibited municipalities in Colorado from banning discrimination against the LGBT community. Followed by President Clinton signing into law the Republican-sponsored Defense of Marriage Act (DOMA). Without question, the Hawaii court decision served to rally anti-gay forces around the country. Nebraska was the first and only state to introduce a pro same sex marriage bill. The litigation in Hawaii was both a focusing event and a symbol of the impending reality of same-sex marriage. The Hawaii Supreme Court's decision in *Baehr v. Lewin* (74 Haw. 530; 852 P.2d 44; 1993) caught the attention of those opposed to same-sex marriage as it was the first legal decision that applied strict scrutiny in a discrimination case against gays and lesbians, making same-sex marriage all but legal in Hawaii. The upcoming trial represented the approaching legalization of same-sex marriage in the first U.S. state. Opponents could use *Baehr v. Miike* (1996 WL 694235, Hawai'i Cir.Ct.) as a symbol of the necessity for a federal policy to address the legal complications that would arise at both the state and

federal level with this new union between couples of the same sex. If the litigation in Hawaii did not exist, it is unlikely that this mobilization against same-sex marriage and its place on Congress's agenda would not have happened at this particular time.

Several courts had previously been forced to wrestle with the issue of same-sex marriage. It was not the first time that couples had pursued litigation in response to the denial of their marriage certificates, and it was not the first time that the courts had ruled on the issue. Prior to the Hawaii case, some states passed laws in the 1970s in response to same-sex marriage cases brought at the time, while others have been part of the marriage statute for far longer. These may be statutes expressly limiting marriage to one man and one woman, and/or statutes explicitly forbidding same-sex marriage; most of these laws were passed contemplating only same-sex marriage contracted within their respective states. Most post-*Baehr* legislation was directed primarily at marriages contracted outside of the state.

The case of *Romer v. Evans*, (1996) where voters, with a vote of 53.4 percent, enacted Amendment 2. The amendment was drafted and promoted by an organization that called itself "Colorado for Family Values," and it would have effectively prevented any laws banning discrimination against gays, thereby nullifying gay rights laws that already existed in Colorado. The state Supreme Court ruled it unconstitutional Colorado appealed to the State Supreme Court, which affirmed the District Court's decision, and subsequently appealed to the U.S. Supreme Court. The case was argued on October 10, 1995 and the court ruled in May, 1996 in a 6-3 vote that Colorado's Amendment 2 was unconstitutional (*Romer v. Evans*, 1996). The

Clinton Administration decided against filing amicus curiae brief in the case. However, 8 states filed briefs in support of the case (California, Alabama, Idaho, Nebraska, South Carolina, South Dakota and Virginia). Seven states filed briefs opposing Amendment 2 (Oregon, Iowa, Maryland, Massachusetts, Minnesota, Nevada, and Washington). The state argued that Amendment 2 enhanced individual freedom by eliminating governmental interference in the choices that people make in religious, familial, personal, and associational matters (*Romer v. Evans*, 1996). These individual liberty interests are at "the heart" of the freedom to make personal choices regarding with which one wishes to associate. Further adding that this interest by eliminating city-by-city and county-by-county battles over the political issue of homosexuality. The campaign asserted that LGBT protection from discrimination is the equivalent of demanding "special rights" that are not available to other citizens (*Romer v. Evans*, 1996).

The message of "special rights" was the key to the passage of Amendment 2 and laid the foundation for its use in other states. Maine was the first state east of the Rocky Mountains where an anti-gay initiative (Question 1) was defeated. A special people's veto referendum in early 1998 was the first state to nullify previously enacted state-wide provisions barring discrimination against LGBT in employment, public accommodations. By a 52 to 48 percent vote, opponents of the gay rights law narrowly succeeded. In October 97, after the Maine legislature passed and Governor Angus King signed the gay rights measure, the Christian Civic League of Maine and the Christian Coalition of Maine announced that they had formed a political action committee to thwart the legislation. Ten percent of Mainers who voted in the previous election were required to put the measure on the ballot. The effort to support the measure was led in part by a Governor King. The effort to kill the sexual orientation statute was augmented by paid visits to Maine by nationally prominent figures such as Alveda King, the niece of Martian Luther King Jr. She protested any link between racism and homophobia when she spoke to gay rights opponents gathered at the State House (People for the American Way, 1997).

Strict scrutiny is the highest level of constitutional review under equal protection doctrine. In order to pass muster, defendants must show a "compelling state interest" being advanced by the legislation under question. Strict scrutiny review is reserved for legislation implicating "suspect classes," or "fundamental rights" (Herman, 1998). The only classification truly qualifying as "suspect" in American law is the category of "race." In the *Romer* case the only way to trigger a strict scrutiny review was if a fundamental right was violated. If not, the measure would be subject to a "rational-basis" review;

meaning there must be some rationality to the measure. In practice, few laws survive strict-scrutiny review, and most emerge unscathed from the rational basis test. Close to two years following the passage of the amendment, the Colorado Supreme Court issued its final decision in favor of those challenging the constitutionality of the amendment. The majority affirmed the position that a fundamental right to participate in the political process existed, and that strict scrutiny analysis was in order. The court then considered the justificatory arguments made by the state in attempt to show the compelling interests to advance Amendment 2. Of note, was the state's position of protecting freedom of religion was served through the amendments enactment. This argument was based on the idea that gay rights laws violate religious freedoms through forcing those with antigay religious views to house or hire gay people. While the court agreed that "freedom of religion…is among the highest values of our society," *(Romer v. Evans,* 1996) the judges did not find the amendment narrowly tailored to meet this interest. Instead, suggested that a religious exemption would be a suitable means of addressing this issue. These religious exemptions, release churches, other religious organizations, and sometimes orthodox individuals from obligations under civil rights law, are often part of gay rights measures (Herman, 1998). As the author of the majority opinion Justice Anthony Kennedy rejected the state's argument that Amendment 2 merely blocked gays from receiving "special rights" saying that

To the contrary, the amendment imposes a special disability upon those persons alone. Homosexuals are forbidden the safeguards that others enjoy or may seek without constraint… that protection offered by antidiscrimination laws was not a "special right" because they protected fundamental rights already enjoyed by all other citizens. (Romer v. Evans, 1996)

Kennedy did not go into depth in rejecting the claims put forward in support of the law because he held that the law was so unique as to "confound this normal process of judicial review" and "defies … conventional inquiry." This conclusion was supported by his assertion that "It is not within our constitutional tradition to enact laws of this sort." Finding that "laws of the kind now before us raise the inevitable inference that the disadvantage imposed is born of animosity toward the class of persons affected," the Court implied that the passage of Amendment 2 was borne of a "bare … desire to harm homosexuals" (*Romer v. Evans*, 1996). Justice Antonin Scalia[Amendment 2] wrote an impassioned dissent, stated that the Court should take no part in what is termed the "culture war" and wrote:

I would not myself indulge in such official praise for heterosexual monogamy, because I think it no business of the courts (as opposed to the political branches) to take sides in this culture war. But the Court today has done so, not only by inventing a novel and extravagant constitutional doctrine to take the victory away from traditional forces, but even by verbally disparaging as bigotry adherence to traditional attitudes... Today's opinion has no foundation in American constitutional law, and barely pretends to. The people of Colorado have adopted an entirely reasonable provision, which does not even disfavor homosexuals in any substantive sense, but merely denies them preferential treatment. Amendment 2 is designed to prevent piecemeal deterioration of the sexual morality favored by a majority of Coloradans, and is not only an appropriate means to that legitimate end, but also a means that Americans have employed before. Striking it down is an act, not of judicial judgment, but of political will. I dissent. (Romer v. Evans, 1996)

Justice Scalia voiced further concerns noting that at stake was the victory in the "culture war" between conservatives and liberals. The amendment symbolized the citizenry's judgement that homosexuality was to be condemned, not protected; its overturn by the courts represented an impermissible taking of sides in this war (Herman, 1998). The cultural impact of *Romer v. Evans* (1996) although only peripherally applied to state laws that ban passage of gay rights laws. It was perceived by God-fearing people in all major religions who believe that homosexuality is wrong, were now deemed to be outside the realm of decency. This was a sweeping condemnation of the deeply-held beliefs of billions of people around the world (Knight, 1996).

The opinion for *Romer v. Evans* (517 U.S. 620; 1996) was announced on May 20, 1996, a week after the Federal Defense of Marriage Act was introduced. The *Romer* case was in obvious tension with the Court's earlier decision in *Bowers v. Hardwick (1986)*, and it laid the groundwork for *Lawrence v. Texas (2003),* which later overturned *Bowers.*

Almost simultaneously, *Lawrence v. Texas* (2003) arguments were presented November, 1999 to a three-judge panel of the Texas Fourteenth Court of Appeals on both equal protection and right to privacy grounds. This 2-1 decision ruled the Texas law was unconstitutional; the full court, however, voted to reconsider its decision, upholding the law's constitutionality (*Lawrence v. Texas*, 2003). On April 13, 2001, the Texas Court of Criminal Appeals was petitioned to hear the case; the Court, the highest appellate court in Texas for criminal matters, denied review. The case then arrived at the U.S. Supreme Court, and attracted much public attention, and it was decried by social conservatives as an example of judicial activism. The Supreme Court granted a writ of certiorari agreeing to hear the case on December 2, 2002. Oral arguments were held on March 26, 2003; and the decision was rendered on June 26, 2003 (*Lawrence v. Texas*, 2003).

In the 6-3 ruling, the justices struck down the criminal prohibition of homosexual sodomy in Texas.

The court had previously addressed the same issue in *Bowers v. Hardwick* (1986), but had upheld the challenged Georgia statute, not finding a constitutional protection of sexual privacy (*Lawrence v. Texas*, 2003). The question before the Supreme Court was whether *Bowers v. Hardwick (1986)* should be overruled. Justice Kennedy delivered the opinion of the Court and cast doubt on the factual findings of the court in *Bowers*, that homosexual sodomy is a historically condemned practice. The Court concluded that, "Bowers was not correct when it was decided, and it is not correct today. It ought not to remain binding precedent. *Bowers v. Hardwick* (1986) should be and now is overruled" (*Lawrence v. Texas*, 2003). Justice Antonin Scalia wrote a sharply worded dissent, which Chief Justice William H. Rehnquist and Justice Clarence Thomas joined. Scalia also said that, State laws against bigamy, same-sex marriage, adult incest, bestiality, and obscenity are likewise sustainable only in light of Bowers' validation of laws based on moral choices. With this decision, Scalia concluded, the Court "has largely signed on to the so-called homosexual agenda." While Scalia said that he has "nothing against homosexuals, or any other group, promoting their agenda through normal democratic means," Scalia argued that the Court has an obligation to decide cases neutrally (*Lawrence v. Texas*, 2003).

In the dissenting opinion is *Bowers* Justice Stevens concluded that a States governing majority has traditionally viewed a particular private as immoral if not a sufficient reason for upholding a law; individual decision…even when not intended to produce offspring are a form of 'liberty' protected by due process. Bowers was not correct when it was decided, and it is not correct today. The right to liberty under the Due Process Clause gives them full right to engage in private conduct without government intervention *(Planned Parthood of Southeastern PA v. Casey*, 1992). The Texas statute furthers no legitimate state interest which can justify its intrusion into the individual's personal and private life (*Lawrence v. Texas,* 2003).

The *(Planned Parthood of Southeastern PA v. Casey*, 1992) decision confirmed that "at the heart of liberty" is the right to make personal decisions without compulsion by the state. Texas attempted to justify its law by arguing that the statute satisfied the rational basis review because it furthered a legitimate government interest of the promotion of morality. Further the State argued that the law only applied to conduct, but the conduct targeted is correlated with being homosexual and branded a class of persons as criminal solely based on the moral disapproval of that class runs contrary to the values of the Constitution equal protection clause. Justice Antonin Scalia dissented stating that "the court has signed on to the so-called homosexual agenda… and taken sides in the culture war" (Gearan, 2003).

Hawaii was not alone its struggles over same-sex marriage in this period. *Baker v. State of Vermont* (1997; 1999) case involved three same-sex Vermont couples filed suit on July 22, 1997 for the right to marry in Superior Court, Burlington, Vermont. Like the Hawaii case, the plaintiff couples sued the Vermont state health department for denying them marriage licenses. In 1999, the Vermont Supreme Court held that denying same-sex couples the rights and protections that come with civil marriage violated the state constitution's equality guarantee. The court ordered the legislature to take steps to end that discriminatory exclusion (*Baker v. Vermont*, 1999).

The Vermont motto of "Freedom and Unity" reflects the historical aspirations and concepts of freedom, justice, independence and unity. All of these ideals relate to the causes and history in which the LGBT community fought continues to fight for protection from discrimination. These ideals of freedom and unity have been evident throughout the culture wars for equality in the state. In the early 1970s, Bill Lippert helped form the state's first gay men's support group and, in 1983, Lippert worked with others to organize Vermont's first gay pride rally in Burlington. In 1989, Lippert helped to establish Outright Vermont, an organization dedicated to serving the needs of lesbian, gay, bisexual, and transgender youth. Howard Dean was a key figure, who grew up on Park Avenue in New York City, educated at Yale and moved to Vermont, where he and his wife practiced medicine. In 1986, Howard Dean was elected lieutenant governor and became Governor when incumbent Republican Richard Snelling died in 1991, this turning point, the state moved more to the left on America's political spectrum.; whereas, Republicans didn't become extinct in Vermont, but the ones who survived tended to be much more moderate than their peers within the national GOP. In April, 1994, Lippert2 was appointed by Governor Howard Dean to fill a vacant seat representing in the Vermont House of Representatives.

Fix it now, the court told the Legislature, either by extending full marriage rights and benefits to all or by creating a parallel status that would essentially do the same. The job to figure it out fell to the House Judiciary Committee, whose members included Lippert, then the only openly gay member of the

Legislature, and Republican Representative John Edwards, a retired longtime state trooper. But Edwards was like most people in the largely rural Green Mountain State and didn't have same-sex marriage on his radar. Edwards knew that a yes vote for civil unions would almost certainly doom his re-election chances. But he says any doubts he harbored about the proposed law were banished when he read accounts of the civil rights debates of the 1960s. The language of that time startled him.

Republican, Nancy Sheltra a fifty-one year old house member from Derby (Derby is on the Canadian border) She had been in office nine years (elected in 1989) and had made a name for herself as one of the legislators most ardent opponents of legalized abortion and gay rights. She heard the news of the *Baker* decision in the middle of the day, and saw it as another sign of the drift if American society toward secular humanism she believed was ruining the nation. God's word, not the ideals of liberal democracy shaped her politics, stating "If you want to be a nation that is blessed, we have to follow biblical teachings…there is no separation of church and state…" (Moats, 2004).

On the day of the court decision, she talked to her Pastor Fred Barker of the United Church of Derby with her friends who were concerned about what the legislature would do in response to the ruling (Moats, 2004). As a devout Assembly of God member she believed the Bible to be the only inspired, inerrant, infallible, authoritative Word of God. Insisting that the Bible condemned homosexuality she saw herself as a voice in the wilderness.

In January, 2000 Bill Lippert was the vice chair of the House Judiciary Committee, and as the General Assembly's only openly gay member, Lippert was central to the work of drafting and passing into law the landmark Vermont civil union law which granted legal recognition to same gender couples. On April 1, 2000 the bill came to a final vote in the House, and opponents would have their last chance to stop it. She was the outspoken conservative expressing her disapproval, "I don't think the state of Vermont should pit its seal of approval on conduct that is unnatural." She was unapologetic of her view that her duty was to serve the word of God, and she led a small contingent of House members who were less concerned about counting votes than in bearing witness and making a statement. Representative Frank M. Mazur a Democrat warned that Vermont's moves toward recognizing same-sex couples left him worried about whether it might hurt the state's business climate and concerned ''about whether there'll be a boycott against the state.'' ''Vermont is not an island,'' Mr. Mazur said. ''We depend upon other states,'' and many of those states have made their views clear by passing Defense of Marriage

Acts that specify that they would not recognize same-sex marriages if another state ever approved them.

A diametrically opposed argument came from Representative Marion C. Milne, a Republican, who contended that the Legislature must respect the State Supreme Court's finding that same-sex couples had been enduring unconstitutional discrimination 'I will vote for this bill because I believe it is constitutionally mandated, but more importantly, because I believe it is the right thing to do,'' Ms. Milne said. She invoked the future, noting that the results of the vote would linger long after she and her fellow lawmakers were gone. Minutes later, Representative, Nancy Sheltra, invoked the future differently: ''It's going to be very hard for me to explain to the next generation why the State Legislature decided to define marriage in a different manner and take away the moral standards we have stood for in this state" (Halloran, 2013).

Bill Lippert, the only openly gay member of the Legislature, offered a vision of a different future:

Those of you who vote no on this bill for a variety of reasons, I'm sorry for your fear, I'm sorry because we gay and lesbian couples are not a threat, as opponents will discover with time. I look forward to living together and to living in growing fairness in the state of Vermont. (Halloran, 2013)

After Lippert spoke that day, Sheltra stood to denounce the legislation as "legalizing sodomy." And then Democratic Representative Mary Mazzariello rose to make an emotional plea for civil unions, revealing for the first time publicly that she has two lesbian daughters and longed for them to have the same opportunities for love and family as her straight son. "They did not choose to be different, their pain and their inability to fit the mold has been our pain, too."

Ultimately, it was Lippert and moderate Republican Representative Thomas Little, House Judiciary chairman at the time, who emerged as catalysts for not only the law's creation, but also its passage. Anti-civil unions forces organized a "Take Back Vermont" effort that helped lead to the defeat in the next election of all but one of the 14 Republican House members who voted for civil unions. Edwards, who had taken office in 1997, was one of the victims. Conservative legislators tried to attach antigay amendments that would have barred Vermont from recognizing same-sex marriages performed in any other states was defeated. Another amendment was defeated that would have required HIV testing for civil unions. But an amendment was adopted that declared that marriage in Vermont is a union between a man and a woman.

That definition previously had existed only in the bills preamble and not in the text of the statute.

This ruling by the Vermont State Supreme court was a legal and cultural milestone. The impact of the decision on the nation depended on whether or not the Vermont Legislature approved marriage of a separately constructed system. Former Representative Karen Milne voted in favor of the civil union bill in 2000 and along with 17 other legislators who voted for the bill lost their seats in the next election (Nelson, 2010). Representative Mazzariello also lost her seat, along with a slew of other Democrats, handing control of the House to Republicans for the first time in 14 years. In 2004, Democrats regained control the House, which they won back when Sheltra and 13 other Republicans lost in what has been described as the "symbolic end of the political convulsions" of the civil unions debate (Delaney, 2004).

For Edwards, there has been a personal change since civil unions. After losing his political career, he received a Bush administration appointment as U.S. marshal, and has remained friendly with Lippert and others whose relationships were sealed during the civil union's upheaval. Edwards jokes that Republicans have since come to him to note that hellfire hasn't rained down on Vermont, that nothing much has changed (Halloran, 2013).Lippert, however, now one of a half-dozen openly gay Vermont legislators, has another take. "This is very emotional for me," he says, standing again on the floor of the House, Edwards at his side." John and my fellow colleagues helped us create civil unions, and John and others gave their political lives for the success of creating the first legal recognition anywhere in the United State for same-sex couples. "Both men are convinced that what Vermont went through — the agonizing conversations, the vitriol and ugliness, the tears and the moments of grace — set a new course for gay rights and reset the conversation for those that would come after across the nation. "John and those who lost," Lippert says, "are my heroes, to this day" (Halloran, 2013).

In response to the Court's decision, the legislature debated and enacted a first-of-its-kind legal status according same-sex couples virtually all the state-law protections, responsibilities, and benefits of civil marriage. "An Act Related to Civil Unions" was signed into Vermont law on April 26, 2000, and went into effect July 1, 2000. Only same-sex couples could enter a civil union, which involved almost identical processes for creation and dissolution as marriage. In 2009, Lippert chaired the House hearings on full Marriage Equality, and led its successful passage by the House on a vote of 94-52.

Despite strong votes and passage by both the Senate (26-4) and the House (94-52), Gov. Jim Douglas vetoed the Marriage Equality bill on April 6, 2009. In Vermont, overriding a governor's veto requires a two thirds majority, not a simple majority of fifty percent. On April 7, 2009, the Senate overrode the veto on a vote of 23-5. Lippert worked with House leadership to marshal enough House votes, and the House followed suit, overriding the governor's veto 100-49. As a result, marriage equality became Vermont law. As a result of the 2016 election, Vermont became one of 19 states under divided government. Shortly after Supreme Court struck down *Bowers*, another significant case commanded attention. This time, Massachusetts stepped into the fray.

SOLUTIONS AND RECOMMENDATION

Same- sex marriage was legalized in 2015 and antigay initiatives at the state level, are snowballing. Where we go from here is really up in the air? With a divided country it seems as if we have a tough road ahead. One possible recommendation aside from moving to Canada is to get involved in the political process. Make a difference by reaching across your own back yard fence and meet your neighbors. Be open to considering others people perspectives. Until we as individuals make an effort to bridge the divides in our own neighborhoods it is going to a challenge to heal our country.

FUTURE RESEARCH DIRECTIONS

Southern states are populated by residents with relatively high religiosity, as are several other states in the middle of the country, stretching from Texas through Oklahoma to Kansas and the two Dakotas. At the same time, states whose residents are least likely to report that religion is important tend to be concentrated in New England and the far West (with the exception of Utah). Levels of religiosity also are lower in several Mid-Atlantic states. The question of why residents of some states (e.g., Mississippi and other Southern states) are highly likely to report that religion is an important part of their lives, while residents of other states (e.g., Vermont and other New England states) are much less likely to report the same is fascinating and thoughts for future research.

CONCLUSION

This chapter presented an overview of Federal and State court cases that prompted state legislators across the country to pass measures that banned same-marriage. Debates within state legislatures are frequently sparked by concerns about judicial activism, as indicated the examination of court rulings related to same-sex marriage. It is not a coincidence that the Northeastern states have been targeted to change the same-sex marriage laws. Advocates for change began a coordinated campaign in the Northeast because it was seen as fertile ground for reform. Three states in the region had passed civil unions, public polling showed that New England residents favored relationship recognition and the region is reported to be the least religious in the country, which is significant given that the opposition to same-sex marriage is often based on religious beliefs (Nelson, 2010).

Not surprisingly, the lower the percentage of hostile religious adherents in a state (such as Baptists, Catholics, and Mormons), the less the controversy that might be expected around same-sex marriage.

There is a strong correlation between the religiosity of a state and its propensity to ban or legalize same-sex marriage, with a particular bonus effect correlating with the number of white evangelicals in a state (Newport, 2009). The United States is generally a religious nation, although the degree of this religiosity varies across states and regions of the country. The relative importance of religion in Americans' lives has interesting geographical differentiation states whose residents are least likely to report that religion is important tend to be concentrated in New England and the far West (with the exception of Utah). Levels of religiosity also are lower in several Mid-Atlantic states. Additional, factors also were important to the effort, higher education levels and for the most part Northeastern states do not have initiative and referendum processes that would allow voters to overturn legislative action, except for Maine.

REFERENCES

Baehr v. Lewin, 74 Haw. 530, 852 P.2d 44 (1993).

Barclay, S. (2010). In search of judicial activism in the same-sex marriage cases: Sorting the evidence from courts, legislatures, initiatives and amendments. *Perspectives on Politics, 8*(1), 111–126. 10.1017/S1537592709992696

Blomquist, W. (2007). The policy process and large-N comparative studies. In P. E. Sabatier (Ed.), *Theories of the policy process*. Boulder, CO: Westview Press.

Bowers v. Hardwick, 478 U.S. 186 (Georgia, 1986). (n.d.). Retrieved from http://caselaw.lp.findlaw.com/scripts/getcase.pl?court=us&vol=478&invol=186

Brewer, P., & Wilcox, C. (2005). Same-Sex Marriage and Civil Unions. *Public Opinion Quarterly, 69*(4), 599-616. DOI: https://doi.org/10.1093/poq/nfi052

Chauncey, G. (2004). *Why marriage? The history shaping today's debate over gay equality*. New York: Basic Books.

Cherlin, A. (2004). The deinstitutionalization of American marriage. *Journal of Marriage and the Family*, *66*(4), 848–861. doi:10.1111/j.0022-2445.2004.00058.x

Coontz, S. (2005). *Marriage, a history: From obedience to intimacy or how love conquered marriage*. New York: Viking.

D'Emilio, J. (1983). *Sexual Politics, sexual Communities: The making of a homosexual minority in the United States 1940–1970*. Chicago: University of Chicago Press.

Defense of Marriage Act, Pub. L. No. 104–199, 110 Stat. 2419.

Delaney, S. (2004 December 30) Year in Review, Part 4: Politics. *VPR*. Retrieved from http://www.vpr.net/news_detail/72433/year-in-review-part-4-politics/

Eskridge, W. N. (1999). *Gaylaw: Challenging the apartheid of the closet*. Cambridge, MA: Harvard University Press.

Goodridge v. Department of Public Health, 748 N.E. 2d 941 (Mass. App. Ct. 2003). (n.d.). Retrieved from http://www.boston.com/news/daily/18/sjc_gaymarriage_decision.pdf

Graber, M. (1993). The nonmajoritarian difficulty: Legislative deference to the judiciary. *Studies in American Political Development*, *7*(1), 35–73. doi:10.1017/S0898588X00000687

Haider-Markel, D. P. (2000). Lesbian and gay politics in the states: Interest groups, electoral politics, and public policy. In C. A. Rimmerman, K. A. Wald, & C. Wilcox (Eds.), *The politics of gay rights*. Chicago: University of Chicago Press.

Haider-Markel, D. P. (2001). Policy diffusion as a geographical expansion of the scope of political conflict: Same-sex marriage bans in the 1990s. *State Politics & Policy Quarterly*, *1*(1), 1–26. doi:10.1177/153244000100100102

Halloran, L. (2013, March 23). How Vermont's 'Civil' War Fueled The Gay Marriage Movement. *NPR All Things Considered*. Retrieved from http://www.npr.org/2013/03/27/174651233/how-vermonts-civil-war-fueled-the-gay-marriage-movement

Herek, G. M. (2006). Legal recognition of same-sex relationships in the United States: A social science perspective. *The American Psychologist*, *61*(6), 607–21. 10.1037/0003-066X.61.6.607

Herman, D. (1998). *The Antigay Agenda: Orthodox vision and the Christian right*. Chicago: University of Chicago Press. doi:10.7208/chicago/9780226327693.001.0001

Knight, R. (1996, May 30). *The impact of Romer v. Evans. Insight*. The Family Research Council.

Lewin, E. (1998). *Recognizing ourselves: Ceremonies of lesbian and gay commitment*. New York: Columbia University Press.

Lovell, G. (2003). *Legislative Deferrals: Statutory Ambiguity, Judicial Power, and American Democracy*. Cambridge, UK: Cambridge University Press.

Moats, D. (2004). *Civil wars: A battle for gay marriage* (1st ed.). Orlando, FL: Harcourt.

Nelson, C. (2010, April). Same Sex Marriage Redux. *State Legislatures*, 31–33.

Newport, F. (2009, January 28). State of the states: Importance of religion. *Gallup*. Retrieved from http://www.gallup.com/poll/114022/state-states-importance-religion.aspx

Pinello, D. R. (2006). *America's Struggle for Same-Sex Marriage*. Cambridge University Press.

Romer v. Evans. 517 U.S. 620. (S. Ct. of Colorado 1996). (n.d.). Retrieved from http://laws.findlaw.com/us/000/u10179.htm

Wilson, A. (Producer). (2004a, February 16). *Prime Time Lawmakers*. Atlanta, GA: Georgia Public Broadcasting.

Wilson, A. (Producer). (2004b, February 26). *Prime Time Lawmakers*. Atlanta, GA: Georgia Public Broadcasting.

Wilson, A. (Producer). (2004c, March 31). *Prime Time Lawmakers*. Atlanta, GA: Georgia Public Broadcasting.

KEY TERMS AND DEFINITIONS

Ballot Initiatives: In political science, an initiative is a means by which a petition signed by a certain minimum number of registered voters can force a public vote. The initiative may take the form of a direct initiative or an indirect initiative.

Civil Union: A legally recognized union of a same-sex couple, with rights similar to those of marriage.

Judicial Activism: The tendency of judges to deviate from past court decision, which allows them to consider their own preferences before issuing a ruling.

States' Rights: Describes the ongoing struggle over political power in the United States between the federal government and individual states as broadly outlined in the Tenth Amendment and whether the USA is a single entity or an amalgamation of independent nations. In modern times the term States Rights has also come to symbolize the opposition of some states to federal mandated laws against racial segregation and discrimination.

Strict Scrutiny: A test for courts that government may not burden or restrict a person's free exercise of religion, unless it demonstrates that the restriction furthers a compelling government interest and is done through the least restrictive means.

Same-Sex Marriage: A legally recognized marriage in which two people of the same gender live together as a family.

ENDNOTES

1. It should be noted that the researcher has been a member of the Georgia House of Representatives since 2001.
2. Lippert was elected to a full term in November, 1994 and has been re-elected biennially ever since.

APPENDIX

Table 1. Statewide votes on same-sex marriage

State	Year	Measure #	Topic Area	Type[a]	CA/S[b]	Pass/Fail
Alabama	2006	Amendment 1	Definition of marriage	L	CA	Pass
Alaska	1998	Measure 2	Definition of marriage	L	CA	Pass
Arizona	2006	Prop. 107	Definition of marriage	I	CA	Fail
Arizona	2008	Prop. 102	Definition of marriage	L	CA	Pass
Arkansas	2004	Amendment 3	Definition of marriage	I	CA	Pass
California	2000	Prop. 22	Definition of marriage	I	S	Pass
California	2008	Proposition 8	Definition of marriage	I	CA	Pass
Colorado	2006	Amend. 43	Definition of marriage	I	CA	Pass
Florida	2008	Amendment 2	Definition of marriage	I	CA	Pass
Georgia	2004	Amendment 1	Definition of marriage	L	CA	Pass
Hawaii	1998	Question 2	Give legislature right to define marriage	L	CA	Pass
Idaho	2006	HJR 2	Definition of marriage	L	CA	Pass
Kansas	2002	Amendment	Definition of marriage	L	CA	Pass
Kentucky	2004	Amendment	Definition of marriage	L	CA	Pass
Louisiana	2004	Amendment 1	Definition of marriage	L	CA	Pass
Maine	2009	Question 1	Reject the legalization of same-sex marriage	PR	S	Pass
Michigan	2004	Proposal 2	Definition of marriage	I	CA	Pass
Mississippi	2004	Amendment 1	Definition of marriage	L	CA	Pass
Missouri	2004	Amendment 2	Definition of marriage	L	CA	Pass
Montana	2004	CI-96	Definition of marriage	I	CA	Pass
Nebraska	2000	Initiative 416	Definition of marriage	I	CA	Pass
Nevada	2002	Question 2	Definition of marriage	I	CA	Pass
North Dakota	2004	ICM 1	Definition of marriage	I	CA	Pass
Ohio	2004	Issue 1	Definition of marriage	I	CA	Pass
Oklahoma	2004	Question 711	Definition of marriage	L	CA	Pass
Oregon	2004	Measure 36	Definition of marriage	I	CA	Pass
S. Carolina	2006	Amendment 1	Definition of marriage	L	CA	Pass
South Dakota	2006	Amendment C	Definition of marriage	L	CA	Pass
Tennessee	2006	Amendment 1	Definition of marriage	L	CA	Pass
Texas	2005	Proposition 2	Definition of marriage	L	CA	Pass
Utah	2004	Amendment 3	Definition of marriage	L	CA	Pass

continued on next page

Table 1. Continued

State	Year	Measure #	Topic Area	Type[a]	CA/S[b]	Pass/Fail
Virginia	2006	Amendment 1	Definition of marriage	L	CA	Pass
Wisconsin	2006	Question 1	Definition of marriage	L	CA	Pass

Source: National Conference of State Legislatures, 2014
[a]Type: L = legislative referendum
I = citizen-initiated
PR = popular referendum (a petition-driven effort to overturn a law passed by the legislature)
[b]CA = constitutional amendment; S = statutory

Table 2. Defense of marriage act statues and constitutional amendments by year of implementation up to 2014

States with Statutes Defining Marriage		States with Constitutional Language Defining Marriage		States with No Provision Prohibiting Same-Sex Marriage	
Alabama	1998	Alabama	2006	Connecticut	
Alaska	1996	Alaska	1998	Massachusetts	
Arizona	1996	Arkansas	2004	New Jersey	
Arkansas	1997	Colorado	2006	New Mexico	
California	2000	Georgia	2004	New York	
Colorado	2000	Hawaii **	1998	Rhode Island	
Delaware	1996	Idaho	2006		
Florida	1997	Kansas	2005		
Georgia	1996	Kentucky	2004		
Hawaii	1997	Louisiana	2004		
Idaho	1996	Michigan	2004		
Illinois	1996	Mississippi	2004		
Indiana	1997	Missouri	2004		
Iowa	1998	Montana	2004		
Kansas	1996	Nebraska	2000		
Kentucky	1998	Nevada	2002		
Louisiana	1999	North Dakota	2004		
Maine	1997	Ohio	2004		
Maryland *	2001	Oklahoma	2004		
Michigan	1996	Oregon	2004		
Minnesota	1997	South Carolina	2006		
Mississippi	1997	South Dakota	2006		
Missouri	2001	Tennessee	2006		
Montana	1997	Texas	2005		

continued on next page

Table 2. Continued

States with Statutes Defining Marriage		States with Constitutional Language Defining Marriage		States with No Provision Prohibiting Same-Sex Marriage	
Nevada	2000	Utah	2004		
New Hampshire	2004	Virginia	2006		
North Carolina	1996	Wisconsin	2006		
North Dakota	1997				
Ohio	2004				
Oklahoma	1996				
Pennsylvania	1996				
South Carolina	1996				
South Dakota	1996				
Tennessee	1996				
Texas	2003				
Utah	1995				
Vermont	2007				
Virginia	1997				
Washington	1998				
West Virginia	2000				
Wisconsin	2007				
Wyoming	2005				
	41	30	5		

Source: National Conference of State Legislators Overview online, 2014

Section 3

State Battle Grounds and Emerging Research Opportunities

This section summarizes how faith moral worldviews have been applied throughout the nation and broadens the understanding of the legislative arena.

Chapter 5
Defenders of Faith

ABSTRACT

In the past few decades, the question of whether and how civil society should recognize committed intimate relationships between two people of the same sex is a prominent and divisive policy issue. This chapter discusses the heightened lawmaking efforts by legislators that are more inclined toward religious claims due to their opposition to homosexuality.

We're elected to represent our constituents when they're right, and to vote our consciences regardless of whether our constituents are right. And our conscience should be telling us to stand up for civil rights regardless of how unpopular it may appear. The Reverend Dr. Martin Luther King Jr. once said, "A time comes when silence is betrayal." Such a time is now. With your no vote on this bill, you can help break the silence and stand with those who have no one to stand with them. ~ Iowa State Representative Ed Fallon

INTRODUCTION

The founders' perspective on the relationship of religion and politics was predicated on a separatist approach. Despite other differences in political theory, the Republican justifications for the exclusion of religion from the political processes are analogous to liberalism's justifications for a similar exclusion of religion (Pangel, 1988). For a considerable time, the two viewpoints of

DOI: 10.4018/978-1-5225-2388-8.ch005

America have created political tension because of the opposing views of the proper Christian society. Conservatives insisted that a Christian state required some official recognition and support for churches. By contrast, Separatists contended that state support of an established denomination infringed upon the freedom of individual conscience and of the other churches (Kammen, 1980).

In fact, some studies of legislative behavior have included measures of religious affiliation to capture the preferences of individual legislators (Benson &Williams, 1982; Gohmann & Ohsfeldt, 1994, 1994; Green & Guth, 1991). As a result, legislators do not simply disagree over an instrumental policy goal; the fundamental issue frame is in dispute. What for one group is clearly a religious wrong, for another is clearly a civil right. In that context, legislators become the defenders of a way of life — a divinely ordained way of life. These arguments represent the type of wedge issues that divide families, parties, states; and challenge governance (Lowi, 1969). These are conflicts over morality issues and are defined by "clashes of first principle" or arguments over fundamental values on "technically simple and salient public policy issues with high citizen participation" (Mooney & Lee, 2000). In the past few decades, the question of whether and how civil society should recognize committed intimate relationships between two people of the same sex has is an example of a prominent and divisive policy issue. This chapter discusses the heightened lawmaking efforts by legislators that are more inclined toward religious claims due to their opposition to homosexuality.

Background

State legislative opposition to court decisions over the recognition of same-sex couples has been intense. Beginning with a Hawaii court decision (*Baehr v. Lewin, 1993*), the prospect of marriage rights being granted to same-sex partners in the Aloha State became a reality. Congress responded by passing the 1996 Defense of Marriage Act (DOMA). DOMA's purpose was to define marriage as the union of one man and one woman and to exempt states from recognizing marriages performed in another state between two people of the same sex (Defense of Marriage Act, 1996). From 1993-2012, states passed multiple versions of their own mini DOMA's (Peterson, 2014). In 2010, House Bill 56 was sponsored by Representative Jim Hill, an Alabama Republican. The bill proposed allowing judges and some state workers to opt out of services that violate their religious beliefs. Hill was the only person to speak in favor of the bill during the hearing, and he told the committee that he was…

…concerned the courts could interpret some language in current law to force judges to perform same-sex marriages. (Moon, 2015)

Even states that were the first to accord legal status to same-sex partners (i.e., Hawaii and Vermont), originally did so mainly to avoid granting full marriage rights to such couples as a consequence of court decisions; supporters of the legal recognition of same-sex marriage have framed their arguments in terms of human rights and justice, whereas opponents have usually invoked religious teachings and tradition to support their position (Price, Nir, & Cappella, 2005). In addition to this clash between deeply felt values, the debate has raised questions about the nature of same-sex couples, their families, and the institution of marriage in general. Interestingly, advocates on both sides have invoked scientific research to support many of their legal and policy arguments, even given the slim likelihood that this type of empirical data could reconcile disputes about faith and the resulting core values implicated by the marriage controversy.

Game Changers

Legalizing same-sex marriage has not been greeted with universal acclaim. Indeed, some claim that the promotion of same-sex marriage contravenes their religious principles and that they should not be forced to violate their consciences by providing services to same-sex couples and their families. As more states accorded rights to sexual minorities, an increasing number of individuals have claimed that the First Amendment immunizes their conscience based refusals to provide goods or services to such allegedly objectionable families. In response, religious conservatives groups supported by faith driven legislators intensified their state-level campaigns across the country to pass statutes allowing religious actors to refuse service based on theological opposition. The political terrain surrounding same-sex marriage and the need for religious accommodations has been part of the public discussion since the passage of initial marriage equality statutes. These provisions were passed in what were considered friendly states and have gone largely unquestioned, since same-sex marriage is now legal nationally. During early years when marriage statutes were drafted, the political need for these accommodations was obvious and carried the weight of precedent (Tebbe, 2015).

Even though these states were perceived as the most protective of LGBT equality and largely unquestioned and were viewed as progress; the impetus behind these early religious accommodations in marriage equality statutes was political—they were included to address concerns of potential opponents and thereby to ensure that the laws were passed. To many, the choice was not between marriage equality with religious accommodations and without, but between marriage equality with religion accommodations and continued exclusion of same-sex couples from civil marriage. The gain in equality was thought to outweigh the cost of exempting certain religious actors (Day, 2016). These exemptions without exception allowed religious actors to refuse service based on theological opposition. Some of the exemptions were so broadly phrased so that religious organizations could discriminate on other grounds.

Within the context of the legislative arena, it is expected that the dynamics of faith driven political debate will be highly partisan and ideological (Haider-Markel & Meier, 1996; Mooney & Lee, 1995). Because morality politics often is organized around religious beliefs (Meier, 1994; Mooney & Lee, 1995), the religious affiliation of legislators should play a role in legislative sponsorship and decision-making on issues perceived to involve morality. Across the nation, legislative measures have been introduced by faith directed lawmakers supported by a network of religious groups; forging a national campaign that would allow people to refuse to provide goods or services to same-sex couples based on religious grounds. Compromise between these competing views is unlikely since the political battle is waged over core beliefs.

California initially altered their marriage statutes in 1977, and Maryland followed suit in 1984, in response to the first wave of same-sex marriage cases that were filed by gay activists in Minnesota, Washington, Kentucky, and New York starting in 1971 (Eskridge, 2002). Wisconsin and California also had couples that sought relationship recognition only to be met with a "no." The issue of gay marriage was impaled on these failures to make any legal headway. Garnering little success, energies were focused on the repeal of state sodomy, and other conduct laws. Like the year 2004, when same-sex couples were first issued marriage licenses in Massachusetts, 2005 was a watershed year in the fight for marriage equality. This year marked the first time that a U.S. legislative body passed a bill granting same-sex couples the freedom to marry (Evans, 2005). Led by Democratic Assembly member, Mark Leno, the California Legislature passed Assembly Bill 849 in September 2005. A few weeks later, Republican Governor Arnold Schwarzenegger vetoed the bill. In 2006 another bill was introduced in California extending the freedom to marry to same-sex couple's and crucial to its passage was Democrat Assembly member Tom Umberg, he abstained from voting and the bill failed. Three months later, Umberg changed his vote to a "yes" vote and is noteworthy for several reasons. He was term-limited and would leave the Assembly in 2006, and his next career move was a run for state Senate. This vote for marriage equality could negatively impact his Senate race. Despite these downsides, Umberg took the floor of the Assembly before his "yes" vote and expounded:

This is one of those times that history looks upon us to be in the lead. This is one of those times when history looks upon us to see where we are. ... Ten years from now there are a handful of issues that history will record where we stood. And this is one of those issues. History will record whether we pushed a bit, whether we took the lead to encourage tolerance, to encourage equality, to encourage fairness ... the constituency I'm concerned about is a very small one — that's the constituency of my three children, should they decide to look back on my record and lookback and reflect on where I was when I could have made a difference. ... If I stood with those who sought to take a leadership role in terms of tolerance, equity and fairness. And I'll be proud to say I did. (Evans, 2005)

However in 2008, a citizen led initiative (Proposition 8) in California proposed an anti-marriage amendment to the state constitution. Complicating the fact that same-sex marriages that took place between June and November, 2008, continued to be defined as marriages. This became the *Hollingsworth v. Perry* (the Proposition 8 case) the U.S. Supreme Court decision in 2013 stated that Proposition 8 was unconstitutional and advanced the argument that marriage is a fundamental right in which same-sex couples are constitutionally entitled to participate.

This was followed by another case in 2013 the *United States v. Windsor* (2013) involving Edith Windsor and Thea Spyer, a same-sex couple residing in New York, were lawfully married in Canada. New York recognized their marriage following a court decision. Spyer died in 2009, leaving her entire estate to Windsor. Windsor sought to claim the federal estate tax exemption for surviving spouses and was barred from doing so by Section 3 of DOMA (codified at 1 U.S.C. § 7), which provided that the term "spouse" only applied to marriages between a man and woman. The Internal Revenue Service found that the exemption did not apply to same-sex marriages, denied Windsor's claim, and compelled her to pay $363,053 in estate taxes. In a 5–4 decision issued on June 26, 2013, the Supreme Court found Section 3 of DOMA to be unconstitutional, (Williams & McClam, 2013; Liptak, 2013; Mears, 2013;

Hurley, 2013) "as a deprivation of the liberty of the person protected by the Fifth Amendment" (Mears, 2013). The Court held that the Constitution prevented the federal government from treating state-sanctioned heterosexual marriages differently from state-sanctioned same-sex marriages, and that such differentiation "demean[ed] the couple, whose moral and sexual choices the Constitution protects" (Barnes, 2013). Justice Kennedy authored the court's decision stating that…

The federal statute is invalid, for no legitimate purpose overcomes the purpose and effect to disparage and to injure those whom the State, by its marriage laws, sought to protect in personhood and dignity. (Socarides, 2013)

In the dissent Justice Scalia argued that the majority opinion characterized opponents of same-sex marriage as "enemies of the human race" (Grieve, 2013) and stated that the ruling would affect state bans on same-sex marriage "by formally declaring anyone opposed to same-sex marriage an enemy of human decency, the majority arms well every challenger to a state law restricting marriage to its traditional definition" (Gerstein, 2013). Scalia concluded by saying that the Supreme Court "has cheated both sides, robbing the winners of an honest victory and the losers of the peace that comes from a fair defeat" (*Windsor v. United States*, 2012).

The warning issued by Justice Scalia in the case *Windsor v. United States*, (2012) was exemplified in *Elane Photography v. Willock*[1], (2013) has been magnified by opponents of same-sex marriage. Elane Photography, a Christian-identified business in New Mexico, Albuquerque, declined to photograph Vanessa Willock's same-sex commitment ceremony based on the business owners' personal beliefs. New Mexico law prohibits any refusal to render business services because of sexual orientation. Willock filed a claim with the New Mexico Human Rights Commission. She argued that Elane Photography is a "public accommodation," akin to a hotel or restaurant, which is subject to the state's anti-discrimination law. The commission found against Elane and ordered it to pay $6,600 in attorney fees. The New Mexico Supreme Court ruled on August 22, 2013 against Jonathan and Elaine. One of the justices said that the Huguenins are "now are compelled by law to compromise the very religious beliefs that inspire their lives," and he declared that this compulsion "is the price of citizenship." Although the Supreme Court reviewed this request at three of its conferences, it declined to review the case on April 7, 2014 (Volokh, 2013).

In response to the *Elane Photography v. Willock*, (2013) decision Arizona Senator Steve Yarbrough sponsored Senate Bill 1062 that would allow any individual or legal entity an exemption from any state law if substantially burdened their exercise of religion, including laws that required public accommodation. The bill was passed along party lines by the Republican controlled state legislature and vetoed by Republican Governor Jan Brewer. State Senator a Democrat Steve Gallaro[2] prompted by the bill publically came out referring to the bill as a "game changer" realizing that this bill affects me" (Pitzl, 2014). Three Republican Senators Majority Whip Adam Driggs, Bob Worsley, Steve Pierce[3] who voted for Senate Bill 1062 said they made a bad decision and are now asking Governor Jan Brewer to veto the right to refuse service bill. In a letter to the Governor stating,

While our sincere intent in voting for this bill was to create a shield for all citizens' religious liberties, the bill has instead been mischaracterized by its opponents as a sword for religious intolerance and are causing our state immeasurable harm. (Pitzl, 2014)

Shortly thereafter, the case of *Burwell v. Hobby Lobby* (2014) was decided by the U.S. Supreme Court. This decision allowed closely held[4] for-profit corporations to be exempt from a law if its owners religiously objected to if there were a less restrictive means of furthering the law's interest, according to the provisions of the Religious Freedom Restoration (RFRA). It was the first time that the court recognized a for-profit corporation's claim of religious belief, but it was limited to closely held corporations (Liptak, 2014). The decision did not address whether such corporations were protected by the free exercise of religion clause of the First Amendment of the Constitution. At issue was whether or not RFRA applied to for-profit corporations, or just individuals and non-profits. While this case was filed as religious freedom case, it ended up being resolved by the Supreme Court as a case about constitutional separation of powers and limited government. Justice Alito wrote for the majority, even though corporate personhood is a "legal fiction," those corporations were formed by human beings and they represented the people who were associated with them and their rights and in protecting the corporation thus protected the people who owned and controlled it (Schwartz, 2014). Justice Ginsburg asserted in her dissent that it seemed odd that, "People from all sides of the political spectrum voted for" RFRA and questioned if Congress had intended the law to mean that for-profit corporations could trump federal civil rights laws. Similarly, Justice Kagan, also expressed disbelief that RFRA could mean what *Hobby Lobby* insisted it must mean "interpretation of [RFRA], essentially subjected the entire U.S. Code to the highest test in constitutional law" *(Burwell v. Hobby Lobby*, 2014).

Contributing to the shifting landscape was the *Obergefell v. Hodges* (2015) decision in which the Court held in a 5-4 decision that the fundamental right to marry is guaranteed to same-sex couples by both the due process and the equal protection clause of the fourteenth the amendment to the US Constitution (Denniston, 2015). In June 2013, following the U.S. Supreme Court's decision in *United States v. Windsor* (2013), James Obergefell and John Arthur decided to get married to obtain legal recognition of their relationship. They married in Maryland after learning that their state of residence, Ohio, would not recognize their marriage, they filed a lawsuit. Because one partner, John Arthur, was terminally ill, they wanted the Ohio Registrar to identify the other partner, James Obergefell, as his surviving spouse on his death certificate, based on their marriage in Maryland. The local Ohio Registrar agreed that discriminating against the same-sex married couple was unconstitutional (Geidner, 2013), but the state attorney general's office announced plans to defend Ohio's same-sex marriage ban (Hastings, 2013; Thompson, 2013).

After a series of lengthy appeals in November 2014, court rulings from the fourth, seventh, ninth, and tenth circuit's stated level bans on same-sex marriage were unconstitutional, the sixth circuit ruled that it was bound by *Baker v. Nelson (1972),* and found such bans to be constitutional. This created a split between the circuits and led to an inevitable Supreme Court review. The Court decision listed four distinct reasons why the fundamental right to marry applies to same-sex couples. First, "the right to personal choice regarding marriage is inherent in the concept of individual autonomy" (*Obergefell v. Hodges, 2015).* Second, "the right to marry is fundamental because it supports a two-person union unlike any other in its importance to the committed individuals," a principle applying equally to same-sex couples (*Obergefell v. Hodges, 2015).* Third, the fundamental right to marry "safeguards children and families and thus draws meaning from related rights of childrearing, procreation, and education"; as same-sex couples have children and families, they are deserving of this safeguard—though the right to marry in the United States has never been conditioned on procreation"(*Obergefell v. Hodges, 2015).* Fourth, and lastly, "marriage is a keystone of our social order", and "[t]here is no difference between same- and opposite-sex couples with respect to this principle"; consequently, preventing same-sex couples from marrying puts them at odds with society, denies them countless benefits of marriage, and introduces instability into their relationships for no justifiable reason" (Obergefell v. Hodges, 2015).

In addressing the states' argument, the Court emphasized that, while the democratic process may be an appropriate means for deciding issues such as same-sex marriage, no individual has to rely solely on the democratic process to exercise a fundamental right *(Obergefell v. Hodges, 2015)*. An individual can invoke a right to constitutional protection when he or she is harmed, even if the broader public disagrees and even if the legislature refuses to act, for "fundamental rights may not be submitted to a vote; they depend on the outcome of no elections" *(Obergefell v. Hodges, 2015)*. Furthermore, to rule against same-sex couples in this case, letting the democratic process play out as "a cautious approach to recognizing and protecting fundamental rights" would harm same-sex couples in the interim" *(Obergefell v. Hodges, 2015*. Lastly, the Court rejected the notion that allowing same-sex couples to marry harms the institution of marriage, leading to fewer opposite-sex marriages through a severing of the link between procreation and marriage, calling the notion "counterintuitive" and "unrealistic" *(Obergefell v. Hodges, 2015)*. Instead, the Court stated that married same-sex couples "would pose no risk of harm to themselves or third parties" stressing that the first amendment protects those who disagree with same-sex marriage. In closing, Justice Kennedy wrote for the Court:

No union is more profound than marriage, for it embodies the highest ideals of love, fidelity, devotion, sacrifice, and family. In forming a marital union, two people become something greater than once they were. As some of the petitioners in these cases demonstrate, marriage embodies a love that may endure even past death. It would misunderstand these men and women to say they disrespect the idea of marriage. Their plea is that they do respect it, respect it so deeply that they seek to find its fulfillment for themselves. Their hope is not to be condemned to live in loneliness, excluded from one of civilization's oldest institutions. They ask for equal dignity in the eyes of the law. The Constitution grants them that right. (Obergefell v. Hodges, 2015)

The *Obergefell v. Hodges (2015)* decision came on the second anniversary of the *US v. Windsor* (2013) ruling that struck down Section 3 of the Defense of Marriage Act (DOMA), which denied federal recognition to same-sex marriages. It also came on the twelfth anniversary of *Lawerence v. Texas,* (2003) which struck down sodomy laws in 13 states.

The Restoration of Justice

It is no surprise that after all of these court decisions within the last several years, legislators would be motivated to respond by passing mini Religious Freedom Restoration Acts (RFRA) and other measures designed to protect religious objectors from same-sex marriage. The state' version applies to individual States and local governments with most of the language identical to the federal statute. Today, twenty states have passed state laws based on the federal Religious Freedom Restoration Act. The protections in an additional thirteen states came through court rulings. These state mini RFRAs were initially enacted in response to Supreme Court decisions and had nothing to do with same-sex marriage. These state court decisions were cases about hunting moose for funeral rites, eminent domain and Amish buggies, an assortment of conflicts between religious practice and regulation.

However, in 2012, the state court decision *Elane Photography, LLC v. Willock,* tried to use religion in court as grounds for refusing to photograph a same-sex wedding. The photographer lost the discrimination lawsuit in 2013. This court ruling and the legalization of same-sex marriage has sparked legislative proposals which continue to shift the definition of when citizens can opt out of providing public or private services based on religious grounds. University of Illinois law professor Robin Fretwell Wilson, who has written letters of support of RFRA to various state legislators, stated that:

...are the RFRAs really trying to do real work for religious minorities? But they've been glommed onto by religious believers who are freaked out by same-sex marriage right now. They're latching onto a vehicle that is just not designed to do what they want it to do, at a time of great social change. (Wilson, 2014)

Legislators who see themselves as "defenders of the faith" argue that without certainty, Christianity will not survive. The effect of this religious mentality is to diminish; making outsiders fit objects for both conversion and missionary activity. Latourette (1943) described the nineteenth century as the greatest period of Christian expansion. When these missionaries came they had the Bible and the native people had the land. Shortly after, the missionaries had the land and the native people had the Bible. This expansion is still ongoing today and is occurring at with state legislatures across the country. The mission of many these legislators are to sponsor bills that persecute minorities to justify their claim in the name of the "one true God. A statement by Mark Tushnet demonstrates this difficulty,

As far as I can tell, I am a Jew down to the ground, and I cannot imagine a political decision that I could make without reference, at some level of my being, to my Jewishness. (Tushnet, 1989)

Religious actions have been justified by appeals to the scriptures, which have been quoted to demonstrate that if people disagree with the "stated faith of the church," then they are actually disagreeing with God's truth (Spong, 2005, p. 215). Religious intolerance has been justified frequently by quoting a group of writings that are designated as the "general epistles" one particular reference is the epistle of Jude, "the faith which was once for all delivered to the saints." The implication is that Christianity is the unchanging truth of God and anyone who questions these core beliefs is questioning God. It is therefore the duty of the church to protect the world from such heresy. This suppresses all lack of uncertainty, deviation and produces claims such as they alone are "the true church" or "our pope is infallible" or "our Bible is inerrant"(Spong, 2005) There is no room for compromise between them, no middle ground, just mutually exclusive points of view. Each side of the church's conflict over homosexuality is to them a life-and-death struggle. If gay people are not welcomed and accepted, then the Christian church becomes nothing more than a sectarian movement; if gays are welcomed and accepted, morality collapses and the system of church authority becomes unrecognizable. It is likely that in the United States, where religious faith is widespread, many individuals, legislators, and political leaders are, like Tushnet, Jews, Catholics, Baptists, Presbyterians, Methodists, Mormons, Muslims, Buddhists, or believers of an almost countless number of religious denominations, are "down to the ground." When threatened religious people command conformity for their own faith assertion, or to put down any challenge to their religious past, as suggested by Senator Brian Ivestor, Democrat from Oklahoma in Senate Joint Resolution 70:

Section 2A.

Whereas Almighty God hath created the mind free; that all attempts to influence it by temporal punishments or burthens, or by civil incapacitations, tend only to beget habits of hypocrisy and meanness, and are a departure

from the plan of the Holy author of our religion, who being Lord both of body and mind, yet chose not to propagate it by coercions on either, as it was in his Almighty power to do;

that the impious presumption of legislators and rulers, civil as well as ecclesiastical, who being themselves but fallible and uninspired men, have assumed dominion over the faith of others, setting up their own opinions and modes of thinking as the only true and infallible, and as such endeavoring to impose them on others, hath established and maintained false religions over the greatest part of the world, and through all time; that to compel a man to furnish contributions of money for the propagation of opinions which he disbelieves, is sinful and tyrannical;

that even the forcing him to support this or that teacher of his own religious persuasion, is depriving him of the comfortable liberty of giving his contributions to the particular pastor, whose morals he would make his pattern, and whose powers he feels most persuasive to righteousness, and is withdrawing from the ministry those temporary rewards, which proceeding from an approbation of their personal conduct, are an additional incitement to earnest and unremitting labors for the instruction of mankind;

that our civil rights have no dependence on our religious opinions, any more than our opinions in physics or geometry; that therefore the proscribing any citizen as unworthy the public confidence by laying upon him an incapacity of being called to offices of trust and emolument, unless he profess or renounce this or that religious opinion, is depriving him injuriously of those privileges and advantages to which in common with his fellow-citizens he has a natural right;

that it tends only to corrupt the principles of that religion it is meant to encourage, by bribing with a monopoly of worldly honors and emoluments, those who will externally profess and conform to it; that though indeed these are criminal who do not withstand such temptation, yet neither are those innocent who lay the bait in their way; that to suffer the civil magistrate to intrude his powers into the field of opinion, and to restrain the profession or propagation of principles on supposition of their ill tendency, is a dangerous fallacy, which at once destroys all religious liberty, because he being of course judge of that tendency will make his opinions the rule of judgment, and approve or condemn the sentiments of others only as they shall square with or differ from his own;

that it is time enough for the rightful purposes of civil government, for its officers to interfere when principles break out into overt acts against peace and good order; and finally, that truth is great and will prevail if left to herself, that she is the proper and sufficient antagonist to error, and has nothing to fear from the conflict, unless by human interposition disarmed of her natural weapons, free argument and debate, errors ceasing to be dangerous when it is permitted freely to contradict them:

Be it enacted by the Legislature, That no man shall be compelled to frequent or support any religious worship, place, or ministry whatsoever, nor shall be enforced, restrained, molested, or burdened in his body or goods, nor shall otherwise suffer on account of his religious opinions or belief; but that all men shall be free to profess, and by argument to maintain, their opinion in matters of religion, and that the same shall in no wise diminish enlarge, or affect their civil capacities.

And though we well know that this Legislature elected by the people for the ordinary purposes of legislation only, have no power to restrain the acts of succeeding assemblies, constituted with powers equal to our own, and that therefore to declare this act to be irrevocable would be of no effect in law; yet we are free to declare, and do declare, that the rights hereby asserted are of the natural rights of mankind, and that if any act shall be hereafter passed to repeal the present, or to narrow its operation, such act shall be an infringement of natural right. (Oklahoma Senate Joint Resolution, 70)

Missouri Representative Brian Nieves, a Republican in 2010, House Joint Resolution 88 also does not equivocate on the "wall of separation" that exists between the "defenders of faith" expressing the following:

2. The state of Missouri shall:

(1) Uphold and defend the Constitution of the United States of America by hereby prohibiting the Missouri legislative, executive, and judicial branches of government from recognizing, enforcing, or acting in furtherance of any federal law, executive order, judicial ruling, administrative ruling, collection of revenue, dispersal of revenue, or other action by the legislative, executive, or judicial branches of the federal government that exceeds the limited powers enumerated and delegated to the federal government;

(2) Not recognize, enforce, or act in furtherance of the following:

(a) Federal actions restricting the right of private citizens to bear arms;

(b) Federal actions legalizing or funding abortions, or the destruction of any embryo containing human DNA from the zygote stage onward through all stages of development;

(c) Any federal action requiring the sale or trade of carbon credits or imposing a tax, fee, fine, or penalty on the release of carbon emissions;(d) Federal actions involving a public option for health care, mandating end of life counseling, rationing health care, dictating or limiting the type of treatment a doctor may provide to his or her patient, authorizing or mandating the collection of a patient's medical record into a database, covering illegal aliens under health insurance or prohibiting enforcement of laws regarding coverage for illegal aliens, mandating the benefits health insurance must cover, requiring insurance providers to cover abortion services, restricting the ability of patients to purchase health insurance in another state, or assessing fees, fines, or penalties on employers who do not provide health insurance to their employees;

(e) Any federal action mandating the recognition of same sex marriage, civil unions, or any relationship other than the marriage of one man and one woman;

(f) Any federal action increasing the punishment for a crime based on the thoughts of the perpetrator or the designation of the crime as a "hate crime";

(g) Any federal action regarding the establishment clause based upon a "wall of separation" between church and state. As Supreme Court Justice William Rehnquist wrote in Wallace v. Jafree, 472 U.S. 38, 99: "It is impossible to build sound constitutional doctrine upon a mistaken understanding of Constitutional history.... The establishment clause has been expressly freighted with Jefferson's misleading metaphor for nearly forty years.... There is simply no historical foundation for the proposition that the framers intended to build a wall of separation [between church and state].... The recent court decisions are in no way based on either the language or intent of the framers.";

(h) Any federal action restricting the right of parents or guardians to home school, enroll their children in a private or parochial school, or placing restrictions on curriculum;

(3) Interpret the Constitution of the United States of America based on its language and the intent of the signers of the Constitution at the time of its passage. The several amendments shall be interpreted by their language and the intent of the congressional sponsor and co-sponsors of the amendment. Any interpretation of the Constitution based on an emerging awareness, penumbras or shadows of the Constitution, a theory of the Constitution being a "living, breathing document", or any interpretation that expands federal authority beyond the limited powers enumerated and delegated to the federal government, without an amendment to the Constitution, shall be deemed to exceed the limited powers enumerated and delegated to the federal government. (Missouri House Joint Resolution, 88)

As noted from the debate about same-sex marriage has been profoundly shaped by both the passage, and the idea, of time. National majorities now support marriage equality in most polls, and the there is still a growing conservative base that objects. The concept of time has been prominently featured in the controversy. Consider two central tropes in the same-sex marriage debate that have been repeated to the point of cliché. One relates to history, and each side has had its version. The very phrase "traditional marriage" used by opponents of change imparts the sanctity of the past, and claims about marriage's history have frequently shaped the oppositional rhetoric. In contrast, those supporting same-sex marriage have commonly responded that opponents of same-sex marriage will be on the "wrong side of history." This retort has become a concise way to express the imprudence of resisting marriage equality after legalization.

Two days after the Texas 2015 legislative session ended, 14 legislators urged Governor Greg Abbott to call a special session "to pass legislation that would defend the Texas Marriage Amendment and that would prevent marriage licenses from being issued to homosexuals in the event the U.S. Supreme Court rules illegitimately in favor of homosexual marriages" (Rangel, 2015). Republican Representative Cecil Bell, introduced House Bill 4105 to prohibit county clerks and state officials from issuing gay marriage licenses or to recognize same-sex marriages from other states. House Democrats opposed to Bell's House Bill 4105 used parliamentary procedures and a delay tactic called "chubbing" to prevent the proposal from coming up for a vote before the deadline to pass House bills. However, Senate Bill 2065 the "Pastor Protection Act," a bill that gives members of the clergy the right to refuse to conduct marriage ceremonies that conflict with their religious beliefs was passed. Governor Abbott signed it saying that…

…freedom of religion is the most sacred of our rights and our freedom to worship is secured by the Constitution. Religious leaders in the state of Texas must be absolutely secure in the knowledge that religious freedom is beyond the reach of government or coercion by the courts. (Rangel, 2015)

During the same session, Democrat Representative Rafael Anchia authored a bill that would have legalized same-sex marriage in Texas. About the only thing opponents and supporters of gay marriage agree on is, that if the court rules in favor of ending the gay marriage ban, it would be a landmark case. In November 2016, Texas Senator Judith Zaffirini letter to the Chair of the Senate Committee on State Affairs stated that:

…by far my most serious concern pertains to the report's discussion of religious liberty. The report recommends that the Legislature enact statewide religious liberty '1protections" whose effect and apparent purpose would be to preempt local ordinances that may be more protective than current state law of persons in the LGBT community. Should such a preemptive statute be enacted, a local ordinance prohibiting a merchant from refusing to serve a person solely on the ground that the person is, for example, transgendered, would be rendered ineffective.

Such legislation understandably would be seen as a symbolic rebuke to a large number of our fellow Texans and, as we have seen in the nation's reactions to comparable laws in other states, it would damage our reputation at great potential cost to our relationships with national corporate citizens and others in the business community. If "religious liberty'' means a liberty to discriminate against gays and lesbians, it ironically can be seen as infringing their religious liberty, insofar as their religions obviously do not condemn their, 2003 sexual orientations or gender identities. Such legislation, then, would offend the very principles of religious tolerance that its proponents purport to extoll, while simultaneously offending principals of local control. (Texas Senate Committee on State Affairs, 2016)

A second time-related reply relates to the "evolution" of attitudes about same-sex marriage. How fitting it seems that one of the most publicly salient issues of our era is steeped in appeals to temporality, given that ideas about time have also long inspired some of the basic battle lines of heterosexual marriage versus contemporary evolution, adaptation to social change, and the call of the future. It sounds not unlike some of the well-worn debates between James Cotton and Roger Williams. The State of Vermont House of Representatives introduced on April 2, 2015 and passed on April 3, 2015; House Resolution 8 by a vote of 119 to 1 in response to the passage of Indiana Religious Freedom bill. Representative Susan Davis, a member the progressive Democrat party, sponsored along with twenty-six other members the moderate partisan House Resolution:

House resolution expressing strong opposition to state religious freedom restoration legislation that authorizes discrimination based on sexual orientation

Whereas, on March 26, 2015, Governor Mike Pence of Indiana signed Senate Bill 101, the Religious Freedom Restoration Act, that addresses public and private sector actions related to religious practices, and

Whereas, many organizations and individuals have interpreted the Indiana legislation, and criticized it strongly, as granting private businesses, based on an owner's religious beliefs, the right to discriminate against individuals who are gay, lesbian, bisexual, or transgender, and

Whereas, the National Collegiate Athletic Association (NCAA), which is headquartered in Indianapolis, has expressed concern how the legislation might affect student-athletes and NCAA employees, and

Whereas, the American Federation of State, County and Municipal Employees has cancelled plans to hold its 2015 Women's Conference in that city, and

Whereas, on Tuesday, March 31, 2015, the Indianapolis Star newspaper ran a front-page editorial with a bold headline stating "FIX THIS NOW," and

Whereas, also on Tuesday, March 31, 2015, Governor Mike Pence announced the law would be amended to clarify that the law "does not give businesses the right to deny services to anyone," and

Whereas, despite this promise, opponents of the law in Indiana are demanding its repeal and not amendment, and Whereas, aside from the enacted Indiana law, there is similar legislation under consideration in approximately a dozen states, and

Whereas, on Monday, March 30, 2015, Governor Dannel Malloy of Connecticut signed Executive Order No. 45 restricting "state funded or state sponsored travel to states" that have enacted legislation such as Indiana's Religious Freedom Act, "unless necessary for the enforcement of state law, to meet contractual obligations or for the protection of public health, welfare and safety;" and also providing the that the travel restriction continues for any state as long as that state's law remains in effect, and

Whereas, on March 31, 2015, Secretary of Administration Justin Johnson sent an e-mail directing all Executive Branch agencies and departments not to send employees on State-funded or State-sponsored trips to Indiana until further notice, now therefore be it

Resolved by House of Representatives:

That this legislative body expresses its strong opposition to Indiana's Religious Freedom Restoration Act as signed into law on March 26, 2015, and expresses its support for, at a minimum, enactment of the proposed clarification and, preferably, for the law's repeal, and be it further Resolved:

That this legislative body requests Governor Peter Shumlin to broaden the application of the directive issued on March 31, 2015, to apply to any state that adopts a law similar to Indiana's Religious Freedom Restoration Act, and urges the Judicial and Legislative Branches of State government to adopt a similar policy, and be it further. (VT HR0008, 2015-2016)

Several amendments were proposed from the floor, Representative Paul Poirier an Independent, offered the following:

Whereas, in 1992, the State of Vermont prohibited discrimination based on sexual orientation, and Whereas, in 2000, the State of Vermont established civil unions, becoming the first state to grant legal recognition to same sex couples, and Whereas, in 2007, the State of Vermont prohibited discrimination based on gender identity, and Whereas, in 2009, the State of Vermont established full marriage equality, becoming the first state to grant this recognition legislatively… (Vermont Journal of the House, 2015)

Thereupon, Republican Representative Anne Donahue moved to amend the recommendation of amendment by adding a new second resolve clause to read:

That this legislative body declares its strong opposition to any federal or state law that discriminates against an individual or group of individuals based on their race, sex, sexual orientation, gender identity, age, marital status, religious creed, color, national origin, or disability… (Vermont Journal of the House, 2015)

Which was agreed to and pending the question, Representative Bill Lippert offered the third amendment by adding a new resolved clause preceding the third resolved clause to read as follows:

That this legislative body encourages all 50 states to enact nondiscrimination statutes to protect their lesbian, gay, bisexual, and transgender citizens… (Journal of the House, 2015)

Which was agreed to. Five House members, 3 Republicans and 2 Democrats explained their vote as follows, Republican Representative Peter Fagan wanted to "ensure that my name was added as a sponsor;" Another, Republican Donald Turner thanked the sponsors for "finding the right balance, addressing initial concerns;" Democrat Michael Mrowicki made clear that "there are significant differences between the Indiana and the Federal law;" Openly gay Democrat Herbert Russell reaffirmed the states motto of 'Freedom and Unity;' Republican Job Tate described that:

On Good Friday when Christians all over the globe are commemorating the crucifixion of Jesus Christ I think it is apropos that we are making this act of love-inclusion and support for peoples of all personal persuasion to, as the Lord Himself said, 'Come whosoever will, let him take the water of life freely.' As a member of our nation's most diverse military in history I applaud any condemnation of discrimination…be it for someone's sexual orientation or be it the persecution and slaughter of my fellow believers all over the world. (Vermont Journal of the House, 2015, p. 967).

RECOMMENDATIONS

Judicial decisions often times get mired down in precedent and miss the major common sense approach necessary for evaluating controlling facts and applying reason. It's not always possible, but to the extent that it can be, the U.S. needs "bright line" or black letter law" decisions, particularly when constitutional rights are in question. If that type of decisive action were possible, our society would be more cohesive and cooperative as a result, with the majority of society understanding what those rights are and where the boundaries lie. There are far too many people yelling that their First Amendment rights or freedoms have been infringed upon when they have little understanding of the origins of those rights, or the precedent-setting case law that shaped them.

FUTURE RESEARCH DIRECTION

Emerging demographic data indicates that non-LGBT millennials are beginning to use LGBT discrimination as a litmus test when deciding where to live and work, this poses a major economic threat to the states and its employers. Further research should continue to evaluate their role in the political process.

CONCLUSION

In summary, this chapter provided a steady stream of examples as to marriage and religion the clashes between different legislators. These differences are based on the concept of separation at the individual level and parallels John Locke's *Two Treatises of Government* view of separate spheres for religion and politics in society. The separation principle appears artificial and impossible. Individuals do, in fact, rely on religious (and non-religious) reasons in their public decision-making (Pangle, 1988). Rethinking the process by which individuals make decisions has implied an attendant rethinking of the deliberative processes of the political community. Religion is "one of the strongest forces in society that affirms traditional values" (Smith &

Tatalovich, 2003, p. 38), and it is directly relevant to the conflict over same-sex marriage and gay rights. In 2015, same-sex marriage was legalized in the U.S and the impact of institutionalized religion on democracy and human rights is profound. Religious authority is transcendental and not, like democracy, based on the will of the people. Religious dogma delineates boundaries and inevitably gives preference to believers over non-believers, fueling outbreaks that can only be considered a holy war and fought by the defenders of faith.

REFERENCES

Baehr v. Lewin (74Haw. 530; 852 P.2d 44; 1993).

Benson, P. L., & Williams, D. (1982). *Religion on Capitol Hill: Myths and Realities*. San Francisco: Harper and Row.

Burwell v. Hobby Lobby, 573 U.S. ___ (2014).

Defense of Marriage Act, Pub. L. No. 104–199, 110 Stat. 2419 (1996).

Denniston, L. (2015 June 26). Opinion Analysis: Marriage Now Open to Same-Sex Couples. *SCOTUS* [Blog]. Retrieved from http://www.scotusblog.com/2015/06/opinion-analysis-marriage-now-open-to-same-sex-couples/

Elane Photography, LLC v. Willock, No. 30,203 (N.M. Ct. App. May 31, 2012). (n.d.). Retrieved from http://caselaw.findlaw.com/nm-court-of-appeals/1611023.html

Eskridge, W. (2002). *Equality practice: Civil unions and the future of gay rights*. New York: Routledge.

Evans, C. (2005, December). *Equality from state to state: Gay, lesbian, bisexual and transgender Americans and state legislation in 2005*. Human Rights Campaign Foundation. Retrieved from http://s3.amazonaws.com/hrc-assets//files/assets/resources/2004statetostate.pdf

Geidner, C. (2013 July 22). Ohio officials ordered to recognize gay couple's marriage. *BuzzFeed News*. Retrieved from https://www.buzzfeed.com/chrisgeidner/ohio-officials-ordered-to-recognize-gay-couples-marriage?utm_term=.wkJzbQRVa#.cwJKVaAyl

Gohmann, S., & Ohsfeldt, R. (1994). Voting in the U.S. house on abortion funding issues: The Role of constituents and legislators ideology, before and after the Webster decision. *American Journal of Economics and Sociology*, *53*(4), 455–474. doi:10.1111/j.1536-7150.1994.tb02618.x

Green, J., & Guth, J. (1991). Religion, representatives, and roll calls. *Legislative Studies Quarterly*, *16*(4), 571–584. doi:10.2307/440018

Haider-Markel, D., & Meier, K. (1996). The politics of lesbian and gay rights: Expanding the scope of the conflict. *The Journal of Politics*, *58*(2), 532–349. doi:10.2307/2960229

Hastings, D. (2013, July 15). Terminally ill Ohio gay man gets dying wish, marries partner after being flown to another state. *New York Daily News*. Retrieved from http://www.nydailynews.com/news/national/terminally-ill-gay-man-ohio-flies-partner-maryland-tarmac-wedding-article-1.1399228

Hollingsworth v. Perry, 133 S. Ct. 2652 (2013).

Hurley, L. (2013 June 26). Gay marriage gets big boost in two Supreme Court rulings. *Reuters*. Retrieved from http://www.reuters.com/article/us-usa-court-gaymarriage-idUSBRE95P06W20130626

Kammen, M. (1980). *People of paradox*. Ithaca, NY: Cornell University Press.

Latourette, K. (1943). *Christianity in a revolutionary age: The 19th century – the great century in the Americas, Australia and Africa, 1800-1914*. New York: Harper and Brothers.

Liptak, A. (2014 March 24). Ruling Could Have Reach Beyond Issue of Contraception. *The New York Times*.

Lowi, T. (1969). *The end of liberalism*. New York: Norton.

Mears, B. (2013 June 27). Supreme Court strikes down federal provision on same-sex marriage benefits. *CNN*. Retrieved from http://www.cnn.com/2013/06/26/politics/scotus-same-sex-doma/

Moon, J. (2015 April 16). Alabama religious protection bill advances in state senate. *The Montgomery (Ala.) Advertiser*. Retrieved from http://www.usatoday.com/story/news/politics/2015/04/16/alabama-religious-freedom-bill/25872887/

Mooney, C., & Lee, M. (1995). Legislating morality in the American states: The case of pre-Roe abortion regulation reform. *American Journal of Political Science*, *39*(3), 599–627. doi:10.2307/2111646

Mooney, C., & Lee, M. (2000). The influence of values on consensus and contentious morality policy: U.S. death penalty reform, 1956–1982. *The Journal of Politics*, *62*, 223–239.

Obergefell v. Hodges, 576 U.S. ___ (2015)

Pangle, T. (1988). *The Spirit of Modern Republicanism: The Moral Vision of the American Founders and the Philosophy of Locke*. Chicago, IL: University of Chicago press.

Peterson, K. (2014, June 30). Supreme court's Hobby Lobby ruling ignites debate over religious-freedom law. *The Wall Street Journal*. Retrieved from https://www.wsj.com/articles/supreme-courts-hobby-lobby-ruling-ignites-debate-over-religious-freedom-law-1404155510

Pitzl, M. J. (2014). 3 GOP senators who voted for SB 1062 asking Brewer to veto bill. *The Republic*.

Price, V., Nir, L., & Cappella, J. (2005). Framing public discussion of gay civil unions. *Public Opinion Quarterly*, *69*(2), 179–212. doi:10.1093/poq/nfi014

Rangel, E. (2015, June 21). Texas Republicans expect 'sad day,' same-sex marriage advocates hopeful for Supreme Court ruling. *Lubbock Avalanche-Journal*. Retrieved from http://lubbockonline.com/local-news/2015-06-21/texas-republicans-expect-sad-day-same-sex-marriage-advocates-hopeful-supreme#.VYgZ1FVViko

Religious Freedom Restoration Act of 1993, Pub. L. No. 103-141, 107 Stat. 1488 (November 16, 1993), codified at 42 U.S.C. § 2000bb through 42 U.S.C. § 2000bb-4

Schwartz, J. (2014, June 30). Between the lines of the contraception decision. *New York Times*. Retrieved from http://www.nytimes.com/interactive/2014/06/30/us/annotated-supreme-court-hobby-lobby-contraception-decision.html?_r=0

Smith, T., & Tatalovich, R. (2003). *Cultures at War: Moral Conflicts in Western Democracies*. Orchard Park, NY: Broadview Press.

Socarides, R. (2013). How the Court Ruled on DOMA and Prop. 8. *The New Yorker*. Retrieved from http://www.newyorker.com/news/news-desk/how-the-court-ruled-on-doma-and-prop-8

Spong, J. (2005). *The sins of scripture: Exposing the bible's texts of hate to reveal the God of love* (1st ed.). San Francisco, CA: Harper.

Tebbe, N. (2015). Religion and Marriage Equality Statutes. *Harvard Law and Policy Review*, *26*, 9–61.

Texas Senate Committee on State Affairs. (2016). *Interim report to the 85th Legislature*.

Thompson, A. (2013, July 19). Cincinnati lawsuit challenges Ohio's same-sex marriage ban. *WVXU Cincinnati*. Retrieved from http://wvxu.org/post/cincinnati-lawsuit-challenges-ohios-same-sex-marriage-ban#stream/0

Tushnet, M. (1989). Religion in Politics. *Columbia Law Review*, 89.

United States v. Windsor, No. 12-307, 570 U.S. (2013, June 26). (n.d.). Retrieved from https://supreme.justia.com/cases/federal/us/570/12-307/

Vermont Journal of the House. (2015 April 3). *House Resolution 8*. Retrieved from http://legislature.vermont.gov/assets/Documents/2016/Docs/JOURNAL/hj150403.pdf#page=5

Volokh, E. (2013, December 13). *Elane Photography v. Willock*. CATO Organization. Retrieved from https://www.cato.org/publications/legal-briefs/elane-photography-v-willock-0

VT HR0008 | 2015-2016 | Regular Session. (2015, April 3). LegiScan. Retrieved January 31, 2017, from https://legiscan.com/VT/bill/HR0008/2015

Williams, P., & McClam, E. (2013, June 26). Supreme Court strikes down defense of marriage act, paves way for gay marriage to resume in California. *NBC News*. Retrieved from http://nbcpolitics.nbcnews.com/_news/2013/06/26/19151971-supreme-court-strikes-down-defense-of-marriage-act-paves-way-for-gay-marriage-to-resume-in-california?lite

Wilson, R. (2014). Marriage of necessity: Same-sex marriage and religious liberty protections. *Case Reserve Law Review*, *64*(3). Retrieved from http://perma.cc/MWL7-8QBH

KEY TERMS AND DEFINITIONS

Chubbing: A kind of talking that's used to stall legislation. With a Republican majority in the House and Senate, Democrats have to rely on something other than their voting strength in a fight. The filibuster is the classic example, but that's allowed only in the Senate.

Defense of Marriage: A United States federal law that defined marriage for federal purposes as the union of one man and one woman.

Family Values: Describes a set of varied and ambiguous moral beliefs in society.

Public Accommodation: Generally defined as entities, both public and private, that are used by the public.

Precedent: A principle or rule established in a previous legal case that is thereafter referred to in deciding similar cases.

ENDNOTES

1. New Mexico: Alliance Defending Freedom[Video] https://www.adflegal.org/detailspages/case-details/elane-photography-v.-willock
2. 3 GOP senators who voted for SB 1062 asking Brewer to veto bill [Video] Retrieved from http://archive.azcentral.com/news/politics/articles/20140224arizona-gop-senators-sb-1062-ask-brewer-veto.html
3. 3 GOP senators who voted for SB 1062 asking Brewer to veto bill [Video] Retrieved from http://archive.azcentral.com/news/politics/articles/20140224arizona-gop-senators-sb-1062-ask-brewer-veto.html
4. Closely held corporations are defined by the Internal Revenue Service as those which a) have more than 50% of the value of their outstanding stock owned (directly or indirectly) by 5 or fewer individuals at any time during the last half of the tax year; and b) are not personal service corporations. By this definition, approximately 90% of U.S. corporations are "closely held", and approximately 52% of the U.S. workforce is employed by "closely held" corporations.

Chapter 6
The Implications of Religious Liberty

ABSTRACT

The political terrain surrounding the legalization of same-sex marriage and the need to accommodate individual's faith based objections have been part of the public discussion since the passage of initial marriage equality statutes. These exemptions played an important part in the bill's passage and have gone largely unquestioned from proponents of marriage equality. This chapter discusses the heightened lawmaking efforts by opponents insisting on broad protection measures for religious claims based on opposition directed towards homosexuality. This Chapter discusses the resulting tension between religious freedom and marriage equality.

Congress shall make no law respecting an establishment of religion, or prohibiting the free exercise thereof.... ~ U.S. Constitution

INTRODUCTION

With the power of judicial review, the U.S. Supreme Court has a profound effect on the policy making environment in the American states. Cannon and Johnson (1999) noted, "The Court's exercise of judicial review of state and local laws is its most important responsibility in modern times." Due

DOI: 10.4018/978-1-5225-2388-8.ch006

to constitutional issues and challenges, policies that raise issues of morality regarding personal liberties such as freedom of speech and expression, privacy, or the separation of church and state are more likely to be challenged at the highest levels of the federal judicial system (Patton, 2007).

The Supreme Court has been active in the past several decades in its review of policies regarding same-sex marriage. These policies that involve morality are referred to as social regulatory or "cultural war" issues and elicit support or opposition based largely upon an individual's core values. Such policies are characterized as a debate over principles where at least one group involved portrays an issue in terms of sin and uses moral arguments to support their policy position (Haider-Markel & Meier, 1996; Mooney, 2001) and the other group depicts their position as seeking equality.

Several studies have examined the impact and/or implementation of state policies following a Supreme Court ruling. Glick (1994) concludes that there is a need to "include Supreme Court decisions…in the study of state policy innovation." Similarly, Canon and Johnson (1999) describe ways that legislatures have attempted to limit the effect of a Court decision by adopting laws that work around the ruling or that do not directly conflict with a decision (e.g. the extension of Religious Freedom bills to limit the implementation of same-sex marriage).

This Chapter focuses on conflicts that have resulted since the anticipated and actual legalization of same-sex marriage. Expanded protections under state mini Religious Freedom Restoration Acts (RFRA) are characterized by many as religious discrimination to resist the recognition of LGBT equal rights. Both religious freedom and equal protection are prized constitutional rights. The dilemma is can these rights coexist in this deeply charged culture war between religious freedom and LGBT rights. The guiding question of the following discussion is whether religious beliefs are so different from non-religious beliefs that they alone can override the state's interest in enforcing the right to non-discrimination.

BACKGROUND

As the public awaited the U.S. Supreme Court's same-sex marriage decision in *Obergefell v. Hodges*, (2015) the country braced itself for the next wave of an ongoing "kultur kampf"—the cultural war—in the name of religion and against LGBT[1] rights (Meckler & Campoy, 2015). On June 26, 2015, the Court issued an historic decision, which extended the constitutionally protected fundamental right to marry to same-sex couples (*Obergefell v. Hodges*, 2015). Although advocates cheered the Court's landmark decision, the social, religious, and moral debate is far from over (Fausset & Blinder, 2015). Having lost in the Court, same-sex marriage opponents have sought legislative remedies to ensure that their religious view of morally is protected.

Long before the Court announced its decision in *Obergefell v. Hodges* (2015), legislative opponents of same-sex marriage sought to minimize or block the aftershock the decision favoring same-sex marriage rights. These legislative responses took center stage at the state level, by either extending or sponsoring state mini Religious Freedom Restoration Acts (RFRAs) (National Conference of State Legislatures, 2015). Although many states had existing RFRA statutes, other states adopted laws are far more protective of religious freedom than the federal RFRA. These legislative efforts include state laws blocking local efforts to pass nondiscrimination ordinances that extend antidiscrimination protections to the LGBT community. The backlash to the *Obergefell v. Hodges* (2015) decision is real the opponents of same-sex marriage have altered their battle strategy. Invoking religious freedom, instead of defending their right to discriminate, they now claim to be the victims of discrimination. Tennessee Republican State Representative Susan Lynn, a Southern Baptist passed House Joint Resolution 529 stating:

WHEREAS, on June 26, 2015, the U.S. Supreme Court issued an opinion in the case of Obergefell v. Hodges, 576 U.S. ___ (No. 14-556, 2015 WL 2473451 (June 26, 2015); and

WHEREAS, two years earlier, in the case of Windsor v. United States, 570 U.S. ___(2013), the U.S. Supreme Court said, "[t]he whole subject of the domestic relations of husband and wife, parent and child, belongs to the laws of the states, and not to the laws of the United States"; and

WHEREAS, the Obergefell decision raises serious constitutional issues regarding the constitutional doctrines of federalism and separation of powers; now, therefore,

BE IT RESOLVED BY THE HOUSE OF REPRESENTATIVES OF THE ONE HUNDREDNINTH GENERAL ASSEMBLY OF THE STATE OF TENNESSEE, THE SENATE

CONCURRING, that this body expresses its disagreement with the constitutional analysis in Obergefell v. Hodges and the judicial imposition of a marriage license law that is contrary to the express will of this body and the vote of the people of Tennessee. (Tennessee House Joint Resolution 529, 2015)

To understand the reason why states have begun rapidly sought to adopt mini RFRAs, one must consider the historical context from which religious exercise challenges to same-sex marriage rights were first invoked. Religious exercise challenges increased as states and municipalities began recognizing rights for nontraditional sexual choices and identities.

Across the nation, these legislative measures have been introduced by lawmakers supported by a network of religious groups forging a national campaign that would allow people to refuse to provide goods or services to same-sex couples based on religious grounds. Within the context of the legislative arena, it is expected that the dynamics of morality politics debate are highly partisan and ideological (Haider-Markel & Meier, 1996; Mooney & Lee, 1995). Because morality politics often is organized around faith beliefs (Meier, 1994; Mooney & Lee, 1995), the religious affiliation of legislators should play a role in legislative sponsorship and decision-making on issues that involve morality. In 2016, state legislators introduced more than 200 anti-LGBT bills in states across the country (Warbelow & Diaz, 2016. While the majority of these bills were vetoed or defeated, states such as Mississippi and North Carolina did adopt discriminatory legislation (Warbelow & Diaz, 2016).

Mississippi Speaker of the House Philip Gunn, an elder in the Baptist church was the sponsor of House Bill 1523 otherwise known as the "Protecting Freedom of Conscience from Government Discrimination Act." The bill bars the state from addressing discrimination when individuals or organizations assert that they discriminate based on their belief that marriage is between one man and one woman, that sexual relations should occur only in the context of such a marriage, or that a person's sex is defined by immutable biological traits (Warbelow & Diaz, 2016). In effect, the bill enables almost any individual or organization to discriminate against LGBT Mississippians at work, at school, and in their communities. The U.S. District Judge Carlton Reeve ruled that the law was unconstitutional, blocking it from taking effect.

North Carolina's House Bill 2 forbids transgender people from accessing shared facilities in accordance with their gender identity causing enormous damage to North Carolina's reputation and economy. Companies responded by scrapping expansions, concerts and conferences were canceled, sporting events have been moved to other states. Shortly thereafter, North Carolina voters ousted one of the most vocal supporters, Republican Governor Pat McCrory, and elected a new Governor. In both instances, these bills were introduced by a partisan group of legislators and federal judges blocked enforcement of parts of those bills.

RFRAs were originally intended to protect religious freedom; many states adopted them in order to override nondiscrimination laws. Legislators are increasingly sponsoring bills that include religion accommodations in a wide variety of areas, including government licensing, employment benefits, even conscience clauses for government employees including judicial officers. Those seeking a defense to violate laws are labeling personal offense as religious freedom to justify imposing discrimination on the LGBT individuals. These new protections under state, mini RFRAs are being characterized as religious discrimination to resist LGBT equality in light of same-sex marriage legalization.

In response, to Mississippi and North Carolina, Governors in four states issued Executive Orders prohibiting discrimination against LGBT people. Montana Governor Steve Bullock signed an Executive Order addressing discrimination on the basis of sexual orientation and gender identity for state employees and recipients of state services, as well state contractors and subcontractors. Louisiana Governor John Bel Edwards and New Hampshire Governor Maggie Hassan issued similar Executive Orders. Pennsylvania Governor Tom Wolf added protections, via Executive Order, for the employees of grantees, contractors, and subcontractors, supplementing prior executive action. Finally, North Carolina Governor Pat McCrory issued an Executive Order stating an intention not to discriminate in state employment on the basis of sexual orientation and gender identity without actually prohibiting such discrimination; he also affirmed the discriminatory restriction on transgender people established by House Bill 2. Georgia and South Dakota, both with Republican governors, vetoed legislation that attacked the LGBT community; in doing so, these leaders show the nation that fairness, equality and justice aren't Democratic or Republican values – they are simply American values. Georgia Governor Nathan Deal vetoed a variation of the Mississippi law, explaining that he wanted to maintain Georgia's status as a welcoming state for everyone (Warbelow & Diaz, 2016).

BALANCING THE INTERESTS: LIBERTY VS. EQUALITY

For many Americans, freedom is the essence of what America is about–it is the reason why the colonists fought for independence and the most fundamental principle at the heart of American democracy. But freedom is no less complex than other values that drive politics. The dilemma of liberty surfaces in public policy around the question of when government can interfere with the choices of its citizens (Stone, 2002). Written in 1859, John Stuart Mill's *On Liberty* essay attempted to find a single criterion for deciding when society should interfere with a person's liberty. Mill believed that deliberation and the exercise of choice are the essence of being human and therefore government should interfere as little as possible. According to Mill, policy issues are cast as a choice between protecting the liberty of individuals and preventing harm to others. This assertion of harm sets one set of interests against the other which generates political contention.

Harms are not objective but are rather political claims which are granted legitimacy by government. Thus a significant political strategy is to define harms as legitimate; these types of harms can be described as an emotional or psychological harm that spill over into the area of spiritual and moral harm. Frequently in history, a group has sought to have government prohibit behavior based on its own religious laws or compelling behavior mandated by its religious tradition.

Despite the tradition of separation of church and state, claims in America about spiritual or moral harms continue to be heard in American politics. The same-sex marriage issue can be understood as a conflict between those who believe that photographers, bakers, ministers, etc. are spiritually or morally harmed if they have to participate in a same-sex marriage. Mills' (1859) strictures against granting legitimacy to claims of spiritual harm are in direct opposition to same-sex marriage challengers who have sought to translate their claims into ones of spiritual injury. Injury results from and is expressed as a "fear of flaunting," in other words while gay people may be more or less tolerated, gay sexuality is not; suggesting that while it may okay to "be gay" it is not okay to "do gay." This status/conduct distinction appears in legal and theological discourse, especially when believers are admonished to "love the sinner but hate the sin." Erotophobia, or "fear of flaunting," is pervasive in a society that is, at one and the same time, both fascinated and repelled by sex. According to Eskridge (1996) "our culture manages to be pervasively prurient and puritanical, tolerant, and judgmental."

Which leads to the questions of liberty as defined by the harm criterion these are inevitable questions of equity, for they include decisions about who bears the harms, whose activities should be curtailed and who bears the cost of prevention? Every society has a pattern of recognized needs and a pattern of recognized harms. It is a matter of cultural history and political choice as to which kinds of harms are privileged in any society. Extending this principle to scenarios in which individuals and businesses refuse services to LGBT persons and families on the basis of religious freedom, those discriminated against will certainly suffer "dignity" harm. Over seventy years ago, the U.S. Supreme Court recognized that segregation in public schools harmed children by "generat[ing] a feeling of inferiority as to their status in the community that may affect their hearts and minds in a way unlikely ever to be undone" (*Brown v. Board of Education*, 1954).The Court took special notice of the fact that segregation in public schools harmed children; similarly, discrimination in other areas of public life against LGBT families also harms children. Children in LGBT families are equally vulnerable and susceptible of sustaining irreversible feelings of inferiority when they and their family members are discriminated against, in the name of faith religion, based on sexual orientation and gender identity. Further, children are not the only victims harmed by efforts against same-sex marriage rights. Justice Kennedy linked the fundamental right to marry, regardless of sexual orientation, to "human dignity" *(Obergefell v. Hodges*, 2015).Condemning same-sex marriage as an offense to religion and, therefore, justifying discrimination certainly inflicts dignitary harm on all members of the LGBT community. In some ways, condoned discrimination in the name of religion gives added legitimacy to discrimination.

Mill (1859) was adamant that religious belief should never be a permissible ground for government regulation of behavior. He claimed that a group that is morally offended or revolted by some practice, such as homosexuality or same-sex marriage should never be recognized by government as a basis for policy; arguing that it is "the logic of persecutor's" to say that we may persecute others because we are right (Mill, 1859). Although not framed as religious liberty versus freedom from discrimination, Justice Ginsburg in her *Burwell v. Hobby Lobby* (2014) dissent re-emphasized her concern that in accommodating free exercise claims, courts should consider the harm caused to third persons who do not share the RFRA claimant's religious beliefs. With the rise of robust mini-RFRAs and other laws protecting religious freedom at the expense of civil rights, the country is at a crossroad the choice between spiritual or dignity harms.

THE LINE BETWEEN SECULAR AND SECTARIAN

Like a pendulum, the country has seen a swing in both directions of the civil rights continuum. Attitudes have changed significantly since states almost universally banned same-sex marriage in the 1970s and 1980s to the post-*United States v. Windsor* (2013) movement when municipalities expanded protections for LGBT individuals through the passage of local anti-discrimination ordinances.

Despite vigorous opposition, same-sex marriage protection continued to spread across the country, and LGBT as anti-discrimination laws increased, causing many to fear that a court might grant civil rights for the LGBT population. Consequently, state mini RFRA laws became the legal missile directed at marriage equality. What followed in conservative states was the proliferation of increasingly robust mini RFRA laws. As the judiciary invalidated bans on same-sex marriage, and as municipalities adopted LGBT-protective antidiscrimination laws, states [legislators] pushed back with the adoption of robust religious freedom laws. Some of the mini RFRA laws mimic the federal RFRAs by reinstating strict scrutiny review for challenges to government regulations that are alleged to substantially burden religious exercise. But other state RFRAs have key provisions that extend far beyond their federal parent.

Against this backdrop, on the last day of the legislative session the Arkansas legislature passed House Bill 1228, known as the "Conscience Protection Act." This legislation represented an expansive religious freedom law that had been the topic of a heated public debate (Berman, 2015). The bill was sponsored by Republicans State Representative Bob Ballinger and State Senator Bart Hector. Both men hold leadership positions within their Baptist churches. In fact, Arkansas's attempt to pass an expansive religious freedom law followed the mini RFRA saga in Indiana, where, after public outcry, Republican Governor Mike Pence sought amendments to the law to appease the concern that the law would open the door to sex and gender discrimination (Bomboy, 2015). These changes clarified that the law would not supersede local ordinances that banned discrimination based on sexual orientation and gender identity.

In March 2014, the Arizona state legislature attempted to pass a very narrow "fix" or amendment to their existing RFRA statute. The bill was intended to make explicitly clear that RFRA laws apply when two people sue each other, in cases where the government would enforce the outcome.

Although Arkansas pulled back their religious freedom laws due to public furor, the proliferation of similar laws in other states continues to be pursued to the added patchwork of robust religious freedom laws. Collectively, these laws threaten to produce a new wave of separate but equal statutes this time affecting the LGBT community.

The Founders regarded the demand for religious uniformity as detrimental to individual liberty and believed that no religion could claim to be the one true way. Realizing that the elevation of one sect would denigrate all others that would create a cycle of resentment and oppression that would culminate in a war of religion, the founders erected a wall of separation between religion and government to protect individual religious conviction from government persecution. Considered equally important was the protection of give-and-take that is required in politics of a free people from the uncompromising demands of orthodoxy. Enshrined in Americans founding is the principle that faith, is a personal, individual matter of belief and not part of public business.

A regime of disestablishment does not mean that religious beliefs may not be brought into secular controversies. Of course not. Most Americans believe in a God, a Creator, a Universal Life Force, or a Higher Power, with the majority subscribing to a particular faith. An individual's moral compass is a critical element of citizenship in a democracy. People bring their faith into politics when they use their own conscience to guide their citizenship.

Any given faith traditions can produce diametrically opposed political positions among individuals. History illustrates these intra-denominational conflicts. The design of the constitution sought to forbid the government from taking sides in the ever-swirling theological and moral controversies to which faith traditions are prone. Religions are partial to theocracy rather than democracy as a political goal when given access to civil power. The gay rights controversy within denominations is evident in the differing ways in which religious groups deal with their openly gay congregants. The traditional condemnation of homosexuality is not highlighted to favor LGBT individuals. Because the issue of homosexuality and religion is evolutionary, that fact makes a strong argument for rejecting dogma as a basis for public policy on the issue.

Religion adherents turn to the public arena, in part, as a move to resolve issues outside the church that the church remains divided about. The inevitability of such an attempt shows how prudent the separation of church and state is as a practical policy. Religions will always resort to external authority to resolve internal disputes. What bothers some legislators are that (at least in principle) in this country, ideas are all equal in the intellectual marketplace.

Believing, as an article of faith, that the revealed truths to which they subscribe supersede all other truths, they find the voices of American pluralism anxiety provoking. A legislator driven by faith characteristically credits their mission and motive as being above the criticism that other political interests take for granted. While other legislators seek to persuade, the faithful want to convert. Persuasion does not require that the person persuaded, abandon all previously held beliefs and subscribe to an entirely different set, nor does it assume that bad faith or perversity on the part of the unpersuaded. It is not necessary for instance, to embrace homosexuality to believe that discrimination against others because of their homosexuality violates their individual freedom. It is possible to dislike gays and believe they are condemned to hell and still respect their right to live life as they choose, holding whatever beliefs they have about themselves, knowing this same freedom protects you.

This perspective differs markedly for some legislators because they allow no distinction between their faith convictions and civil law. Based on their beliefs, if their own faith tradition condemns homosexuality, then the law must reflect this condemnation. This reluctance to compromise, combined with the belief that a different standard applies to their political activity, explains again the importance for the constitutional separation of church and state.

Establishment is as natural to religious impulse in politics, as monopoly is to business impulse. But while businesses may be willing to settle for less, it is against the nature of religious interests to compromise. For this reason, even freedom that promotes and protects religious expression cannot be left to religion. The freedom to seek spiritual truth, by other expressions of individual freedom are not welcomed by churches. They look askance at the very climate of pluralism and individual choice that enabled their own growth.

This view of freedom exists for the sole purpose of establishing their views. This strain of faith intolerance has constantly intruded into American political life. The point is that while their targets may change, the purpose of the faith driven [legislators] is the denigration of differing points of view and silence of those who hold them. The goals of the LGBT community and those of the faithful are not commensurate. One group aims to extend citizenship and its protections to a community excluded from them for no acceptable constitutional reason, while the other wishes to suppress unwelcome neighbors and their way of life by denying them equal protection of the law. But equal protection is not determined by majority vote *(Obergefell v. Hodges*, 2015), and much less by religious certainty, however vociferously expressed. It exists in part to prevent majorities from imposing their will in a way that subverts the liberties of everyone (Nava & Dawidoff, 1994)

Accommodation

The term accommodation[2] as used by the Supreme Court refers to the facilitation of religious liberty and its exercise, usually through exemptions from general laws. The principle of accommodation implies two forms of discrimination: it confers a right to discriminate on religious institutions, and it withholds this right from non-religious employers. Non-religious employers can neither invoke the right to freedom of association nor the right to freedom of conscience to refuse complying with non-discrimination employment provisions, even if their wish to discriminate is based on a comprehensive moral worldview or otherwise sincerely held beliefs. As conservatives and liberals continue to be splintered over LGBT rights, there is increasing evidence regarding the tension between religious freedom and civil rights. The flash point between religious liberty and the legalization of same-sex marriage is in the goal of using the law to refuse to support a particular lifestyle that their religious beliefs deem immoral.

This tension between religious freedom and civil rights has and will continue to play out in the courtroom. The New Mexico Supreme Court's 2006 decision in *Elane Photography v. Willock* (2013) provides a prime illustration. Elane Photography spelled the start of a new era—an era in which the LGBT community would find itself unfairly pitted against an increasingly conservative religious community. The tension caused by this division grew as similar cases arose including the case of *State v. Arlene's Flowers, Inc*. (2015) where a gay couple and the State of Washington sued a flower shop owner for refusing to create the flower arrangements for the couple's same-sex wedding after the owner claimed that serving the couple conflicted with her religious belief that marriage should "only be between a man and a woman." These types of cases contributed to the further dissension throughout the country over the issue of LGBT civil rights and businesses' religious beliefs and practices.

Neither New Mexico nor Washington states had mini RFRA laws on the books at the time of these cases. The conflict in Elane Photography and Arlene's Flowers foreshadows the real-life impact of an overly protective state RFRA. With all of the cards stacked in favor of religious freedom and no express antidiscrimination protections for same-sex patrons, in many states across the nation the balance between religious exercise and civil rights tilts heavily in favor of religious freedom advocates. Keeping RFRA in check, is to expressly prohibit discrimination on the bases of sexual orientation, gender identity, and gender expression. Otherwise, state, mini RFRAs could provide a pernicious shield in discrimination suits. In Louisiana, groups that had backed RFRA in 1993 when the original was first passed have since changed their views, realizing that laws they really cared about were being attacked under RFRAs. The title of the law—the Religious Freedom Restoration Act, was misleading. It claimed to "restore" something, but was instead, is a grab for new rights.

As many are acknowledging, there is an element in RFRA a "less restrictive means" test, never before seen in religious liberty cases in the United States, and it is a game-changer. RFRA is simply restoring prior law, with its implicit premise suggesting that if it is the standard we have always had, it can't hurt. It's not the same, and it does hurt. RFRA today is motivated by legislators and religious organizations that embrace agendas deeply at odds with civil rights, to the detriment of those whose faith differs. RFRA presents a public-policy problem, for it creates a presumption against every law, in favor of the religious actor. Laws exist to protect the vulnerable. When a religious actor gets wide latitude to ignore the law, as RFRA invites, it is the vulnerable get hurt. After the *City of Boerne v. Flores* (1997), decision religious groups scrambled to get a new, revised federal RFRA re-enacted, and to push state versions in all 50 states. About a dozen state RFRAs were passed in relatively short order before opponents were able slow the pro-RFRA movement.

Given the frequency with which Courts are involved in disputes over policies that involve moral issues, state legislators are attentive when weighing the adoption of these decisions. Glick (1970) notes that judicial review "establishes a direct policy-making link between courts and other officials." Similarly, Vanberg (2001) stated "Legislative behavior may be conditioned by anticipation of constitutional review." The Supreme Court decisions influence the policy-making environment in state legislatures and thus affect the adoption of morality policies. Over a 22-year period, state legislatures have come increasingly under single-party control. Where Republicans control a sizable majority of legislatures, there's already a push for measures which are discriminatory; attempting to stem the tide of support for LGBT- expanding civil rights, the anti-same-sex marriage movement galvanized efforts to win legislative victories on the state level that would neutralize, or even block, this growing pro-LGBT rights' trend.

However, swinging too far in favor of religious freedom may impose burdens on nonbelievers and threaten violation of the Establishment Clause. The First Amendment religion clauses require a balance between government neutrality and accommodation. In mediating this latest culture war between religious freedom and LGBT rights, the interplay between accommodation laws and granting defenses to compliance through RFRA religious freedom claims must honor this fine balance. The courts will be called on to perform this delicate balancing act. In doing so, the courts should distinguish between offense and religious belief. When denial of services is based on offense (even if grounded in religious doctrine), then enforcing public accommodation laws is not at odds with religious freedom.

Defenders of accommodation, that is, defenders of the facilitation of religious liberty through exemptions from general laws, need to offer reasons that go beyond the religion to explain why religion is special enough to qualify for such a treatment. Conversely, if religion is not special, there is no reason for legislators and courts to favor religion over non-religion by deferring to religious consciences but not to their secular counterparts.

Steven Gey, in a 1990 University of Pittsburgh Law Review, titled "*Why Is Religion Special?*" states that while it is constitutionally legitimate that the government cannot "force a church to accept a nonbeliever [or a homosexual] as a priest," it is unclear why the government can force non-religious private employers to respect non-discrimination provisions, but has to show deference to religious employers who adopt discriminatory policies for purely secular employment positions. Why are religious objections to homosexuality so special that they should be accommodated by a simple appeal to the Constitution? Although the U.S. Constitution does single out religion in the First Amendment, it does so ambiguously, which means that it can be used by both defenders and opponents of religious exemptions from general laws (Schmidt, 2015). Those who consider religion to be especially beneficial and therefore deserving of protection "refer only to the free exercise clause, to which they subordinate the establishment clause" (Gey, 1990). By contrast, those who politicized religion to be especially dangerous insist on the secular values of the establishment clause and downplay the importance of the "free exercise clause" (Gey, 1990).

This raises the question of why homosexual discrimination is tolerated when it is grounded in religious reasons. The case of same-sex is relevant since gay rights continue to be controversial. There are many non-religious employers who oppose homosexuality and would like to continue discriminating on the basis of sexual orientation. Such special treatment seems to be incompatible with the neutrality principle that underlies the religion clauses. At the same time, defenders of religion's special status are right since the second prong, the free exercise clause, applies only to religions. Extending accommodation to non-religious moral viewpoints and lifestyles requires opponents of religion's special status to show that secular, moral viewpoints and lifestyles bear sufficient resemblance to their religious counterparts to fall under the protection of the free exercise clause.

In other words, they have to explain why and how religious and non-religious individuals are 'similarly situated' with regard to their beliefs about right and wrong. By contrast, if religion is special, then it might be legitimate to treat it differently from non-religion (provided that the accommodation is compatible with liberal democratic principles). The fact that certain individuals or groups could benefit more than others from a law, or that they are differently affected by it, does not necessarily undermine the law's legitimacy.

Conservatives frequently describe the gay agenda as a campaign for special rights unavailable to others. It suffices to say that the meaning of 'equal rights' and 'equal treatment' must be considered. Enforcing these principles does not require identical or similar treatment of all individuals, but only of those who are, in one particular respect, similarly situated. Consequently, is not whether accommodation creates "a category of social benefits to which nonpractitioners have no access" (Gey, 1985) but whether believers and non-believers are differently situated with regard to their 'sincerely-held beliefs' (based on the accommodation principle), such that it might be legitimate to treat them differently. Proponents of accommodation claim that religious beliefs are special and may require various forms of accommodation, contrary to non-religious moral beliefs. In discussing the case of *Estate of Thornton v. Caldor, Inc.* (1985), Michael W. McConnell (1985) argues that the special treatment of religion does not unduly favor practitioners over non-practitioners since religious duties are burdens that non-believers simply do not face. Justice O'Connor explains that,

All employees, regardless of their religious orientation, would value the benefit which the statute bestows on Sabbath observers -- the right to select the day of the week in which to refrain from labor. Yet Connecticut requires private employers to confer this ... benefit only on those employees who adhere to a particular religious belief. The statute singles out Sabbath observers for special ... protection without according similar accommodation to ethical and religious beliefs and practices of other private employees. (Estate of Thornton v. Caldor, Inc., 1985)

McConnell (1985) takes exception, stating that Sabbath observers do not 'select the day of the week in which to refrain from labor' – the day is imposed on them by their religion. This belief places religious employees in a double bind about whether to comply with the instructions of their employers or to obey their God incurring possible negative employment consequences. This situation means that they have no real choice, (i.e. the possibility to opt between two outcomes that are more valuable or bearable for them). For the state to require private employers to accommodate practicing believers without giving the impression of favoring religious over non-religious workers, the language of 'choice' needs to be abandoned when referring to religious beliefs and practices. Michael Sandel (1989) opposes the voluntarist conception of religious liberty which "confuses the right to exercise a duty with the right to make a choice." Implicit in this conception of the person is 'the unencumbered self,' i.e. a self that is not defined by religion but chooses it freely.

Koppelman (2006) suggests that, the battle of so-called culture wars, both sides of the debate should be taken seriously and that the same standards must apply to everyone equally; antigay views should not be silenced, because "as gay people know so well, the closet is not a healthy place to be." Thus, leftists and secularists who have fought against the closet need to take religious individuals and groups seriously when they lament the privatization of religion or antigay views. This alone cannot justify exemptions from employment anti-discrimination provisions, but it can explain why voicing objections to homosexuality should not always be conceived of as hate speech. All this is just to say that for accommodation (in the form of exemptions from anti-discrimination provisions) to have a principled foundation, it has to be granted to all those who intensely and sincerely hold a certain moral position, whether religious or not.

RECOMMENDATION

RFRA was copied directly from the Supreme Court cases that impose the strictest level of scrutiny known in all of constitutional law. The claimant must prove that the law impose a "substantial burden"; if this succeeds then the burden shifts to the government; which then must defend its law by proving that the law serves a "compelling interest" and does so by employing the "least restrictive means" available. These are tough standards to apply to neutral laws that apply to every actor in society (Hamilton, 2010). With that history in mind, the next wave of state RFRAs can be more fully understood. These laws demand and deserve harsher public scrutiny, for these new RFRAs go even further than their predecessors.

FUTURE RESEARCH DIRECTIONS

Scholarship on morality issues includes a discussion of relevant U.S. Supreme Court decisions. Future research on issues of morality should include empirical consideration involving state policy adoption as a result of court decisions.

CONCLUSION

America was founded by pilgrims who came here to escape religious tyranny and to practice their faiths freely. This is among the myths of America's founding – that the nation, even before its inception, was a bastion of religious freedom and tolerance. This view has remained one of the most enduring slants on American history. The pilgrims left Europe to escape religious persecution. Ironically, from the moment they landed, they showed no intention of granting religious freedom to those faiths not deemed orthodox. This intolerance paved the way for religious the clauses in the Bill of Rights. When James Madison warned that "the diabolical Hell-conceived principle of persecution rages," he was talking about Anglicans attacking Baptists (*National Archives, n.d.*). The Framers intended for the United States to have the benefit of ordered liberty, which included the common-sense insight that there is such a thing as too much liberty.

This modern kulturkampf pits religious freedom against nondiscrimination principles and is reminiscent of an era when governors blocked efforts to integrate public schools. Just as governors and segregationists defied the U.S. Supreme Court's edict that "separate is NOT equal," the present war to stifle LGBT civil rights has the potential to create a new wave of separate but not equal in the delivery of goods and services. RFRA was never intended to be a shield to those who discriminate in places of public accommodation or in violation of ethical standards. The RFRA variants go well beyond those boundaries.

The First Amendment religion clauses require a fine balance between religious life and secular life. Some religions and religious observers believe that marriage between two individuals of the same sex is a sin, and, undoubtedly, the First Amendment protects their right to this belief. However, at some point, a religious belief cannot be imposed on others in the secular realm. Respect for secular consciences does not imply undermining the rule of law by extending exemptions to innumerable organizations. However, when it comes to anti-discrimination laws for secular employment positions that require individuals to act in a way that is contrary to their beliefs, religious and non-religious persons are similarly situated. Both groups feel that they need to obey the duties of their conscience, whether these duties derive from a transcendent source or not. Religion cannot claim a special status when it comes to moral issues such as abortion, contraception, or homosexuality. If exemptions are granted for religious reasons, they should also be granted for non-religious conscientious objections

Although religious freedom is indeed important, the voluntary embrace of same-sex marriages permits legislators to consider competing considerations, including ways to permit those who adhere to a traditional view of marriage to continue to do so and balancing others civil rights.

REFERENCES

Berman, M. (2015, March 31). Arkansas lawmakers approve religious liberty bill despite firestorm over Indiana law. *Washington Post*. Retrieved from http://www.washingtonpost.com/news/post-nation /wp/2015/03/31/after-a-firestorm-over-indianas-religious-law-is-arkansas-next/

Bomboy, S. (2015, April 1). *Explaining the Indiana RFRA Controversy in Five Minutes*. National Constitutional Constitution Center. Retrieved from http://blog.constitutioncenter.org/2015/04/explaining-the-indiana-rfra-controversy-in-five-minutes/

Brown v. Board of Education of Topeka, 347 U.S. 483 (1954)

Burwell v. Hobby Lobby, 573 U.S. ___ (2014)

Canon, B., & Johnson, C. (1999). *Judicial policies: Implementation and impact*. Washington, DC: CQ Press.

City of Boerne v. Flores, 521 U.S. 507 (1997). (n.d.). Retrieved from http://caselaw.findlaw.com/us-supreme-court/521/507.html

Elane Photography, LLC v. Willock, 284 P.3d 428,432 (N.M. Ct. App. 2012), aff'd, 309 P.3d 53 (N.M. 2013).

Eskridge, W. (1996). *The case for same-sex marriage: From sexual liberty to civilized commitment*. New York: Free Press.

Estate of Thornton v. Caldor, Inc., 472 U.S. 703 (1985).

Fausset, R., & Blinder, A. (2015, January 25). States Renew Fight To Stop Same-Sex Marriage. *New York Times*. Retrieved from http://www.nytimes.com/2015/01/29/us/battles-over-same-sex-marriage-roilstatehouses-ahead-of-supreme-courts-decision.html?_r=1

Gey, S. (1990). Why is religion special? Reconsidering the accommodation of religion under the religion clauses of the first amendment. *University of Pittsburgh Law Review. University of Pittsburgh. School of Law*, *52*(75), 92.

Glick, H. (1994). The impact of permissive judicial policies: The U.S. Supreme Court and the right to die. *Political Research Quarterly*, *47*, 207–222.

Hamilton, M. (2010, October 14). The new wave of extreme state Religious Freedom Restoration Act (RFRA) legislation: Why it's dangerous. *FindLaw*. Retrieved from http://writ.news.findlaw.com/hamilton/20101014.html

McConnell, M. W. (1985). Accommodation of Religion. *The Supreme Court Review*, *1985*, 10. doi:10.1086/scr.1985.3109496

Meckler, L., & Campoy, A. (2015, April 1). Arkansas governor calls for changes to 'Religious Freedom' bill. *Wall Street Journal*. Retrieved from http://www.wsj.com/articles/arkansas-governor-calls-forchanges-to-religious-freedom-bill-1427904740

Meier, K. (1994). *The politics of sin: Drugs, alcohol and public policy*. Armonk, NY: Shar.

Mill, J. (1974). On Liberty. Penguin. (originally published 1859)

Mooney, C. (2001). *The Public Clash of Private Values: The Politics of Morality*. Thousand Oaks, CA: Sage Publishing.

Mooney, C., & Lee, M. (1995). Legislating morality in the American states: The case of pre-Roe abortion regulation reform. *American Journal of Political Science*, *39*, 599–627.

National Archives. (n.d.). *The Papers of James Madison*. University of Chicago Press. Retrieved from https://founders.archives.gov/about/Madison

Nava, M., & Dawidoff, R. (1994). *Created equal: why gay rights matter to America* (1st ed.). New York: St. Martin's Press.

Obergefell v. Hodges, 576 U.S. ___ (No. 14-556, 2015 WL 2473451 (June 26, 2015)

Patton, D. J. (2007). The supreme court and morality policy adoption in the american states: The impact of constitutional context. *Political Research Quarterly*, *60*(3), 468–488. doi:10.1177/1065912907303844

Religious Freedom Restoration Act of 1993, Pub. L. No. 103-141, 107 Stat. 1488 (November 16, 1993), codified at 42 U.S.C. § 2000bb through 42 U.S.C. § 2000bb-4

Sandel, M. (1989). Religious liberty - Freedom of conscience or freedom of choice? *Utah Law Review*, *597*, 598.

Schmidt, N. (2015). The right to discriminate: Why religion is not special with regard to secular employment. *International Journal of Religion and Spirituality in Society*, *4*(75), 1–14.

State of Washington v. Arlene's Flowers, SCT No. 91615-2 (2017)

Stone, D. A. (2002). *Policy paradox: the art of political decision making* (Rev. ed.). New York: Norton.

United States v. Windsor, 570 U.S. ___ (2013) (Docket No. 12-307).

Vanber, G. (2001). Legislative-judicial relations: A game-theoretic approach to constitutional review. *American Journal of Political Science*, *45*(2), 346–361. doi:10.2307/2669345

Warbelow, S., & Diaz, B. (2016). *State Equality Index*. Human Rights Campaign Foundation/Equality Federation Institute. Retrieved from http://www.hrc.org/campaigns/state-equality-index

KEY TERMS AND DEFINITIONS

Accommodation: A settlement or compromise.

Establishment Clause: A clause in the First Amendment that prevents government from establishing an official religion. Treating one religion preferable to another, or promoting religion over non-religion.

Equality: The value that all Americans should be treated the same under the law, be able to influence government, and have an equal opportunity to succeed in life.

Free Exercise Clause: A clause in the First Amendment that prohibits government from interfering with individual religious practice.

Judicial Activism: The tendency of judges to deviate from past court decision, which allows them to consider their own preferences before issuing a ruling.

Liberty: The beliefs that government should allow people the freedom to do as they please with interference from the government.

Sectarian: Believes in the idea that the particular sect to which he belongs is the right and proper one, and that others belonging to other sects, even if they're still of the same religious group are completely wrong.

Secular: A concept wherein a state or country promotes to be officially neutral in the matters of religion.

ENDNOTES

1 Initials that stand for Lesbian, Bisexual, Gay and Transgendered individuals.

2 Zorach v. Clauson, 343 U.S. 306, 314 (1952).

Related Readings

To continue IGI Global's long-standing tradition of advancing innovation through emerging research, please find below a compiled list of recommended IGI Global book chapters and journal articles in the areas of faith, religion, and legislation. These related readings will provide additional information and guidance to further enrich your knowledge and assist you with your own research.

Adeyanju, A. (2016). Symbols and Not Manifestoes Are the Selling Point Here: A Multimodal Critical Discourse Analysis of Two Contemporary Nigerian Political Parties' Images and Slogans. In D. Orwenjo, O. Oketch, & A. Tunde (Eds.), *Political Discourse in Emergent, Fragile, and Failed Democracies* (pp. 265–285). Hershey, PA: IGI Global. doi:10.4018/978-1-5225-0081-0.ch015

Aham-Anyanwu, N. M., & Li, H. (2017). E-State: Realistic or Utopian? *International Journal of Public Administration in the Digital Age*, *4*(2), 56–76. doi:10.4018/IJPADA.2017040105

Akpojivi, U. (2017). Rethinking Information Privacy in a "Connected" World. In N. Mhiripiri & T. Chari (Eds.), *Media Law, Ethics, and Policy in the Digital Age* (pp. 268–285). Hershey, PA: IGI Global. doi:10.4018/978-1-5225-2095-5.ch015

Almobarraz, A. (2016). Investigating the Seeking Behavior for Religious Information in Social Media. *International Journal of Information Systems and Social Change*, *7*(4), 67–79. doi:10.4018/IJISSC.2016100104

Alphin, H. C. Jr, Lavine, J., Croome, R. J., & Hocker, A. J. (2016). Higher Education and Current E-Learning Potential in the MENA Region: Analysis of the Current Challenges and Opportunities for E-Learning in the MENA Region. In J. Prescott (Ed.), *Handbook of Research on Race, Gender, and the Fight for Equality* (pp. 68–89). Hershey, PA: IGI Global. doi:10.4018/978-1-5225-0047-6.ch004

Alsaç, U. (2017). EKAP: Turkey's Centralized E-Procurement System. In R. Shakya (Ed.), *Digital Governance and E-Government Principles Applied to Public Procurement* (pp. 126–150). Hershey, PA: IGI Global. doi:10.4018/978-1-5225-2203-4.ch006

Assay, B. E. (2017). Intellectual Property Rights and the Protection of Africa's Traditional Knowledge. In N. Mhiripiri & T. Chari (Eds.), *Media Law, Ethics, and Policy in the Digital Age* (pp. 122–145). Hershey, PA: IGI Global. doi:10.4018/978-1-5225-2095-5.ch007

Atlan, H. (2014). Foundations of Interreligious Dialogue. In I. Nahon-Serfaty & R. Ahmed (Eds.), *New Media and Communication Across Religions and Cultures* (pp. 1–15). Hershey, PA: IGI Global. doi:10.4018/978-1-4666-5035-0.ch001

Baasanjav, U. B. (2016). "A Girl Move": Negotiating Gender and Technology in Chess Online and Offline. In J. Prescott (Ed.), *Handbook of Research on Race, Gender, and the Fight for Equality* (pp. 198–211). Hershey, PA: IGI Global. doi:10.4018/978-1-5225-0047-6.ch009

Bilimoria, E. (2017). The Alchemy of Religion: From Inner Illumination to Love and Service in Action. In A. Pascal (Ed.), *Multiculturalism and the Convergence of Faith and Practical Wisdom in Modern Society* (pp. 16–61). Hershey, PA: IGI Global. doi:10.4018/978-1-5225-1955-3.ch002

Bishop, J. (2017). Overcoming the Legal Challenges of News Reporting: A Case Study of a Start-Up News Corporation. In N. Mhiripiri & T. Chari (Eds.), *Media Law, Ethics, and Policy in the Digital Age* (pp. 146–163). Hershey, PA: IGI Global. doi:10.4018/978-1-5225-2095-5.ch008

Blom, R. (2017). Naming Crime Suspects in the News: "Seek Truth and Report It" vs. "Minimizing Harm. In N. Mhiripiri & T. Chari (Eds.), *Media Law, Ethics, and Policy in the Digital Age* (pp. 207–225). Hershey, PA: IGI Global. doi:10.4018/978-1-5225-2095-5.ch012

Brice, T. S. (2016). Race Relations in the Churches of Christ: Strategies towards Reconciliation. In B. Glimps & T. Ford (Eds.), *Gender and Diversity Issues in Religious-Based Institutions and Organizations* (pp. 184–199). Hershey, PA: IGI Global. doi:10.4018/978-1-4666-8772-1.ch008

Brown, M. D. (2017). Religion and the Social Economy: Elective Affinities. In A. Pascal (Ed.), *Multiculturalism and the Convergence of Faith and Practical Wisdom in Modern Society* (pp. 220–235). Hershey, PA: IGI Global. doi:10.4018/978-1-5225-1955-3.ch010

Calvo, N., Bastida, M., & Feás, J. (2016). Is Gender Equality a Reality after a Change in the Political Agenda?: Dynamic Analysis for Higher Management Levels. In J. Prescott (Ed.), *Handbook of Research on Race, Gender, and the Fight for Equality* (pp. 539–558). Hershey, PA: IGI Global. doi:10.4018/978-1-5225-0047-6.ch023

Cannon, D. F. (2014). All in the Family: How Should Religion Communicators Understand Relationships When Conflicts Arise? In I. Nahon-Serfaty & R. Ahmed (Eds.), *New Media and Communication Across Religions and Cultures* (pp. 129–160). Hershey, PA: IGI Global. doi:10.4018/978-1-4666-5035-0.ch009

Carr-Ruffino, N. (2016). Leadership Opportunities for Managing Diversity. In J. Prescott (Ed.), *Handbook of Research on Race, Gender, and the Fight for Equality* (pp. 298–320). Hershey, PA: IGI Global. doi:10.4018/978-1-5225-0047-6.ch013

Carter, S. D. (2016). Increased Workforce Diversity by Race, Gender, and Age and Equal Employment Opportunity Laws: Implications for Human Resource Development. In J. Prescott (Ed.), *Handbook of Research on Race, Gender, and the Fight for Equality* (pp. 398–423). Hershey, PA: IGI Global. doi:10.4018/978-1-5225-0047-6.ch018

Chania, A., & Demetrashvili, K. (2017). Public Procurement Reform in Georgia: The Way from Paper-Based Procurement to an E-Procurement System. In R. Shakya (Ed.), *Digital Governance and E-Government Principles Applied to Public Procurement* (pp. 151–169). Hershey, PA: IGI Global. doi:10.4018/978-1-5225-2203-4.ch007

Chari, T. (2017). Ethical Pitfalls in the Digital Age: When the Desire to "Serve Hot" Gets in the Way of Verification. In N. Mhiripiri & T. Chari (Eds.), *Media Law, Ethics, and Policy in the Digital Age* (pp. 25–43). Hershey, PA: IGI Global. doi:10.4018/978-1-5225-2095-5.ch002

Chollier, M., & Tassinari, M. (2017). Multiculturalism, Morality, and Secondary Secularisation: CoSA or Common Good in Practice. In A. Pascal (Ed.), *Multiculturalism and the Convergence of Faith and Practical Wisdom in Modern Society* (pp. 297–314). Hershey, PA: IGI Global. doi:10.4018/978-1-5225-1955-3.ch015

Choudhury, M. A. (2014). Bringing God into the Banking System: Contrasting Meaning of Ethics in Socio-Scientific Reasoning. In *Socio-Cybernetic Study of God and the World-System* (pp. 100–142). Hershey, PA: IGI Global. doi:10.4018/978-1-4666-4643-8.ch004

Choudhury, M. A. (2014). Conclusion. In *Socio-Cybernetic Study of God and the World-System* (pp. 339–348). Hershey, PA: IGI Global. doi:10.4018/978-1-4666-4643-8.ch012

Choudhury, M. A. (2014). Corporate Social Consciousness and Responsibility with an Ethico-Economic Idea of Productivity and Efficiency. In *Socio-Cybernetic Study of God and the World-System* (pp. 173–191). Hershey, PA: IGI Global. doi:10.4018/978-1-4666-4643-8.ch006

Choudhury, M. A. (2014). Financial Interest and Human Depravity: Emergence of the Theory of Interest from the Philosophical Roots of Occidental Epistemological Thought. In *Socio-Cybernetic Study of God and the World-System* (pp. 219–247). Hershey, PA: IGI Global. doi:10.4018/978-1-4666-4643-8.ch008

Choudhury, M. A. (2014). How is God Studied in Relation to Science and the World-System? In *Socio-Cybernetic Study of God and the World-System* (pp. 1–31). Hershey, PA: IGI Global. doi:10.4018/978-1-4666-4643-8.ch001

Choudhury, M. A. (2014). Money, Price, Output, Interest Rate, and Factor Employment: Comparative Theory. In *Socio-Cybernetic Study of God and the World-System* (pp. 284–306). Hershey, PA: IGI Global. doi:10.4018/978-1-4666-4643-8.ch010

Choudhury, M. A. (2014). Productivity Analysis in Ethically Induced Financing Environment: A Case Study of Indonesian Islamic Banks. In *Socio-Cybernetic Study of God and the World-System* (pp. 192–218). Hershey, PA: IGI Global. doi:10.4018/978-1-4666-4643-8.ch007

Choudhury, M. A. (2014). Social Reconstruction by Replacing Interest Rates with Trade Instruments. In *Socio-Cybernetic Study of God and the World-System* (pp. 248–283). Hershey, PA: IGI Global. doi:10.4018/978-1-4666-4643-8.ch009

Choudhury, M. A. (2014). The Future of Monetary Reform and the Real Economy: The Ethics of 100 Percent Reserve Requirement Monetary System. In *Socio-Cybernetic Study of God and the World-System* (pp. 307–338). Hershey, PA: IGI Global. doi:10.4018/978-1-4666-4643-8.ch011

Choudhury, M. A. (2014). The Idea of God in Relation to the Social System: Banking as a Social System. In *Socio-Cybernetic Study of God and the World-System* (pp. 32–64). Hershey, PA: IGI Global. doi:10.4018/978-1-4666-4643-8.ch002

Choudhury, M. A. (2014). The Moral Content of Monetary History. In *Socio-Cybernetic Study of God and the World-System* (pp. 65–99). Hershey, PA: IGI Global. doi:10.4018/978-1-4666-4643-8.ch003

Choudhury, M. A. (2014). The Moral Possibility of Islamic Banking System as Institution: Contrasting Cases. In *Socio-Cybernetic Study of God and the World-System* (pp. 143–172). Hershey, PA: IGI Global. doi:10.4018/978-1-4666-4643-8.ch005

Cohen, R. I. (2014). Media Policy, Co-Existence, and Freedom of Speech. In I. Nahon-Serfaty & R. Ahmed (Eds.), *New Media and Communication Across Religions and Cultures* (pp. 176–190). Hershey, PA: IGI Global. doi:10.4018/978-1-4666-5035-0.ch011

Cooper, L., Nash, M., & Umugwaneza, A. (2016). Social Work with Refugee Women: Narrative and "Empowerment". In J. Prescott (Ed.), *Handbook of Research on Race, Gender, and the Fight for Equality* (pp. 559–579). Hershey, PA: IGI Global. doi:10.4018/978-1-5225-0047-6.ch024

Cotton, K., Green, D. O., Beckman, S. A., Hussain, A., Robb, A., & Green, M. D. (2016). Leveraging New Media as Social Capital for Diversity Officers: How Equity, Diversity, and Inclusion Professionals Can Use Social Media to Foster Equality. In J. Prescott (Ed.), *Handbook of Research on Race, Gender, and the Fight for Equality* (pp. 113–141). Hershey, PA: IGI Global. doi:10.4018/978-1-5225-0047-6.ch006

da Rosa, I., & de Almeida, J. (2017). Digital Transformation in the Public Sector: Electronic Procurement in Portugal. In R. Shakya (Ed.), *Digital Governance and E-Government Principles Applied to Public Procurement* (pp. 99–125). Hershey, PA: IGI Global. doi:10.4018/978-1-5225-2203-4.ch005

Davis, D. C., & Lopuch, V. S. (2016). Learning Organizations: Connections between Diversity and Innovation. In J. Prescott (Ed.), *Handbook of Research on Race, Gender, and the Fight for Equality* (pp. 267–297). Hershey, PA: IGI Global. doi:10.4018/978-1-5225-0047-6.ch012

Dietz, J. E. (2014). Cultural and Religious Dialogue: A Legacy of Religious Art. In I. Nahon-Serfaty & R. Ahmed (Eds.), *New Media and Communication Across Religions and Cultures* (pp. 232–245). Hershey, PA: IGI Global. doi:10.4018/978-1-4666-5035-0.ch014

Dube, B. (2017). To Lie or Not to Lie: Interrogating Codes of Conduct on Photo Ethics in the Era of Digital Technologies. In N. Mhiripiri & T. Chari (Eds.), *Media Law, Ethics, and Policy in the Digital Age* (pp. 44–63). Hershey, PA: IGI Global. doi:10.4018/978-1-5225-2095-5.ch003

Eid, M. (2014). Religious Sphere in Canada: Public Manifestations and Media Representations. In I. Nahon-Serfaty & R. Ahmed (Eds.), *New Media and Communication Across Religions and Cultures* (pp. 48–65). Hershey, PA: IGI Global. doi:10.4018/978-1-4666-5035-0.ch004

Endong, F. P. (2017). Reconciling Homosexuality and Spirituality in Africa as a Heresy and Survival Strategy: A Critical Study of House of Rainbow (LGBT Church) in Nigeria. In A. Pascal (Ed.), *Multiculturalism and the Convergence of Faith and Practical Wisdom in Modern Society* (pp. 331–353). Hershey, PA: IGI Global. doi:10.4018/978-1-5225-1955-3.ch017

Eraso, A. B., & Cid, D. D. (2016). The Role of Women in the Development of New Religious Movements in Latin America: The Case of Pentecostalism. In B. Glimps & T. Ford (Eds.), *Gender and Diversity Issues in Religious-Based Institutions and Organizations* (pp. 224–247). Hershey, PA: IGI Global. doi:10.4018/978-1-4666-8772-1.ch010

Eze, U. C., & Poong, Y. S. (2016). Investigating the Moderating Roles of Age and Ethnicity in Mobile Commerce Acceptance. In J. Prescott (Ed.), *Handbook of Research on Race, Gender, and the Fight for Equality* (pp. 90–112). Hershey, PA: IGI Global. doi:10.4018/978-1-5225-0047-6.ch005

Fanaian, T. (2017). The Theocratic Deception Trap: Khomeini's Persuasion Techniques and Communication Patterns in His Books, Guardianship of the Jurist 1979 and Testament 1989. In E. Lewin, E. Bick, & D. Naor (Eds.), *Comparative Perspectives on Civil Religion, Nationalism, and Political Influence* (pp. 62–105). Hershey, PA: IGI Global. doi:10.4018/978-1-5225-0516-7.ch003

Fayoyin, A. (2017). Electoral Polling and Reporting in Africa: Professional and Policy Implications for Media Practice and Political Communication in a Digital Age. In N. Mhiripiri & T. Chari (Eds.), *Media Law, Ethics, and Policy in the Digital Age* (pp. 164–181). Hershey, PA: IGI Global. doi:10.4018/978-1-5225-2095-5.ch009

Finol, J. E., & Finol, D. E. (2014). Capillitas: Religion, Communication, and Syncretism in Small Roadside Communities in Venezuela. In I. Nahon-Serfaty & R. Ahmed (Eds.), *New Media and Communication Across Religions and Cultures* (pp. 221–231). Hershey, PA: IGI Global. doi:10.4018/978-1-4666-5035-0.ch013

Fisherman, S. (2016). Body Image and Wellbeing in Religious Male and Female Youth in Israel: An Educational Challenge. In B. Glimps & T. Ford (Eds.), *Gender and Diversity Issues in Religious-Based Institutions and Organizations* (pp. 51–79). Hershey, PA: IGI Global. doi:10.4018/978-1-4666-8772-1.ch003

Ford, T. N., & Glimps, B. J. (2016). A Comparison of "Inclusiveness" in Two Liberal Arts Catholic Universities: What Nurtures an Inclusive Campus Climate? In B. Glimps & T. Ford (Eds.), *Gender and Diversity Issues in Religious-Based Institutions and Organizations* (pp. 159–183). Hershey, PA: IGI Global. doi:10.4018/978-1-4666-8772-1.ch007

Gachigua, S. G. (2016). Legislating for a De Jure One-Party State in 1982 and "Party Hopping" in 2012: Reconstructing Elite Discourse on Political Parties in Kenya. In D. Orwenjo, O. Oketch, & A. Tunde (Eds.), *Political Discourse in Emergent, Fragile, and Failed Democracies* (pp. 286–305). Hershey, PA: IGI Global. doi:10.4018/978-1-5225-0081-0.ch016

Garrido, N. L. (2014). Blasphemy and Outrage in a Secular State: Venezuela's Illegitimate Restrictions to Speech Based on a Republican Religion. In I. Nahon-Serfaty & R. Ahmed (Eds.), *New Media and Communication Across Religions and Cultures* (pp. 191–219). Hershey, PA: IGI Global. doi:10.4018/978-1-4666-5035-0.ch012

Gillath, N. (2017). Avoiding Conscription in Israel: Were Women Pawns in the Political Game? In E. Lewin, E. Bick, & D. Naor (Eds.), *Comparative Perspectives on Civil Religion, Nationalism, and Political Influence* (pp. 226–256). Hershey, PA: IGI Global. doi:10.4018/978-1-5225-0516-7.ch009

Green, S. (2017). China and Europe from Confucius and Aristotle to Now: Old Histories, New Challenges. In A. Pascal (Ed.), *Multiculturalism and the Convergence of Faith and Practical Wisdom in Modern Society* (pp. 1–15). Hershey, PA: IGI Global. doi:10.4018/978-1-5225-1955-3.ch001

Greer, B. M. (2016). Minority-Owned Suppliers A Growing Global Supply Base. In J. Prescott (Ed.), *Handbook of Research on Race, Gender, and the Fight for Equality* (pp. 472–490). Hershey, PA: IGI Global. doi:10.4018/978-1-5225-0047-6.ch021

Günay, S. (2016). Geography of Female Suicide: For Suicide Prevention Policy (Case of Turkey, in 2002-2011 Period). In J. Prescott (Ed.), *Handbook of Research on Race, Gender, and the Fight for Equality* (pp. 580–613). Hershey, PA: IGI Global. doi:10.4018/978-1-5225-0047-6.ch025

Harper, L., & Sanchez, D. (2017). Electronic Government Procurement in Latin America and the Caribbean. In R. Shakya (Ed.), *Digital Governance and E-Government Principles Applied to Public Procurement* (pp. 203–228). Hershey, PA: IGI Global. doi:10.4018/978-1-5225-2203-4.ch009

Harris-Smith, Y. J. (2016). Spiritual Health Identity: Placing Black Women's Lives in the Center of Analysis. In B. Glimps & T. Ford (Eds.), *Gender and Diversity Issues in Religious-Based Institutions and Organizations* (pp. 1–23). Hershey, PA: IGI Global. doi:10.4018/978-1-4666-8772-1.ch001

Heuva, W. E. (2017). Deferring Citizens' "Right to Know" in an Information Age: The Information Deficit in Namibia. In N. Mhiripiri & T. Chari (Eds.), *Media Law, Ethics, and Policy in the Digital Age* (pp. 245–267). Hershey, PA: IGI Global. doi:10.4018/978-1-5225-2095-5.ch014

Higgs, E. T. (2016). Becoming 'Multi-Racial': The Young Women's Christian Association in Kenya, 1955-1965. In B. Glimps & T. Ford (Eds.), *Gender and Diversity Issues in Religious-Based Institutions and Organizations* (pp. 24–50). Hershey, PA: IGI Global. doi:10.4018/978-1-4666-8772-1.ch002

Igah, F. (2016). Changing the Traditional Education of Igbo Females: The Role of Religion in Colonial Education. In B. Glimps & T. Ford (Eds.), *Gender and Diversity Issues in Religious-Based Institutions and Organizations* (pp. 291–305). Hershey, PA: IGI Global. doi:10.4018/978-1-4666-8772-1.ch013

Ilhan, N., & Rahim, M. M. (2017). Benefits of E-Procurement Systems Implementation: Experience of an Australian Municipal Council. In R. Shakya (Ed.), *Digital Governance and E-Government Principles Applied to Public Procurement* (pp. 277–294). Hershey, PA: IGI Global. doi:10.4018/978-1-5225-2203-4.ch012

Imbert, P. (2014). Transculturality and the Included Third. In I. Nahon-Serfaty & R. Ahmed (Eds.), *New Media and Communication Across Religions and Cultures* (pp. 29–46). Hershey, PA: IGI Global. doi:10.4018/978-1-4666-5035-0.ch003

Ionita, C. L. (2017). Religious Themes in Contemporary Art. In A. Pascal (Ed.), *Multiculturalism and the Convergence of Faith and Practical Wisdom in Modern Society* (pp. 188–218). Hershey, PA: IGI Global. doi:10.4018/978-1-5225-1955-3.ch009

Ionita, P. (2017). The Mystical Experience, or the Way to Transformative Union. In A. Pascal (Ed.), *Multiculturalism and the Convergence of Faith and Practical Wisdom in Modern Society* (pp. 149–169). Hershey, PA: IGI Global. doi:10.4018/978-1-5225-1955-3.ch007

Jakaza, E., & Visser, M. W. (2016). Argumentation and Appraisal in Divergent Zimbabwean Parliamentary Debates. In D. Orwenjo, O. Oketch, & A. Tunde (Eds.), *Political Discourse in Emergent, Fragile, and Failed Democracies* (pp. 126–142). Hershey, PA: IGI Global. doi:10.4018/978-1-5225-0081-0.ch007

Jennings, M. A. (2017). Great Risk for the Kingdom: Pentecostal-Charismatic Growth Churches, Pastorpreneurs, and Neoliberalism. In A. Pascal (Ed.), *Multiculturalism and the Convergence of Faith and Practical Wisdom in Modern Society* (pp. 236–248). Hershey, PA: IGI Global. doi:10.4018/978-1-5225-1955-3.ch011

Joshua-Gojer, A. E., Allen, J. M., & Huang, T. (2016). Workforce Diversity in Volunteerism and the Peace Corps. In J. Prescott (Ed.), *Handbook of Research on Race, Gender, and the Fight for Equality* (pp. 453–471). Hershey, PA: IGI Global. doi:10.4018/978-1-5225-0047-6.ch020

Kalagy, T. (2017). Values, Constraints, and Maneuvers: Processes of Academization among Ultra-Orthodox Women and Beduin Women in Israel. In E. Lewin, E. Bick, & D. Naor (Eds.), *Comparative Perspectives on Civil Religion, Nationalism, and Political Influence* (pp. 257–284). Hershey, PA: IGI Global. doi:10.4018/978-1-5225-0516-7.ch010

Kamalu, I. (2016). Politics and Promises: A Multimodal Social Semiotic Interpretation of Political Party Emblems and Slogans as Discourse of Hope in a Democratic Nigeria. In D. Orwenjo, O. Oketch, & A. Tunde (Eds.), *Political Discourse in Emergent, Fragile, and Failed Democracies* (pp. 112–125). Hershey, PA: IGI Global. doi:10.4018/978-1-5225-0081-0.ch006

Kankara, I. S. (2016). Impediments to Nigerian Democracy: Ambivalent Role of Vigilante Groups in Maintaining Security in the Wake of the Boko Haram Insurgence in Northern Nigeria. In D. Orwenjo, O. Oketch, & A. Tunde (Eds.), *Political Discourse in Emergent, Fragile, and Failed Democracies* (pp. 240–251). Hershey, PA: IGI Global. doi:10.4018/978-1-5225-0081-0.ch013

Kasemsap, K. (2017). Mastering Electronic Procurement, Green Public Procurement, and Public Procurement for Innovation. In R. Shakya (Ed.), *Digital Governance and E-Government Principles Applied to Public Procurement* (pp. 29–55). Hershey, PA: IGI Global. doi:10.4018/978-1-5225-2203-4.ch002

Kim, S. (2016). Digital Equity and Policy: Case of Korea. In J. Prescott (Ed.), *Handbook of Research on Race, Gender, and the Fight for Equality* (pp. 30–48). Hershey, PA: IGI Global. doi:10.4018/978-1-5225-0047-6.ch002

Kim, Y. K., Edens, D., Parra, O. E., & Lopez, K. M. (2016). Sense of Belonging in Religious-Based Colleges and Universities: Predictors and Patterns among Students of Color and White Students. In B. Glimps & T. Ford (Eds.), *Gender and Diversity Issues in Religious-Based Institutions and Organizations* (pp. 269–290). Hershey, PA: IGI Global. doi:10.4018/978-1-4666-8772-1.ch012

Knoblock, N. (2016). Sarcasm and Irony as a Political Weapon: Social Networking in the Time of Crisis. In D. Orwenjo, O. Oketch, & A. Tunde (Eds.), *Political Discourse in Emergent, Fragile, and Failed Democracies* (pp. 11–33). Hershey, PA: IGI Global. doi:10.4018/978-1-5225-0081-0.ch002

Kumar, M. (2017). Dynamics of the E-Procurement Process and Key Implementation Issues in India. In R. Shakya (Ed.), *Digital Governance and E-Government Principles Applied to Public Procurement* (pp. 249–276). Hershey, PA: IGI Global. doi:10.4018/978-1-5225-2203-4.ch011

Kunock, A. I. (2017). Boko Haram Insurgency in Cameroon: Role of Mass Media in Conflict Management. In N. Mhiripiri & T. Chari (Eds.), *Media Law, Ethics, and Policy in the Digital Age* (pp. 226–244). Hershey, PA: IGI Global. doi:10.4018/978-1-5225-2095-5.ch013

Lando, A. L. (2017). Media-Invented Stories and Outright Lies a Threat to Journalism Ethics and Media Credibility. In N. Mhiripiri & T. Chari (Eds.), *Media Law, Ethics, and Policy in the Digital Age* (pp. 64–77). Hershey, PA: IGI Global. doi:10.4018/978-1-5225-2095-5.ch004

Lawler, J. A., & Mir, G. (2016). Women, Faith, and Social Cohesion. In B. Glimps & T. Ford (Eds.), *Gender and Diversity Issues in Religious-Based Institutions and Organizations* (pp. 200–223). Hershey, PA: IGI Global. doi:10.4018/978-1-4666-8772-1.ch009

Leon, N. (2017). The Haredi Scholar-Society and the Military Draft in Israel: Counter-Nationalism and the Imagined Military Symbiosis. In E. Lewin, E. Bick, & D. Naor (Eds.), *Comparative Perspectives on Civil Religion, Nationalism, and Political Influence* (pp. 210–225). Hershey, PA: IGI Global. doi:10.4018/978-1-5225-0516-7.ch008

Lévy, P. (2014). An Exercise in Inter-Religious Conceptualization: Towards Online Creative Conversations. In I. Nahon-Serfaty & R. Ahmed (Eds.), *New Media and Communication Across Religions and Cultures* (pp. 82–98). Hershey, PA: IGI Global. doi:10.4018/978-1-4666-5035-0.ch006

Lewin, E., & Bick, E. (2017). Introduction: Civil Religion and Nationalism on a Godly-Civil Continuum. In E. Lewin, E. Bick, & D. Naor (Eds.), *Comparative Perspectives on Civil Religion, Nationalism, and Political Influence* (pp. 1–31). Hershey, PA: IGI Global. doi:10.4018/978-1-5225-0516-7.ch001

Linden, I. (2014). Border Crossings: Secular versus Religious Arguments in the Public Domain. In I. Nahon-Serfaty & R. Ahmed (Eds.), *New Media and Communication Across Religions and Cultures* (pp. 16–28). Hershey, PA: IGI Global. doi:10.4018/978-1-4666-5035-0.ch002

Luoch, T. O. (2016). The Verbal Fuel for Ethnic Hatred and Political Violence in Kenya. In D. Orwenjo, O. Oketch, & A. Tunde (Eds.), *Political Discourse in Emergent, Fragile, and Failed Democracies* (pp. 1–10). Hershey, PA: IGI Global. doi:10.4018/978-1-5225-0081-0.ch001

Marchessault, G. (2014). Is Religion Compatible with Media Entertainment? In I. Nahon-Serfaty & R. Ahmed (Eds.), *New Media and Communication Across Religions and Cultures* (pp. 66–80). Hershey, PA: IGI Global. doi:10.4018/978-1-4666-5035-0.ch005

Margaritis, K. (2016). Are We All Equal?: Immunity of Parliament Members and Criminal Responsibility of Cabinet Members in Greece. In D. Orwenjo, O. Oketch, & A. Tunde (Eds.), *Political Discourse in Emergent, Fragile, and Failed Democracies* (pp. 360–372). Hershey, PA: IGI Global. doi:10.4018/978-1-5225-0081-0.ch020

Mhiripiri, N. A., & Chikakano, J. (2017). Criminal Defamation, the Criminalisation of Expression, Media and Information Dissemination in the Digital Age: A Legal and Ethical Perspective. In N. Mhiripiri & T. Chari (Eds.), *Media Law, Ethics, and Policy in the Digital Age* (pp. 1–24). Hershey, PA: IGI Global. doi:10.4018/978-1-5225-2095-5.ch001

Mpiima, D. M. (2016). Multilayered Political Systems and the Politics of Monitoring Local Government Programmes for Engendered Service Delivery: A Case of Apac District in Northern Uganda. In D. Orwenjo, O. Oketch, & A. Tunde (Eds.), *Political Discourse in Emergent, Fragile, and Failed Democracies* (pp. 220–239). Hershey, PA: IGI Global. doi:10.4018/978-1-5225-0081-0.ch012

Muñoz, L. A., Bolívar, M. P., & Quiles, F. J. (2016). Policies and Strategies for Digital Inclusion: Regional Governments in Spain. In J. Prescott (Ed.), *Handbook of Research on Race, Gender, and the Fight for Equality* (pp. 1–29). Hershey, PA: IGI Global. doi:10.4018/978-1-5225-0047-6.ch001

Musiyiwa, M., & Visser, M. W. (2016). Of Drag and Push Democracies: The Construction of Zimbabwe as a Failed-Partially Resuscitated State in Popular Songs. In D. Orwenjo, O. Oketch, & A. Tunde (Eds.), *Political Discourse in Emergent, Fragile, and Failed Democracies* (pp. 34–60). Hershey, PA: IGI Global. doi:10.4018/978-1-5225-0081-0.ch003

Nettleton, K. F., & Lennex, L. C. (2016). Technodiversity: Lessons Learned From Diversity Exchanges. In J. Prescott (Ed.), *Handbook of Research on Race, Gender, and the Fight for Equality* (pp. 49–67). Hershey, PA: IGI Global. doi:10.4018/978-1-5225-0047-6.ch003

Neugröschel, M. (2017). Anti-Semitism as a Civil Religion: Progressive Paradigms in the Anti-Semitic Construction of German National Identity. In E. Lewin, E. Bick, & D. Naor (Eds.), *Comparative Perspectives on Civil Religion, Nationalism, and Political Influence* (pp. 106–124). Hershey, PA: IGI Global. doi:10.4018/978-1-5225-0516-7.ch004

Neupane, A., Soar, J., Vaidya, K., & Aryal, S. (2017). Application of E-Government Principles in Anti-Corruption Framework. In R. Shakya (Ed.), *Digital Governance and E-Government Principles Applied to Public Procurement* (pp. 56–74). Hershey, PA: IGI Global. doi:10.4018/978-1-5225-2203-4.ch003

Nyam, E. (2016). Revolutionary Politics and Theater of Semiotics: Challenges and Solutions in Northern Nigeria. In D. Orwenjo, O. Oketch, & A. Tunde (Eds.), *Political Discourse in Emergent, Fragile, and Failed Democracies* (pp. 349–359). Hershey, PA: IGI Global. doi:10.4018/978-1-5225-0081-0.ch019

Okezie, C. E., Alhamisi, J., & Glimps, B. J. (2016). The Promise for African American Male Students in Teacher Education at Marygrove College. In B. Glimps & T. Ford (Eds.), *Gender and Diversity Issues in Religious-Based Institutions and Organizations* (pp. 137–158). Hershey, PA: IGI Global. doi:10.4018/978-1-4666-8772-1.ch006

Ortuzar, G. B., Sevillano, E. M., Castro, C. L., & Uribe, C. (2017). Challenges in Chilean E-Procurement System: A Critical Review. In R. Shakya (Ed.), *Digital Governance and E-Government Principles Applied to Public Procurement* (pp. 170–202). Hershey, PA: IGI Global. doi:10.4018/978-1-5225-2203-4.ch008

Palmer, S. (2014). Cult Wars on the Internet: Virtual Battles and the Challenges of Cyberspace. In I. Nahon-Serfaty & R. Ahmed (Eds.), *New Media and Communication Across Religions and Cultures* (pp. 99–108). Hershey, PA: IGI Global. doi:10.4018/978-1-4666-5035-0.ch007

Panda, P., & Sahu, G. P. (2017). Public Procurement Framework in India: An Overview. In R. Shakya (Ed.), *Digital Governance and E-Government Principles Applied to Public Procurement* (pp. 229–248). Hershey, PA: IGI Global. doi:10.4018/978-1-5225-2203-4.ch010

Pandey, A. D. (2017). Women and Religion in the Indian Diaspora. In A. Pascal (Ed.), *Multiculturalism and the Convergence of Faith and Practical Wisdom in Modern Society* (pp. 250–264). Hershey, PA: IGI Global. doi:10.4018/978-1-5225-1955-3.ch012

Pascal, A. (2017). Offerings: The Metaphysics of Giving. In A. Pascal (Ed.), *Multiculturalism and the Convergence of Faith and Practical Wisdom in Modern Society* (pp. 99–134). Hershey, PA: IGI Global. doi:10.4018/978-1-5225-1955-3.ch005

Petraru, G. (2017). Religion, Church, and Public Space. In A. Pascal (Ed.), *Multiculturalism and the Convergence of Faith and Practical Wisdom in Modern Society* (pp. 136–148). Hershey, PA: IGI Global. doi:10.4018/978-1-5225-1955-3.ch006

Popoola, T. (2017). Ethical and Legal Challenges of Election Reporting in Nigeria: A Study of Four General Elections, 1999-2011. In N. Mhiripiri & T. Chari (Eds.), *Media Law, Ethics, and Policy in the Digital Age* (pp. 78–100). Hershey, PA: IGI Global. doi:10.4018/978-1-5225-2095-5.ch005

Riccò, R. (2016). Diversity Management: Bringing Equality, Equity, and Inclusion in the Workplace. In J. Prescott (Ed.), *Handbook of Research on Race, Gender, and the Fight for Equality* (pp. 335–359). Hershey, PA: IGI Global. doi:10.4018/978-1-5225-0047-6.ch015

Röschenthaler, U. M. (2017). Copying, Branding, and the Ethical Implications of Rights in Immaterial Cultural Goods. In N. Mhiripiri & T. Chari (Eds.), *Media Law, Ethics, and Policy in the Digital Age* (pp. 101–121). Hershey, PA: IGI Global. doi:10.4018/978-1-5225-2095-5.ch006

Roth, K. R., & Ritter, Z. S. (2016). Channeling Race: Media Representations and International Student Perceptions. In J. Prescott (Ed.), *Handbook of Research on Race, Gender, and the Fight for Equality* (pp. 172–197). Hershey, PA: IGI Global. doi:10.4018/978-1-5225-0047-6.ch008

Roth, K. R., & Ritter, Z. S. (2016). Racial Spectacle and Campus Climate: Media Representations and Asian International Student Perceptions at U.S. Colleges. In J. Prescott (Ed.), *Handbook of Research on Race, Gender, and the Fight for Equality* (pp. 142–171). Hershey, PA: IGI Global. doi:10.4018/978-1-5225-0047-6.ch007

Rumano, M., & Sommers, R. (2016). Navigating the Terrain of Diversity: Lessons and Insights for Religious Institutions and Faculty from Diverse Backgrounds. In B. Glimps & T. Ford (Eds.), *Gender and Diversity Issues in Religious-Based Institutions and Organizations* (pp. 248–268). Hershey, PA: IGI Global. doi:10.4018/978-1-4666-8772-1.ch011

Sabao, C., & Chingwaramusee, V. R. (2017). Citizen Journalism on Facebook and the Challenges of Media Regulation in Zimbabwe: Baba Jukwa. In N. Mhiripiri & T. Chari (Eds.), *Media Law, Ethics, and Policy in the Digital Age* (pp. 193–206). Hershey, PA: IGI Global. doi:10.4018/978-1-5225-2095-5.ch011

Sanchez-Apellaniz, M., & Triguero-Sánchez, R. (2016). New Trends in Leveraging Workforce Diversity through Human Resource Management Initiatives. In J. Prescott (Ed.), *Handbook of Research on Race, Gender, and the Fight for Equality* (pp. 360–379). Hershey, PA: IGI Global. doi:10.4018/978-1-5225-0047-6.ch016

Santillan, C., & Horwitz, S. K. (2016). Application of Collaboration Technology to Manage Diversity in Global Virtual Teams: The ThinkLet-Based CE Approach. In J. Prescott (Ed.), *Handbook of Research on Race, Gender, and the Fight for Equality* (pp. 240–266). Hershey, PA: IGI Global. doi:10.4018/978-1-5225-0047-6.ch011

Sasson, K. (2017). Religion and Politics: A Troubled Relationship in a Volatile World. In E. Lewin, E. Bick, & D. Naor (Eds.), *Comparative Perspectives on Civil Religion, Nationalism, and Political Influence* (pp. 32–61). Hershey, PA: IGI Global. doi:10.4018/978-1-5225-0516-7.ch002

Semujju, B. (2017). Digital Media in Uganda: Where Regulation and Freedom of Expression Contradictions Are Sharpest. In N. Mhiripiri & T. Chari (Eds.), *Media Law, Ethics, and Policy in the Digital Age* (pp. 182–192). Hershey, PA: IGI Global. doi:10.4018/978-1-5225-2095-5.ch010

Shahpari, H., & Hojjat, T. A. (2016). An Investigation of Creatio Ex Nihilo, Islam, Sociality and Inequality. In *Islamic Economy and Social Mobility: Cultural and Religious Considerations* (pp. 27–68). Hershey, PA: IGI Global. doi:10.4018/978-1-4666-9731-7.ch002

Shahpari, H., & Hojjat, T. A. (2016). Foundations of Islamic Economy, Islamic Scholarship, Mass Media, Linguistic Turn, and Social Mobility. In *Islamic Economy and Social Mobility: Cultural and Religious Considerations* (pp. 234–249). Hershey, PA: IGI Global. doi:10.4018/978-1-4666-9731-7.ch009

Shahpari, H., & Hojjat, T. A. (2016). Functionalism and Stratification, Socio-Cultural Evolution and Revolution. In *Islamic Economy and Social Mobility: Cultural and Religious Considerations* (pp. 107–130). Hershey, PA: IGI Global. doi:10.4018/978-1-4666-9731-7.ch004

Shahpari, H., & Hojjat, T. A. (2016). Islam, Islams and Stratifications: Problematics of Theory, Methodology and Subject Matter. In *Islamic Economy and Social Mobility: Cultural and Religious Considerations* (pp. 1–26). Hershey, PA: IGI Global. doi:10.4018/978-1-4666-9731-7.ch001

Shahpari, H., & Hojjat, T. A. (2016). Middle East Studies and Muslim Experience after September 11th, 2001: Rebellion against Islamic Ideology and the New Counter-Jihadis. In *Islamic Economy and Social Mobility: Cultural and Religious Considerations* (pp. 272–291). Hershey, PA: IGI Global. doi:10.4018/978-1-4666-9731-7.ch011

Shahpari, H., & Hojjat, T. A. (2016). Pathologies and Transition of Socio-Political Conditions and Economies of Islamic Societies with Philosophical Considerations. In *Islamic Economy and Social Mobility: Cultural and Religious Considerations* (pp. 175–197). Hershey, PA: IGI Global. doi:10.4018/978-1-4666-9731-7.ch007

Shahpari, H., & Hojjat, T. A. (2016). Religious Economies and Religious Mobility: The Christian West and the Islamic East and Africa. In *Islamic Economy and Social Mobility: Cultural and Religious Considerations* (pp. 292–327). Hershey, PA: IGI Global. doi:10.4018/978-1-4666-9731-7.ch012

Shahpari, H., & Hojjat, T. A. (2016). Re-Stratification in the Name of God. In *Islamic Economy and Social Mobility: Cultural and Religious Considerations* (pp. 131–158). Hershey, PA: IGI Global. doi:10.4018/978-1-4666-9731-7.ch005

Shahpari, H., & Hojjat, T. A. (2016). Revisiting Companionship and the Socio-Economy of the Islamic Guilds: Sufism, the Guilds' Vertical and Horizontal Structure of Communication, and the Islamic Economic System. In *Islamic Economy and Social Mobility: Cultural and Religious Considerations* (pp. 198–233). Hershey, PA: IGI Global. doi:10.4018/978-1-4666-9731-7.ch008

Shahpari, H., & Hojjat, T. A. (2016). Stratification and Social Mobility, Slavery in Islam: A Critical Structural-Functionalism Approach. In *Islamic Economy and Social Mobility: Cultural and Religious Considerations* (pp. 250–271). Hershey, PA: IGI Global. doi:10.4018/978-1-4666-9731-7.ch010

Shahpari, H., & Hojjat, T. A. (2016). Structural-Functionalism, Stratification and Historical Background of Islamic Economic Thought: Transitions and Ruptures. In *Islamic Economy and Social Mobility: Cultural and Religious Considerations* (pp. 159–174). Hershey, PA: IGI Global. doi:10.4018/978-1-4666-9731-7.ch006

Shahpari, H., & Hojjat, T. A. (2016). Two Sociological Outlooks: Shi'ite-Sunni Imperatives on Ascription and Achievement Statuses, the Bases for Socio-Cultural and Religious Stratification. In *Islamic Economy and Social Mobility: Cultural and Religious Considerations* (pp. 69–106). Hershey, PA: IGI Global. doi:10.4018/978-1-4666-9731-7.ch003

Shahriar, A. (2017). Struggle for Inclusion: The Narratives of Religious Converts from Pakistan. In A. Pascal (Ed.), *Multiculturalism and the Convergence of Faith and Practical Wisdom in Modern Society* (pp. 282–295). Hershey, PA: IGI Global. doi:10.4018/978-1-5225-1955-3.ch014

Shakya, R. K., & Schapper, P. R. (2017). Digital Governance and E-Government Principles: E-Procurement as Transformative. In R. Shakya (Ed.), *Digital Governance and E-Government Principles Applied to Public Procurement* (pp. 1–28). Hershey, PA: IGI Global. doi:10.4018/978-1-5225-2203-4.ch001

Sheiner, D. Z. (2017). National-Liberty Reflections of the Exodus Myth in Palestine-Israel Print Media Advertisements, 1923-1958. In E. Lewin, E. Bick, & D. Naor (Eds.), *Comparative Perspectives on Civil Religion, Nationalism, and Political Influence* (pp. 190–209). Hershey, PA: IGI Global. doi:10.4018/978-1-5225-0516-7.ch007

Shiran, P. (2017). Literary History as National History: The Sufi Tradition in Iranian Culture and Identity. In A. Pascal (Ed.), *Multiculturalism and the Convergence of Faith and Practical Wisdom in Modern Society* (pp. 265–281). Hershey, PA: IGI Global. doi:10.4018/978-1-5225-1955-3.ch013

Smith, R. S. (2017). Rethinking the Fact-Value Split: A Place for Religion in the Public Square? In A. Pascal (Ed.), *Multiculturalism and the Convergence of Faith and Practical Wisdom in Modern Society* (pp. 63–80). Hershey, PA: IGI Global. doi:10.4018/978-1-5225-1955-3.ch003

Sterling, R. S. (2016). Promoting Diversity Leadership: Strategies and Tools to Improve Equity and Access. In J. Prescott (Ed.), *Handbook of Research on Race, Gender, and the Fight for Equality* (pp. 321–334). Hershey, PA: IGI Global. doi:10.4018/978-1-5225-0047-6.ch014

Strelluf, C. (2016). Media Coverage of the 2009 Afghan Presidential Election. In D. Orwenjo, O. Oketch, & A. Tunde (Eds.), *Political Discourse in Emergent, Fragile, and Failed Democracies* (pp. 143–164). Hershey, PA: IGI Global. doi:10.4018/978-1-5225-0081-0.ch008

Tan, M. Y. (2016). Authenticity in Online Religion: An Actor-Network Approach. *International Journal of Actor-Network Theory and Technological Innovation, 8*(1), 44–54. doi:10.4018/IJANTTI.2016010104

Teper, Y. (2017). How Civic is Russia's New Civil Religion and How Religious is the Church? In E. Lewin, E. Bick, & D. Naor (Eds.), *Comparative Perspectives on Civil Religion, Nationalism, and Political Influence* (pp. 125–155). Hershey, PA: IGI Global. doi:10.4018/978-1-5225-0516-7.ch005

Tilson, D. J. (2014). Public Relations and Religious Diversity: Toward the Common Good. In I. Nahon-Serfaty & R. Ahmed (Eds.), *New Media and Communication Across Religions and Cultures* (pp. 110–128). Hershey, PA: IGI Global. doi:10.4018/978-1-4666-5035-0.ch008

Tran, B. (2016). A History of How U.S. Academics, Laws, and Business Have Created the Current Approach to Organizational Diversity: Visual, Innovative, and All-Inclusive Multiculturalism. In J. Prescott (Ed.), *Handbook of Research on Race, Gender, and the Fight for Equality* (pp. 380–397). Hershey, PA: IGI Global. doi:10.4018/978-1-5225-0047-6.ch017

Trinh, M. P. (2016). Which Matters More?: Effects of Surface- and Deep-Level Diversity on Team Processes and Performance. In J. Prescott (Ed.), *Handbook of Research on Race, Gender, and the Fight for Equality* (pp. 213–239). Hershey, PA: IGI Global. doi:10.4018/978-1-5225-0047-6.ch010

Tsygankov, S., & Gasanova, E. (2017). Electronification of the Public Procurement System: A Comparative Analysis of the Experience of the Russian Federation and Ukraine. In R. Shakya (Ed.), *Digital Governance and E-Government Principles Applied to Public Procurement* (pp. 295–305). Hershey, PA: IGI Global. doi:10.4018/978-1-5225-2203-4.ch013

Tunde, A. H., & Orwenjo, D. O. (2016). On The Threshold of Democratic Fragility: A Macrospeech Act Explication of Media Representation of the Nigerian 2011 Post-Presidential Election News Reports. In D. Orwenjo, O. Oketch, & A. Tunde (Eds.), *Political Discourse in Emergent, Fragile, and Failed Democracies* (pp. 328–348). Hershey, PA: IGI Global. doi:10.4018/978-1-5225-0081-0.ch018

Tuttle, T. M. (2016). Laborare est Orare: Starting a Gay-Straight Alliance at a Rural, Private, Catholic College. In B. Glimps & T. Ford (Eds.), *Gender and Diversity Issues in Religious-Based Institutions and Organizations* (pp. 124–136). Hershey, PA: IGI Global. doi:10.4018/978-1-4666-8772-1.ch005

Vassilopoulou, J., April, K., Da Rocha, J. P., Kyriakidou, O., & Ozbilgin, M. (2016). Does the Ongoing Global Economic Crisis Put Diversity Gains at Risk?: Diversity Management during Hard Times – International Examples from the USA, South Africa, and Greece. In J. Prescott (Ed.), *Handbook of Research on Race, Gender, and the Fight for Equality* (pp. 424–452). Hershey, PA: IGI Global. doi:10.4018/978-1-5225-0047-6.ch019

Walsh, C. R. (2017). The Passion of Port Talbot: The Sacred Heart of a Secular Narrative. In A. Pascal (Ed.), *Multiculturalism and the Convergence of Faith and Practical Wisdom in Modern Society* (pp. 170–187). Hershey, PA: IGI Global. doi:10.4018/978-1-5225-1955-3.ch008

Webster, R. S. (2017). Making the Unbearable Bearable through Existential Spirituality. In A. Pascal (Ed.), *Multiculturalism and the Convergence of Faith and Practical Wisdom in Modern Society* (pp. 81–98). Hershey, PA: IGI Global. doi:10.4018/978-1-5225-1955-3.ch004

Wedderburn, N. V., & Carey, R. E. (2017). Forgiveness in the Face of Hate. In A. Pascal (Ed.), *Multiculturalism and the Convergence of Faith and Practical Wisdom in Modern Society* (pp. 315–330). Hershey, PA: IGI Global. doi:10.4018/978-1-5225-1955-3.ch016

Wendo, N. (2016). Ethnic Stereotyping on Kenyan Blog Sites in the 2013 Political Elections: A Spurious Harbinger of Ethnic Discord. In D. Orwenjo, O. Oketch, & A. Tunde (Eds.), *Political Discourse in Emergent, Fragile, and Failed Democracies* (pp. 252–264). Hershey, PA: IGI Global. doi:10.4018/978-1-5225-0081-0.ch014

Wiseman, R. R. (2014). Media Narratives of the Interactions between Religions and Cultures in Canada. In I. Nahon-Serfaty & R. Ahmed (Eds.), *New Media and Communication Across Religions and Cultures* (pp. 161–174). Hershey, PA: IGI Global. doi:10.4018/978-1-4666-5035-0.ch010

Wittmer, J. L., Werth, P. M., & Rudolph, C. W. (2016). Career Transitions and Trajectories for a Diverse Workforce: A Special Focus on Women and Older Workers. In J. Prescott (Ed.), *Handbook of Research on Race, Gender, and the Fight for Equality* (pp. 492–538). Hershey, PA: IGI Global. doi:10.4018/978-1-5225-0047-6.ch022

Wright, R. J., & Shiner, J. M. (2017). Managing Collaboration in E-Procurement. In R. Shakya (Ed.), *Digital Governance and E-Government Principles Applied to Public Procurement* (pp. 75–98). Hershey, PA: IGI Global. doi:10.4018/978-1-5225-2203-4.ch004

Yang, K. C., & Kang, Y. (2016). Real-Name Registration Regulation in China: An Examination of Chinese Netizens' Discussions about Censorship, Privacy, and Political Freedom. In D. Orwenjo, O. Oketch, & A. Tunde (Eds.), *Political Discourse in Emergent, Fragile, and Failed Democracies* (pp. 61–87). Hershey, PA: IGI Global. doi:10.4018/978-1-5225-0081-0.ch004

Yefet, B. (2017). The Clash of Civil Religions in Post-Revolutionary Egypt. In E. Lewin, E. Bick, & D. Naor (Eds.), *Comparative Perspectives on Civil Religion, Nationalism, and Political Influence* (pp. 156–189). Hershey, PA: IGI Global. doi:10.4018/978-1-5225-0516-7.ch006

Young, S. (2016). Psychological Essentialism: Diversity and the Religious Experience. In B. Glimps & T. Ford (Eds.), *Gender and Diversity Issues in Religious-Based Institutions and Organizations* (pp. 80–123). Hershey, PA: IGI Global. doi:10.4018/978-1-4666-8772-1.ch004

Ziadeh, R. (2016). Islam and Modernity: Considering Shafi'i's Perspective on How Islamic Thought Dealt with the Question of Renewal. In H. Shahpari & T. Hojjat (Eds.), *Islamic Economy and Social Mobility: Cultural and Religious Considerations* (pp. 328–343). Hershey, PA: IGI Global. doi:10.4018/978-1-4666-9731-7.ch013

About the Author

Karla L. Drenner is a lead professor in the Public Administration department at Kaplan University. Her research focuses on women in public service, religion and politics and social equity issues. She is in her 9th term serving in the Georgia House of Representatives and sits on five legislative committees including: Rules; Health and Human Services; Natural Resources and the Environment; Energy, Utilities and Telecommunications; and, Small Business Development. She was elected as the first openly gay legislator in the southeast and through this book seeks to share her first-hand experience of the legislative process and the importance of bridging the divides between our differences. She has written a book titled: *One: The True Story of Politics, Prayer, and the Power of One* in which she discussed her experiences. Her leadership, courageousness, and compassion for equality has earned her recognition from numerous organizations such as: National Foundation for Women Legislators, *Women of Excellence Award*; the *Dan Bradley Humanitarian Award* from the Human Rights Campaign; *Legislator of the Year* by the Southeast Association of Telecommunications, Nine-time winner of the Georgia League of Conservation Voters' Environmental Leadership Award; the "*Legislative Service Award*" from the Georgia Opticians Association for her work on improving the education requirements for opticians; the "*Voices of Note Award*" from the Atlanta Gay Men's Chorus; she has been named a "*Diva for Life*" by Business-to-Business magazine; the Advocate named her a "*Ballotbox Trailblazer;*" and she received the "*Legislator of the Year*" from the Organization of DeKalb Educators; Georgia Psychological Association honoured her for her "*LGBT Advocacy*" along with Stonewall Bar Association who presented her with the "Courageous Service Award. And from Georgia Equality she was named "*Champion for Equality.*" Other honours' include "*Excellence in Partnership Award*" from the Community Action Program, for her work on refugee microenterprise initiatives and the AIDS Survival Project named her a "*Legislative Hero*" for her efforts in combatting AIDS.

Index

A

Accommodation 123-124, 142, 153-158, 162

B

Ballot Initiatives 113

C

Chubbing 133, 142
Civil Union 11, 75, 106, 108, 113
Conservative 2, 8, 13, 16, 18, 22, 30-31, 33, 39, 42-44, 51-52, 59, 63, 66, 72, 98, 106-107, 132, 150, 153
Cultural Cleavage 59, 64, 66, 89

D

Defense of Marriage 43, 70, 72, 74, 76, 93-94, 98-100, 103, 106, 119, 126, 142
Denominations 7, 29, 31, 59-60, 77, 79, 128, 151

E

Equality 2, 23, 34, 49, 51-52, 70-71, 75, 96, 105, 108-109, 120-122, 132, 136, 143-144, 147-148, 150, 162
Establishment Clause 131, 154-155, 162
Evangelical 8, 16, 22, 26, 29-31, 33-34, 37-38, 42-43, 45, 51, 60, 77, 79, 83

F

Family Values 8, 27, 98, 100, 142
Federalism 14, 23, 145
Free Exercise Clause 33, 155-156, 162
Fundamentalism 29, 60

G

Gay issues 26, 29, 64, 66-67, 83

I

Ideology 15, 60, 63, 77, 80
Individualism 2, 23

J

Jesus Christ 29-30, 35, 42, 60, 136
Judicial Activism 94, 104, 110, 113, 162

L

Liberal 8, 13, 23, 26, 28, 30, 37-38, 42-43, 106, 156
Liberty 2, 4-5, 8-9, 23, 31-32, 34, 48, 51, 75, 101, 104, 123, 129, 133, 143, 148-149, 151, 153-155, 157-158, 162

M

Moral Worldview 15, 31, 36-38, 42, 44, 83, 89, 153

Morality 4, 10, 14, 26-28, 36, 39, 42, 44, 60, 63, 80, 103, 105, 119, 121, 128, 144, 146, 154, 158

N

national debate 96-98
Nullification 23

P

Pluralism 19, 23, 29, 152
Polarization 1, 12-13, 17, 23, 67
Post-Millennialism 60
Precedent 32, 104, 120, 137, 142
Pre-Millennialism 60
Protestant Reformation 3, 23
Protestantism 29-30, 37, 60
Public Accommodation 123-124, 142, 155, 158

R

Religious Freedom 3, 5-7, 9, 23, 33, 38, 40, 44, 50, 66-67, 69-70, 75-79, 82-83, 124, 127, 133-135, 143-145, 147, 149-151, 153, 155, 158-159
Roll Call Vote 89

S

same-sex couples 32, 50-51, 64, 70-71, 74, 92-94, 97, 99, 105-108, 119-122, 125-126, 145-146
Same-Sex Marriage 9, 11, 15, 27, 29, 31-34, 36-39, 42, 44-45, 48-50, 63-66, 70-72, 74, 76-77, 79-80, 82-83, 92-94, 97-100, 104-106, 110, 113, 120-121, 123, 125-127, 132-134, 138, 143-150, 153
Sectarian 84, 128, 150, 162
Secular 6, 14, 18, 52, 66, 84, 106, 150-151, 155-156, 158-159, 162
sexual orientation 28, 41, 44-49, 51, 74, 83, 96, 101, 123, 134-136, 147, 149-150, 153, 155
state legislatures 1, 8, 12-13, 16-18, 65, 70, 84, 94, 110, 127, 145, 154
States' Rights 93-94, 113
Strict Scrutiny 33, 67, 69, 100-102, 113, 150
Supreme Court 32-33, 38-39, 45, 64-65, 67, 69, 71, 75, 92, 97, 99-100, 102-105, 107-109, 122-125, 127, 131-132, 143-145, 149, 153-154, 157-158

T

Term Limits 12-13, 18, 23, 84
Traditionalism 26, 29, 42, 66-67, 79, 89

U

U.S. Supreme Court 32-33, 45, 67, 97, 99-100, 103, 122, 124-125, 132, 143-145, 149, 158
United States 2-4, 6, 8, 10, 18, 26, 31-32, 34, 64-65, 67, 69-70, 75, 92-93, 96, 99, 110, 113, 122-123, 125, 128, 130, 132, 142, 145, 154, 158

W

Whip 66, 89, 124
Worldview 9, 15, 31, 35-38, 42, 44, 60, 83, 89, 153

IGI Global
Proudly Partners with
eContent Pro
eContent Pro specializes in the following areas:
Academic Copy Editing
Our expert copy editors will conduct a full copy editing procedure on your manuscript and will also address your preferred reference style to make sure your paper meets the standards of the style of your choice.
Expert Translation
Our expert translators will work to ensure a clear cut and accurate translation of your document, ensuring that your research is flawlessly communicated to your audience.
Professional Proofreading
Our editors will conduct a comprehensive assessment of your content and address all shortcomings of the paper in terms of grammar, language structures, spelling, and formatting.
IGI Global Authors, Save 10% on eContent Pro's Services!
Scan the QR Code to Receive Your 10% Discount
The 10% discount is applied directly to your eContent Pro shopping cart when placing an order through IGI Global's referral link. Use the QR code to access this referral link. eContent Pro has the right to end or modify any promotion at any time.
Email: customerservice@econtentpro.com
econtentpro.com

www.ingramcontent.com/pod-product-compliance
Lightning Source LLC
LaVergne TN
LVHW062124200926
848484LV00007B/1757
9781522523888